THE MAN WHO WOULD BE BOGART
BY STONE WALLACE

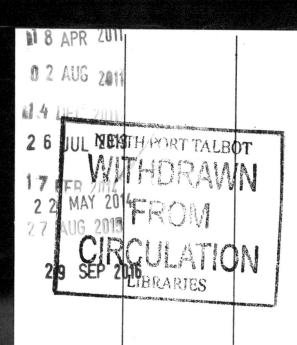

Published in the USA by:
BearManor Media
P O Box 71426
Albany, Georgia 31708
WWW.BEARMANORMEDIA.COM

ISBN 1-59393-123-9

Printed in the United States of America.
Book design by Brian Pearce.

TABLE OF CONTENTS

To fellow author, John O'Dowd, whose friendship and unwavering encouragement during the writing of this book helped make it possible.

ACKNOWLEDGMENTS

Long before I conceived of the idea to write a biography of George Raft, I had the opportunity while on trips to California to meet and speak with some of the people who had either worked with Raft or knew him socially. In each case my fascination with, and admiration for, George Raft prompted me at some point in each conversation to ask questions concerning professional and/or personal feelings toward Raft. Little did I know that some thirty-plus years later some of those generous comments and observations would find a permanent home in this project. In that category of contributor I gratefully acknowledge: the late Jack LaRue, the late Mike Mazurki and, most especially, the late Lloyd Nolan. Movie tough guys each, but gentlemen all.

To those who graciously offered recollections of Raft during the writing of this book, I thank: Margia Dean, Dolores Fuller, Coleen Gray, the late Kevin Hagen, Sybil Jason, the late Frances Langford, the late Marc Lawrence, the late Janet Leigh, Harry Morgan, Nehemiah Persoff, the late Liz Renay, Francesca Robinson-Sanchez, the late Frankie Thomas, Michelle Phillips, Audrey Totter and special thanks to Dr. Lewis Yablonsky for his generous insights into the George Raft he knew.

I'd like to extend a very special thank you to Mack and Joe Gray's nephews Robert Davidson and Martin Abrahams, along with Al Smiley and Lucille Casey's daughter Luellen Smiley. Your generosity is much appreciated.

I also want to extend my appreciation for the help, support and encouragement of Silver Screen Audio host Joel Blumberg; Dr. Philip Chamberlin, former director of the Academy of Motion Picture Arts and Sciences; Kit Parker of Kit Parker Films, who provided information on Raft's Lippert pictures; my fellow biographers John O'Dowd, Robert Nott and Alan K. Rode (thanks, guys!); Tracy Toutant, who helped with the technical requirements of many of the photographs; my publisher Ben Ohmart (the best!); and to my darling Cindy, who is the wind beneath my wings. I love you.

FOREWORD

My mother, who grew up in Hollywood during the so-called "Golden Age," told me a story once about a friend of hers that was smitten with George Raft. The punch line was that after years of silver screen idol worship, Mother's girlfriend was waiting under a bus stop in a driving rainstorm when Raft suddenly pulled up in a coupe and gentlemanly offered her a ride home. As if struck by lightning, the lady became a vocal paralytic and frantically signaled Raft that she was okay and didn't require a lift. After determining that the woman wasn't having an epileptic fit, George finally shrugged and drove off, leaving one of his biggest fans to wait in a downpour. I asked how anybody could be that taken with George Raft; after all, everyone knew he was a terrible actor. Mother's answer was telling. "George Raft was a big star."

George Raft's movie career was an emblematic outcome of the studio system jump-starting a career for a most reluctant actor. While Raft's acting is universally viewed by contemporary critics through a prism of sarcastic contempt, his popularity during the 1930s through the war years was undeniable. Once Howard Hawks had him flip that coin in *Scarface* (1932), George Raft became cemented in the public eye with Paramount and then Warner Brothers eagerly laying the iconic brickwork.

While the studio PR build-up leveraged his visual appeal into stardom, Raft knew from day one that he was no actor. After watching Paul Muni wrench his guts out during *Scarface*, Raft reportedly said, "If I had to do that to be an actor, I'd quit." He protected himself accordingly. Although he picked up some vocational tradecraft through his considerable dancing skills and rote iteration, moving well, touching his hat, and snapping off pithy dialogue, George Raft's major career concern was not to look like a fool. Peter Lorre called movie acting "face making." Raft strove to present a solitary visage to the public; visually striking yet monosyllabically robotic. If John Barrymore was "The Great Profile," George Raft could be dubbed "The Cigar Store Indian."

Many film historians, not unjustly, have made the case that Raft mismanaged his acting career with his prominent rejections of *Dead End, The Maltese Falcon, High Sierra,* and *Double Indemnity*. (Note: the story that Raft turned down playing Rick in *Casablanca* is a bum rap — it never happened. The picture was designed by Hal Wallis specifically for Humphrey Bogart from day one.) Raft retrospectively divided the blame for his career obtuseness between his agent and own lack of professional foresight. After becoming a star, Raft seemingly navigated his way through his chosen profession as if a blindfolded man traversing a minefield. But it wasn't really a choice. One has to possess both the opportunity and desire in a given career in order to screw it up. He certainly had the opportunity to become a respected film actor, but assiduously avoided anything that smacked of risk, taint or effort. For George Raft, avoidance of acting was a guarantee of continued success.

Much of Raft's Armageddon-like career management was rooted in his unshakeable image of himself, which was also how he thought the public would perceive him. George Raft was an urban child spawned during the nineteenth century who came up the hard way. Somewhat analogous to the cinematic hard-boiled private eye, he lived by his own uncompromising standards of conduct and behavior. Raft couldn't play the cuckolded lover who teams up with Barbara Stanwyck to murder her husband in *Double Indemnity* any more than he could get divorced from a loveless, forgotten wife to marry the love-of-his-life, Betty Grable. With an eye cocked on his image and fear of professional risk governing his career decisions, Raft's personal life became his virtual role of a lifetime, eclipsing any part that he essayed on screen.

From growing up in Hell's Kitchen and palling around with Owney Madden to being a dancing gigolo and later hobnobbing in Hollywood with the notorious "Bugsy" Siegel, Raft's curriculum vitae became comprised not of memorable movie performances but the *Guy and Dolls* adventures of a legit star-gangster-lover. The backroom stories were never about the historic proportions of a ruthless, super-charged ego in quest of epic film roles. George Raft gossip concerned the censurable adventures of a loyal, friendly gentleman whose fuel-injected libido was complemented by legendary genitalia. It is somehow poetically ironic that Raft's fulsome life would get made into a cheaply trite movie, *The George Raft Story* in 1961. Hollywood never could get the real thing done right, even for as distinguished an alumnus as Raft, who sold off the rights to himself when he was desperate for cash.

By the time the cinematic version of his life hit the screen, George Raft was reduced to self-parody in order to earn a living. He had been a relentless high-liver: big houses, endless dames, betting the ponies, propping up friends and always picking up the check. The huge sums he earned as a movie star were relentlessly consumed by a fantastic lifestyle with Raft starring in dual roles as Robin Hood and Bacchus. His true-life gangster image was always a front, but in the latter stages it was parlayed into work as a greeter at mob-controlled casinos in Cuba and England with occasional cameo roles in mostly forgettable pictures. In the end, it was the four packs a day of Luckies for sixty years that finally did him in. Unlike his friend, Ben Siegel, Raft died both with dignity and in bed.

George Raft left us with a legacy of films that are representative of an era, many of which continue hold up well. Nearly three decades after his death,

Raft on screen is frequently imbued with a quality that eluded him during his lifetime: authenticity. It is the reality brought not by an actor, but a personage. As Stone Wallace brings to life in his superb biography, Raft's persona in the public consciousness has outlived his studious avoidance of serious acting while transcending surfeit criticism. George Raft endures as a seminal American movie star whose life and films are worthy of our attention.

Alan K. Rode is a film historian, journalist and author of Charles McGraw, Biography of a Film Noir Tough Guy.

AUTHOR'S NOTE

My admiration for George Raft began in Chicago during the summer of 1972, when I caught a late night televised showing of *Each Dawn I Die*. Even though I'd long been a fan of James Cagney's work, watching this movie introduced me to the effective sinister underplaying of his co-star George Raft – and I was impressed. I admit that right away I was hooked on Raft — who to a fifteen-year-old boy epitomized a word then still in vogue: "Cool" — and from that point on never missed the opportunity to catch one of his movies, or devour any information I could uncover about both the actor and the man. It didn't take me long to discover that Raft not only played the quintessential movie gangster, there was a strong possibility that he was also one in real life. This, of course, only increased my fascination with him. From my earliest years I was enamored with the Real McCoys: Capone, Dillinger, Karpis and the rest. While Bogart, Cagney and Robinson were completely convincing movie hoods, George Raft was the real article.

About a year later I caught an ultra-rare showing of *Scarface* on a French television network here in Canada. Naturally, I watched it through, even though I don't understand a word of the language. It hardly mattered. Raft had few lines of dialogue – but that presence. Man, that presence! To quote Raft biographer Lewis Yablonsky, "He was a magnificent hood."

But I soon discovered that Raft could be equally as convincing in less hard-edged roles: *Souls at Sea, They Drive by Night, Manpower* and *Background to Danger*. He even wasn't bad in comedy: *She Couldn't Take It*.

Raft was rarely a "great" actor onscreen (certainly when it came to talent I preferred Bogie, Jimmy and Eddie G.), but he still remained – and remains – my favorite movie performer simply because he radiated masculine toughness (so appealing to a fatherless boy in his adolescence) and commanded attention in a way that few film stars could. Cliché as it may sound, when he walked into a scene, he dominated it. Raft was physically not a big man, but he filled the screen … and even later when he was relegated to inconsequential cameos, he still instantly caught and held the audience's focus.

Sadly, when I started writing this biography and was asked by people what I was working on, and I'd answer "a book about George Raft," invariably their reply would be: "Who?" I understand that with the passage of time and with today's moviegoers fixated on the heavily-hyped "flavor of the month," many of the early Hollywood stars are rarely thought of, or their classic work acknowledged (except, of course, through the wonderful efforts of Turner

Classic Movies). But while Bogart, Cagney, Cooper, Davis or Gable may elicit recognition, the name George Raft, at least in my experience, often leaves a person scratching his or her head. To mention *Scarface, Each Dawn I Die, They Drive by Night* or *Some Like it Hot* likewise does little to jog the memory. This is not only unfortunate ... but unfair — both to the man and his impressive screen legacy.

So – that is the hope and intention of this book. To reintroduce George Raft and his contribution to motion picture history to a contemporary audience. Two previous books were written about Raft in the mid-'70s, when he was still living and could enjoy some of the benefits of his rediscovery. But these fine books are now long out of print. *George Raft: The Man Who Would be Bogart* is the first biography to be written since Raft's death in 1980. Therefore, it will also cover the years following the publications of the James Robert Parish/Steven Whitney and Lewis Yablonsky books (to both of which I am indebted). I feel the title to this book is appropriate, because if not for Raft, one wonders how far Humphrey Bogart's film career would have progressed. The flip side of the coin (forgive the pun) is that once Bogart achieved his enormous success, audiences and the film industry had little use for Raft.

The time is long-overdue to correct this injustice.

Stone Wallace

PROLOGUE

239 North Bristol Avenue
Los Angeles, California

After several months' correspondence, tough guy character actor Lloyd Nolan — he of the beady eyes and cynical demeanor — welcomed me as a visitor to his home during a long anticipated trip to Los Angeles in October of 1974. The meeting with Lloyd occurred exactly one day before a round-the-world trip the versatile actor would be embarking upon with his wife Mell.

Despite the unexpected with last-minute packing and the like, Lloyd was a patient, altogether gracious host. He shook my hand vigorously and never once made me feel that my presence during this hectic time was an intrusion. After pleasantries and an introduction to his charming wife, Lloyd (he refused to have me call him "Mr. Nolan") escorted me into a separate second-story room, his study, where I instantly realized that our conversation had the potential to become a full-fledged journalistic endeavor.

While Lloyd Nolan's film career had spanned forty years and certainly included a wealth of showbiz stories, he began our talk by apologetically admitting that he suffered from a faulty memory.

"Not advanced age. I've always had it," he said with good-natured humor, though this revelation did make me wonder how he had ever been able to remember the lengthy and often complex dialogue he delivered with both clarity and conviction in such stage roles as Captain Queeg in *The Caine Mutiny Court Martial.*

Of course, the answer was simple. Lloyd Nolan was a professional. While he himself could not understand how his memory could service him during his preparation for a part and then elude him almost immediately upon completion of the role, he could, with some effort, recall certain specifics about the people with whom he had worked during his lengthy motion picture career. Fortunately, he had almost total recall when he discussed working with George Raft.

The previous year I had written a letter to the Academy of Motion Picture Arts & Sciences requesting they consider George Raft for an honorary Oscar in recognition of his enormous contribution to the history of cinema. I received a nice reply from the Academy informing me that my recommendation would be voted on by their Board of Directors.[1] During my talk with Lloyd I mentioned this acknowledgment from AMPAS.

Lloyd laughed in that inimitable fashion of his. "I liked George," he said. "We made three pictures together. I can't remember the names, but I know Tay Garnett and Archie Mayo were two of the directors."[2] I furnished Lloyd with the titles: *Stolen Harmony, She Couldn't Take It* (1935) and *The House Across the Bay* (1940). Interesting in light of George Raft's gangster image, in each of these pictures it was Lloyd Nolan who played the principal heavy.

"Jimmy Cagney's brother Bill played one of your gang in *Stolen Harmony*," I reminded Lloyd. "He had a key scene where he fondly reminisces about prison life at San Quentin." Lloyd's memory quickly serviced him. "And I worked with Cagney [James] in one of the first films I did."

"That was *"G" Men*. You played an FBI agent who gets killed by Barton MacLane's mob.

"And George Raft?" I asked.

Lloyd paused for a few moments, and then he offered a co-player's insight. "He wasn't a stage-trained actor. I remember he didn't like a lot of dialogue and had trouble interpreting lines. George? Maybe a little insecure as an actor. But at the time I first worked with him he was probably the biggest star on the [Paramount] lot next to [Gary] Cooper."

"One of Raft's best roles at Paramount was as Gary Cooper's sidekick Powdah in *Souls at Sea* (1937). But initially he didn't want to do the part and both you and Anthony Quinn were then considered for the role," I told him.

Lloyd seemed at a loss. "I did a lot of pictures with Tony," he said reflectively. "But I honestly don't remember that ever happening."

"Regardless of his gifts as an actor, Lloyd, do you feel that if George Raft had not turned down those great screen roles inherited by Humphrey Bogart, he perhaps could have become the huge star that Bogie became?"

Lloyd became silent as he considered my question. Apparently, he again found it difficult to give a definite answer. He merely responded with a smile and offered a general observation. "In my experience, I've found that sometimes luck is more important than talent."

Lloyd Nolan never became the big star that his colleague George Raft had been during the Golden Age of Hollywood. In fact, Lloyd probably enjoyed his greatest popular success as pulp detective Michael Shayne in a series of B-pictures he made during the 1940s. His bigger-budgeted offerings usually found him giving solid support to such co-stars as Ray Milland, Fred MacMurray and Alan Ladd. However, in 1974, at age 72, Lloyd was still in celluloid demand while George Raft had been largely forgotten. I didn't think it appropriate to comment on that fact.

My conversation with Lloyd Nolan took place six years before George Raft's death in 1980. Twenty years before the journeyman actor whom George Raft had inadvertently catapulted into superstar status was recognized by the American Film Institute as the "Greatest Male Screen Actor of the Century." It was an honor due in no small part to this screen player's most famous character walking off with Claude Rains into a soundstage fog. A thick, swirling *noirish* mist that, legend has it, George Raft had refused to enter — yet from which, after the release of 1942's *Casablanca*, the former Hollywood A-list tough guy could never totally emerge.

George Raft's film career possesses all the elements of a Hollywood success story turned sour. At his height during the 1930s and into the mid-'40s, Raft was one of the industry's biggest and highest paid stars, earning an annual income in excess of a quarter million dollars. During his years at Warner Brothers (1939-42), it was said that he was offered more movie roles than any other actor on the lot, including James Cagney. The great director John Huston remembered: "Everything was intended for George Raft at the time," though he was quick to add, "And I was not among George Raft's greatest admirers."

Perhaps Huston's statement is not difficult to understand. Raft was apparently every bit as tough as his screen image. He'd engaged in well-publicized on-set punch fests with Wallace Beery, Edward G. Robinson and (though one-sided) Peter Lorre. He could be equally as pugnacious outside the studio. Jimmy Cagney called him "The only really tough man I knew in the business." Studio boss Jack L. Warner remembered, "There was a time when he was tougher on the set than the gangsters he was playing on film." Quite a tribute coming from two guys who had spent a lifetime dealing with rough characters both on and off the soundstage.

Yet sadly, Raft's placement among the greats in movie history has been overshadowed by the missed opportunities that all but removed him from the pantheon of popular culture and relegated him to a virtual obscurity. The true tragedy is that it was George Raft himself who, through career mismanagement and a naive but perverse sense of loyalty to his "shady" personal associations, terminated his own career. The irony is that it was precisely those underworld connections that sponsored George Raft's entry into motion pictures and, indirectly, were responsible for his subsequent screen success. Raft was the first to admit that he patterned many of his famous movie hoods on the gangsters he had known and admired during his speakeasy days in New York. Each of these roles, ranging from the murderous Guino Rinaldo in *Scarface* (1932) to the noble "Hood" Stacey in *Each Dawn I Die* (1939) to the utterly vicious Dan Beaumonte in *Rogue Cop* (1954), benefited from styles and personality traits Raft had borrowed from real-life mobsters, such as Dutch Schultz, Vincent "Mad Dog" Coll and pals Owney Madden and Benjamin "Bugsy" Siegel. Whether projecting pure onscreen evil or essaying a character imbued with sympathetic qualities, George Raft captured perfectly the essence of the slick urban criminal.

Visually, as well, George was the ideal hood. Glossy, slicked-back hair framing a narrow, intriguingly sinister face accentuated by dark, snake-like eyes and thin cold lips. An often immobile face that rarely betrayed emotion. A "fantastic, arresting mask," as Edward G. Robinson called it. Of course, Raft's natty wardrobe was an integral part of the character. Form-fitting suit jackets, wide lapels, high-waist trousers and long roll shirt collars. Even his hats perfectly complemented the character. Few movie mobsters could don a snap-brimmed fedora to the same effect.

The George Raft image proved so effective that, unlike Bogart, Cagney and Robinson, he had his share of admirers who attempted to imitate him. Former middleweight boxing champion Rocky Graziano admitted that as a young man he and his pals emulated Raft both in their cool, tough attitude and choice of attire. Of course, some real-life tough guys received their early inspiration from George Raft. New York gangster "Crazy Joe" Gallo was remembered by neighbors as a boy who grew up wanting to be like George Raft, even to standing on the street corner tossing a half dollar. Many of the gangsters of Raft's own generation also began to adopt his mannerisms and style once he'd hit it big in the movies.

Yet despite this distinction, George Raft has been consigned to footnote status among many film historians, while contemporaries James Cagney and Humphrey Bogart have become movie icons and Edward G. Robinson is still critically regarded as one of the screen's most distinguished performers.

Why the neglect? Undoubtedly, three factors must be considered. First, while George Raft was absolutely convincing as a deadpan movie mobster and equally believable as a hard-working "man of the people" (*They Drive by Night* and *Manpower*), his acting range suffered in comparison to Cagney, Bogart and Robinson. For example, although considered one of Hollywood's finest dancers (an opinion shared by James Cagney and Fred Astaire), Raft never could have brought the necessary buoyancy to the role of showman extraordinaire George M. Cohan in Cagney's crowning achievement, *Yankee Doodle Dandy* (1942). Nor could have he handled the biographical integrity of Dr. Paul Ehrlich or the complexities of the insurance investigator Barton Keyes, both played to perfection by Edward G. Robinson in *Dr. Ehrlich's Magic Bullet* (1940) and *Double Indemnity* (1944), respectively. Finally and most significantly given the focus of this book, one is hard-pressed to imagine George Raft attempting the dramatic range of dementia displayed in two of Bogart's greatest roles: Fred C. Dobbs (*The Treasure of the Sierra Madre*, 1948) and Captain Philip Francis Queeg (*The Caine Mutiny*, 1954). While Raft possessed a certain defined ability as an actor, he never quite understood or took the time to explore the intricacies of his craft.

Secondly, because George Raft was unsure of himself as an actor, he allowed these insecurities to cloud his judgment regarding scripts that were later turned into classics of the cinema. In hindsight, it seems inconceivable that any actor could not have recognized the merits of *Dead End* (1937), *High Sierra*, *The Maltese Falcon* (1941), and *Double Indemnity*. Yet, apparently,

Raft couldn't see himself in these roles. He had his own idiosyncratic reasons for turning down each of these projects, based primarily on his desire to be perceived by movie audiences as the "good guy" and, to a lesser extent, not to die onscreen. In his later years he would come to regret some of these decisions.

Finally, Raft's well-publicized hair-trigger temper, rows with directors and studio heads, and his association with both reel and real gangsters typed him in the mind of the public, if not to his employers. Whereas Cagney became George M. Cohan and Bogart — indeed, the most prolific of the '30s film heavies — picked up some valuable Raft rejects and was soon displaying a versatility that had previously been denied him, George Raft remained ... George Raft. A strong, commanding image, granted, yet one so indelibly imprinted upon movie audiences that it eventually became dated and proved redundant. Throughout the early days of Raft's career, the movie hoodlum was appreciated by audiences still intrigued by the exploits of Prohibition racketeers and Depression-era gunmen. But with American gangsters fast becoming a faded memory during the years of World War II, Raft's most profitable image likewise suffered. As the decade progressed post-war, and crime dramas evolved into the period of *film noir*, a new breed of tough guy appeared. The cynical, world-weary antihero replaced the smooth nightclub gangster exemplified by George Raft. Actors such as Kirk Douglas, Burt Lancaster, Robert Mitchum and Richard Widmark were fresh and exciting screen personalities, their on-camera creations down and dirty and plagued with psychoses and neuroses that rarely if ever found their way into a George Raft character. It was a new realism, one which afforded Raft limited opportunity since his coin-flipping movie gangster had by now become a virtual caricature.

And Raft himself perpetuated the image. Although despairing of his criminal typecasting, Raft never denied his indebtedness to or his friendship with New York beer baron Owney Madden. He also maintained a very public friendship with Benjamin "Bugsy" Siegel that lasted until the latter's bullet-ridden demise. Although this association was frowned upon by industry men such as Jack Warner, Raft openly socialized with "The Bug" at racetracks and nightclubs. He even went a step further when he defied studio pressure during the declining period of his career and took the stand to defend Siegel when the latter went to trial on an L.A. bookmaking charge.

To a public eager to associate actors' off-screen lives with their film roles, Raft proved the ideal example of fiction merging with fact. The tough-talking, hard-drinking Humphrey Bogart had finally settled into a more sedate lifestyle with his fourth wife Lauren Bacall (and had taken to wearing a rather incongruous bowtie in public, perhaps in an effort to soften his tough reputation). Farmer James Cagney and intellectual art collector Edward G. Robinson had always been quiet homebodies, completely at odds with their rough-and-tumble image. But George Raft, while mellowing in temperament during his advancing years, still lived up to the public's perception of him as a gangster. He continued to frequent nightspots and racetracks, often in questionable company. Occasionally, he would find himself "starring" in the tabloids for trouble stemming from these associations — both current and from his early days. (Appropriately, when a several-installment print series on Raft appeared in *The Saturday Evening Post*, bylined by journalist Dean Jennings, the feature was titled "Out of My Past.") Naturally, the public accepted and absorbed these accusations, even as Raft desperately tried to divorce himself professionally if not personally from being looked upon as a gangster.

Such contradictions perhaps offer the most telling clue to the fascinating story of George Raft's lofty professional ascension and his precipitous cinematic decline.

CHAPTER ONE

"NO BOYS ON MY STREET WANTED TO BE PRESIDENT. THEY JUST WANTED TO BE TOUGH. AND THEY WERE."

GEORGE RAFT

If there was ever a lousy place for a turn-of-the-century kid to be born, it was Hell's Kitchen, New York, which perhaps could best be described as the tenement's tenement.

Hell's Kitchen was a poverty- and crime-infested piece of the Manhattan landscape whose borders extended from 23rd Street to 57th Street, between Eighth Avenue and the Hudson River. Many immigrants who passed through the gates of Ellis Island were dismayed to discover that the promised "streets of gold" they had naively expected to find waiting them in America extended no further than the brick confines of their tenement environment. It was a congested neighborhood, hot and humid during the summer months and frigidly cold in the winter, with families forced to exist in cramped cold-water quarters, and to co-exist in a socio-economic climate where nationalities clashed and prejudiced hostilities festered. These immigrant families tried to maintain an outlook of optimism while they endured their daily struggles, firm in the belief that their adopted country truly was the land of opportunity, and that the elusive brass ring was still within their grasp. But the children quickly grew wise to the reality of slum life as they witnessed their parents' ongoing despair and discouragement. Most families found themselves destitute; either unemployed, or, if lucky, working long hours at hard labor for starvation wages. Their children's hope for prosperity in the New World quickly turned into a bitterness that frequently found release through thievery, vandalism, and violence.

The legend goes that Hell's Kitchen got its name when two policemen, a veteran and a rookie, were on patrol and preparing to break up a bloody street altercation. The nervous, pale-complexioned rookie remarked, "This place is Hell itself." The beefy, red-faced veteran supposedly replied, "Hell's a mild climate compared to this. This is Hell's Kitchen."

Whether this story is true or apocryphal, it was into this desperate environment further polluted by political corruption and escalating racial tensions that the first of Conrad and Eva Ranft's ten children, a boy they named George, was born.

Although later studio biographies would cite George Raft's birth year as 1901 or 1903, the future screen tough guy actually entered the world on September 26, 1895. His parents lived on the third floor of a ten-family tenement on 41st Street, between Ninth and Tenth Avenues.

Conrad Ranft had been heir to a potential fortune, but he had chosen to abdicate his inheritance for the love of a woman. His father Martin had emigrated from Germany to the United States in 1875, settling in Boston, Massachusetts, where he introduced to the country the merry-go-round and other amusement park rides. Martin's success prompted him to move his family to New York City, where he intended to leave his prosperous enterprise to his son.

But Conrad bitterly disappointed his parents when he announced his intentions to marry Eva Glockner, a girl of mixed German and Italian parentage, though highlighted on the maternal side, who possessed striking beauty but whose family was of minimal means. Conrad was given an ultimatum — and he chose love over riches.

Conrad was now forced to find any kind of a job to support his new wife, and he obtained meager employment delivering packages for the John Wanamaker Department Store. George later recalled, "My father stayed at Wanamaker's for twenty-seven years, eventually becoming a warehouse supervisor, and if there was any fun in life, he missed it."

Almost from the day George Raft was born there was a kind of estrangement between father and son. Part of the reason may have been genetic. George did not inherit his father's blond, light-complexioned Teutonic appearance. Instead, the infant favored his mother in looks: Mediterranean features, highlighted by dark hair and eyes, and olive skin.

Both Conrad and Eva (between pregnancies) were required to hold down jobs to support their growing brood. Within three years, George had two younger brothers, Anthony and Michael, both of whom resembled their father both in looks and temperament. Meanwhile, George was growing ever more independent and rebellious. His stubborn self-reliance inevitably widened the gap between his father and himself. "I never understood my father, and I guess the feeling was mutual," George said.

Frequently confronting his son for his delinquency and truancy, Conrad admonished George by calling him a lazy kid. One time during a heated argument with his father, George heaved a milk bottle at his head. George then ran from the house and kept away for several days.

"You got bad blood somewhere," Conrad later scolded his errant son. "Someday you'll kill somebody with that hot head of yours."

George never denied he had a temper, and as a boy he had plenty of opportunity to display it. He never backed down from a fight with other tough kids in the neighborhood. But just as often he was the instigator. He admitted that he had a bad attitude and quick, combative nature and that even the wrong word or look could provoke him into anger. "It was a rare day that I didn't come home bruised and bloody from a street fight," George recalled.

Yet, he also later admitted to having another philosophy for handling a potential altercation. "Be friendly. That was the big thing. Because if worse comes to worst, it's better to be friendly than unfriendly — and if they just won't leave you alone, a friendly guy has a better chance to run or get in one quick kick to the stones before they bust his face ..."

George soon developed the reputation as a tough sidewalk scrapper. He also found other outlets for his hostility, such as joining his pals on tenement rooftops to drop flowerpots, bricks or milk bottles on passing policemen. To the rough kids in the neighborhood, cops and school were considered the enemy. By now he was running with a gang and participated in petty break-ins where they would later fence their stolen goods for a small payoff.

George Ranft had become a peripheral member of the notorious Gopher (pronounced "Goofer") Gang, which earned the reputation as the toughest street club in all of New York. The gang prospered under the leadership of a most unlikely candidate: a thin, frail British import named Owen (Owney) Madden.

Owney — or "Duke" Madden, born in Liverpool, England in 1892, proved himself the roughest kid of the bunch, but he took a liking to the younger George and the two would remain lifelong friends.

Owney's decision to become a criminal was precipitated by a simple incident. Within weeks of arriving in New York with his parents, young Owen and his mother were walking home from grocery shopping through the streets of Hell's Kitchen. Suddenly one of the neighborhood thieves rushed up from behind, cut the string handles on the bag with scissors and ran off with the groceries. Owney would later explain to George, "When I saw what that kid got away with and how easy it was, I decided I'd be a sucker not to do it myself."

Owney had many hurdles to overcome in his quest for leadership of the Gophers. Besides his delicate physique, he also "talked funny." But appearances are often deceiving, and through cunning, courage, and outright murder, Owney Madden achieved his goal and was on his way to his eventual destiny as the undisputed gang boss of New York.

Gang brawls were an almost everyday occurrence among the neighborhood toughs. These "street beefs" frequently escalated into violent episodes where weapons ranged from a roll of coins or a gas-pipe coupling concealed in a fist (in lieu of costly brass knuckles) to broken bottles and knives. George was an able, if not always eager participant in these gang battles. He said, "I got along. There was a dustup or two, sure. But I could run good — and I carried a rock in the toe of an old sock, see ..."

Also, on occasion, he was caught alone in a vicious confrontation. Perhaps the most potentially deadly of George's encounters occurred when he went against a skilled switchblade-fighter named Sammy Schwartz. The two squared off around dusk in a tenement yard on Tenth Avenue, and within about ten minutes of their battle George's left ear was slashed and bloody and barely hanging to his face. George was defending himself with a bone-handled Boy Scout camping knife, which he finally tossed dead-on into Sammy's shoulder, hastily retreating while his adversary screamed in pain.

Obviously, such an environment did not foster academic incentive and George would later admit that he rarely saw the inside of a classroom. He attended P.S. 169, but education held no interest to the youth. It also had little value. George could see only two ways to escape the urban jungle of Hell's Kitchen: Sports or crime.

Of course, George's decision to leave school did not sit well with either of his parents, especially his father. While Conrad understood that the neighborhood streets were violently competitive, he maintained the hope that his eldest son would overcome their influence. But that didn't mean he'd intercede when George got into a scrap.

George recalled the day when his father was returning home from work and saw both him and another boy beating each other to a pulp. Rather than breaking up the fight, Conrad pulled his son aside long enough to say, "If you don't win, I'll take care of you myself." Such cold, stern words coming from his own father helped foster in young George the fierce independence he would carry throughout his life.

Even though George's appearances at home were becoming scarcer and based primarily on a need to fill a famished stomach, Conrad still attempted to exude a semblance of parental control over his son, and arranged with the boy's uncle to put George to work in his barbershop. George endured such menial duties as sweeping the floors, cleaning the shop, and even shining customers' shoes. It proved a strict, stifling environment, of which the rebellious boy quickly tired.

If young George possessed any passion, it was for baseball. He loved the game and was proud to hold down the job of mascot for the New York Highlanders ball club (later to become the Yankees). Again, it consisted of menial chores, including carrying the bats and carting off dirty uniforms for cleaning. But more important to George was that he got to hang around the ballpark and watch his favorite players both at practice and participating in home games.

Yet not even the allure of baseball could curb George's larcenous tendencies. He so wanted a baseball bat from his idol Hal Chase that, when he was not presented with one, he simply stole a couple. He later added that he didn't dare keep them around the apartment for fear his father would find them and think he was going to use them on someone's head.

The pre-adolescent George also discovered a passion of a different kind when at age twelve he had his first sexual encounter with a pretty nurse several years older. Both so enjoyed the experience that, according to George, they met regularly for the next few months when she got off work.

With George no longer attending P.S. 169 and refusing to show up for work at his uncle's barbershop, his father decided to confront the boy. His uncle was also present. The argument became so heated that George stuffed wads of paper into his ears to drown out the loud, angry words. Later, he had to rush himself to a hospital emergency ward to have the paper removed. The experience was so traumatic that George steadfastly tried to avoid loud arguments the rest of his life.

The confrontation with his father proved to be the turning point in the life of thirteen-year-old George Ranft. He left home for good and learned to depend on himself to survive the mean streets of New York.

Although he couldn't guess where his life was heading, he was sure of two things. "I did know definitely I wanted people to know my name, and I wanted them to be glad when I came around," he said.

But for the next three years, George's goals were far from being realized as he slept in subways, pool halls, empty lofts, or in mission halls. Occasionally he would sneak his way into a comfortable night's slumber in the lobby of a nickelodeon at closing time. For eating money he worked a variety of menial jobs, including shoveling snow, selling newspapers, helping in a grocery store, ushering at the Rialto Theater, and, briefly, apprenticing as an electrician. He even rode the rails to Upstate New York counties where he would pick cherries for twenty-five cents a day.

Ironically, this last attempt at honest employment resulted in George's one and only brush with jail, when he was locked up by a railroad cop for vagrancy in Troy, New York.

Often George's circumstances became so dire that he was forced to resort to the petty crime skills he had learned to perfect. He devised a method to cheat the telephone company by slipping coins into the slot which he'd then pull back with a piece of string. He covered his transportation needs by acquiring counterfeit subway tokens and even police badges. When he needed quick meal money, he wasn't averse to rolling a drunk.

George managed to eke out a survival on his hustling and thievery skills, but as he matured he realized that his limited education and lack of marketable skills assured him of a likewise desperate future.

George thought that sports might be the answer. At age seventeen, he decided to take a shot at a baseball career. "I would have traded ten years of my life for a chance to play professional baseball," George later said.

He had played some semi-pro ball, and finally talked his way into a tryout with a minor-league club in Springfield, Massachusetts. George lasted just two days as an outfielder before the manager told him that while he was an okay fielder, he couldn't bat. George was released from his dream and, discouraged and depressed, returned to New York.

Once again, George found himself contemplating a bleak future — and then he saw another opportunity to maybe earn quick money in sports. He'd spent many a night watching the fights at the New Polo Athletic Club on 129th Street. George was an enthusiastic spectator, often seen mimicking the jabs and punches of the more promising club fighters. He had proved himself a skilled street fighter, with a lightning-fast left. Perhaps he could become a prizefighter.

He expressed his interest to a penny-ante fight manager named Maxie Greenburg, who, impressed with the kid's enthusiasm, one night offered George five dollars to appear as a substitute. Much to George's surprise, he won the decision. George's subsequent ring career was marginally distinguished. Adopting various names such as George LaSalle, George Brown and Brownie Ranft, he continued as a substitute in four-round preliminary matches — and out of the fourteen fights recorded in *Ring* magazine, he won nine matches, with three defeats and two draws. George's hope of becoming a professional pugilist ended the night he went up against a "windmill" named Frank Dougherty. George was knocked out in one round, but the damage inflicted upon him was such that it looked as though he'd been pummeled for the distance. Dougherty, soon to change his name to Frankie Jerome, left George with two black eyes, a broken nose, swollen jaw and an ear (the one that had almost been severed by Sammy Schwartz) that required twenty-two stitches to keep it attached to his head. George would later say with irony that the only reason he kept at boxing for so long was that he wanted a cauliflower ear to make him look like a pro.

Besides receiving the loser's purse of five dollars, the only benefit that came out of George's ring career was his association with Maxie Greenberg, who would later shorten his name to Mack Gray and become George's closest friend and confidante during Raft's Hollywood career.

Broke and unemployed, George was back on the street, supporting himself by pick pocketing and hustling. He frequented a pool hall on 166th Street called Crenshaw's where many a night he could beat a sucker for eating money.

One night he was challenged to a game by a short guy with a cocky attitude named William ("Billy") Rosenberg. Billy shot pool like a rookie, but it was George who ended up the chump when, by the end of the evening, he had lost every game and was now broke. Instead of being sore, the enterprising George decided to team up with Billy to work the hustle on unsuspecting "yokels." George would talk some sucker into betting against Billy, who made the wager more attractive by appearing clumsy and awkward with a pool stick, and then he and Billy would clean up.

"He was a real Houdini with a cue," George remembered. But Billy Rosenberg didn't have his sights set on becoming a professional pool hustler. One night while he and George were celebrating a score at Lindy's, a popular

"BIG EDDIE MEADE" (RIGHT) VISITS RAFT IN HOLLYWOOD. MEADE WAS RAFT'S FIGHT MANAGER WHEN HE WAS A BOXER BRIEFLY IN NEW YORK

Broadway delicatessen, Billy watched with awe and envy as two top songwriters of the time, Con Conrad and Ray Henderson, came into the restaurant and were given the deluxe treatment by the maitre d'.

"What d'ya figure those guys make a year?" Billy asked his pal. When George over bites of his pastrami sandwich estimated that their annual income was probably between seventy-five to a hundred grand, Billy became instantly fired with a new enthusiasm — one destined to leave a mark on the history of Broadway entertainment.

William Rosenberg soon stopped hanging around Crenshaw's. Instead, he concentrated on writing song lyrics. Among his many compositions were "That Old Gang of Mine," "It's Only a Paper Moon," "Me and My Shadow" and "Barney Google with the Goo Goo Googley Eyes." George Ranft's old pool partner would later enjoy even greater fame as the legendary Broadway producer Billy Rose. George was genuinely pleased with his friend's success, even if it meant that he again had to resort to picking pockets for meal money. He began hanging around dance halls because they provided the right atmosphere and certainly the ideal physical contact necessary for wallet lifting.

But collecting "pocket" change was not enough to satisfy George's craving for wealth. He remembered sitting around the Audubon Dance Hall and growing wild with envy watching the young hoods in candy-striped silk shirts flashing their rolls and having their pick of any girl in the place.

George's desire to own a candy-striped shirt was so great that he admitted to often being tempted to pull one off the first guy he could catch alone in a dark alley.

In his desperation for cash, George worked out a scam with a drugstore night clerk named Benny Lieberman, whereby George would go about the store shoplifting small but valuable items while Benny kept any customers who might come into the store occupied with small talk. George would later sell the merchandise at a discount to patrons at the dance hall and split the take with Benny. Eventually, with his share of the earnings, George happily purchased a half-dozen candy-striped silk shirts.

Another way George pocketed quick cash was by betting dance hall patrons that he could snap a belt around his chest just by inhaling a deep breath. George made a few bucks with this little stunt, but he also suffered a lot more by developing a chest hernia that contributed to the onset of the emphysema that was to plague him in later years.

George's long hours sitting around the Audubon or the Manhattan Casino waiting for the right "mark" eventually produced a less debilitating and more profitable side benefit. He began to study the dance techniques of many of the more-skilled patrons, and was soon copying their styles.

George had a natural aptitude for dancing: he was smooth, sexy — maybe even a little dangerous. He began to capitalize on this ability, and would practice for hours, exhibiting a tireless dedication that soon began to pay dividends as he entered and began to win dance contests.

George Ranft from Hell's Kitchen was finally beginning to make a legitimate name for himself.

But rather than acknowledge his son's success, Conrad Ranft was bitterly disappointed. With World War I raging across Europe, three of George's younger brothers, Michael, Joseph and Anthony, had responded to their father's patriotic fervor and joined America in its fight against his fatherland of Germany, only to be killed in combat.

George would later endure two more family tragedies when his brother William, too young to serve overseas, later took a job as a construction laborer and was killed when he fell from a skyscraper scaffold. Perhaps the death that most affected George, however, was when his sister Catherine, a sickly child for whom he had a particular fondness, finally succumbed to the tuberculosis that she had contracted in 1920.

Such hardships often bring families closer — and while it was too late for a bond to be forged between George and his father, there would always be a deep and special love between Eva and her son. Although she was often critical of his wayward lifestyle and concerned about his future, she remained his greatest supporter and was very proud once George began to achieve recognition as a dancer.

George loved to experiment with his dancing, and he re-stylized a favorite dance number of the time, the Charleston. George wowed audiences with his triple-time rendition of the song, and it wasn't long before many of New York's more upscale dance clubs such as Rector's and Healy's were requesting George as an entertainer.

George didn't just dance expertly, he also created a "look." He would dress in tight-fitting clothes, slick his hair back with a whole jar of Vaseline and maintain an immobile, mask-like expression on his face that suggested both mystery and eroticism. The combination proved wildly irresistible to the ladies in attendance.

Although his evenings were profitably booked, George, ever hungry for money, needed a way to fill his days and began working as a "taxi-dancer" in Churchill's tea room. Here, he would be paid $2.00 an afternoon plus tips to dance with lonely and often-homely patrons, who on occasion might request a more intimate after-hours rendezvous. Through this work, George would later acquire a reputation he despised, and one that would follow him into Hollywood: as a "gigolo." Conversely, he would enjoy the acquaintance of his fellow tea room dancer Rodolpho Guglielmo, only a few years from becoming one of the movies' first romantic superstars, Rudolph Valentino.

Valentino would achieve screen immortality as *The Sheik* (1921) and *The Son of the Sheik* (1926), along with starring in such silent screen triumphs as *The Four Horsemen of the Apocalypse* (1921) and *Blood and Sand* (1922). Sadly, his career, if not his fame, would be short-lived. Rudolph Valentino died of peritonitis after an appendix operation on August 23, 1926 at age 31. George Raft remembered seeing him only weeks before his death when Valentino invited him for a visit at the Long Island estate he was renting. Valentino was professionally successful, but George remembered him this day as a terminally unhappy man.

"It's all been great," Valentino sadly said to him, "but I am a lonely man."

Valentino's untimely death would later provide George with many offers from entrepreneurs eager to cash in on George's striking resemblance to the sexy star. George was once offered $1,500 per week if he would agree to tour with Valentino's widow Jean Acker. But, to his credit, George refused to accept these ghoulish propositions.

After leaving Churchill's, George decided to put even more serious effort into his dancing, honing his skills as well as supplementing his income by continuing to participate in weekend dance competitions, or performing dance exhibitions either at Palisades Park in New Jersey or Staten Island. This, of course, in addition to playing his regular evening shows at Rector's and Healy's.

It was a dizzying existence, but George loved every minute of it. Since he was never a big eater and did not require much sleep, George maintained his hectic schedule fueled by a sheer enthusiasm for his work.

George would later say that during this period his whole life revolved around dancing. As a basically shy, insecure man, he wasn't after the fame. He wanted the money. As he remembered, "I got ten dollars for those solos in New York, not counting anything I could steal. Fifteen bucks in Brooklyn, and twenty-five if I had to go to Jersey. "

By 1920, George had become a dance headliner. Life was moving along smoothly, if busily, for the ambitious young hoofer, and he was pleased that with his earnings he was able to provide at least a few comforts for his mother.

With his small Wanamaker promotions, Conrad had finally been able to move his family away from Hell's Kitchen and into a flat on 166th Street. But Conrad never welcomed George's visits. He was especially hurt and upset that George had decided to shorten his surname to Raft. George knew this, and so whenever he wanted to drop by to see his mother for coffee cake and cocoa, he'd always first make sure that his father wasn't home.

Eva delighted in listening to George talk about his latest dancing triumphs. On occasion, she even partnered him in flatfoot waltz competitions where the object was to glide across the floor without losing the dime placed under the heel.

It appeared as if Eva's fears concerning her son's future were proving unfounded. This was further emphasized when an agent signed George to dance in his first legitimate theater, the Union Square Theater, on 14th Street. George admitted to being nervous as a cat, but once the music started he instantly fell into the rhythm and ultimately received five curtain calls.

Dancer Vi Kearney worked with George around this time and said, "Oh yes, I knew him. We were in a big show together. Sometimes, to eke out our miserable pay, we'd do a dance act after the show at a club and we'd have to walk back home because all the buses had stopped for the night by that time. He'd tell me how he was going to be a big star one day and once he said that when he'd made it how he'd make sure to arrange a Hollywood contract for me. I just laughed and said: 'Come on, Georgie, stop dreaming. We're both in the chorus and you know it.'"

But George was persistent in his ambitions. He continued to seek out new dance styles. He began frequenting Harlem clubs, where he studied and perfected the dance steps of such great African-American entertainers as Bill "Bojangles" Robinson. When George performed these dances along Broadway, he was wildly applauded.

George's next career upswing occurred in 1920, when he was asked to audition for a job with Elsie Pilcer and Dudley Douglas, two of the top dancers of the day. George passed his tryout and found himself booked into the Orpheum and the B.F. Keith Circuits, where the trio played vaudeville engagements across the country, eventually returning to headline in top Broadway clubs.

George Raft's amazing footwork soon had him billed as "The Fastest Dancer in the World." His signature dance tune was "Sweet Georgia Brown." Besides the Charleston, George soon mastered the intricate steps of a dance called the Peabody. His commitment to perfection was so total that, to prevent the pain of an injury that might halt or inhibit his performance, he laced his shoes with piano wire, tying them tightly to cut off the circulation to his feet and numb all feeling. George recalled once breaking a toe during a fast number and not realizing it until the next day because his feet were so deadened from the tight constriction.

Years later when chastised by another noted hoofer named James Cagney about the dangers of such a technique, George admitted that he would sometimes get pale green around the mouth, as if he were suffering a mild heart attack. However, at this point, George was so heady with success there wasn't much he wouldn't do to further his career.

Despite Eva Ranft's joy over her son's achievements, she felt that George's own happiness would not be complete without the love of the right woman. George's erotic dances, accentuated by his slick, patent-leather Valentino look, left him with no shortage of potential amours, but he was not ready to settle in to a permanent relationship. He was committed to his work, and was earning good money, although he had already developed the reputation of being a lavish spender.

Life had finally taken a positive turn for the former street kid who just a few short years earlier often didn't know where he would sleep or where his next meal was coming from.

And then, George Raft's professional world was dealt a sudden blow when, at 12:01 a.m. on January 17, 1920, a new law came into effect that would change the lives of Americans for over a decade. The ratification of the 18th Amendment to the Constitution of the United States, thereafter known as the National Prohibition Act, forbade the manufacture, import or distribution of all alcoholic beverages. The passing of this unpopular law would be swiftly exploited by the nation's criminal element throughout a violent, reckless decade. A turbulent period that would provide a surprising career transition for a street hustler-turned-athlete-turned-professional Broadway dancer named George Raft.

CHAPTER TWO

"I WAS TOUGH AND I WAS COCKY BECAUSE I CARRIED A GUN IN MY POCKET AND WORKED FOR THE GANG BOSS OF NEW YORK."

GEORGE RAFT

During George Raft's later years, he was often given to sleepless nights of introspection, and he would pad into the bathroom of his modest Beverly Hills bachelor apartment for a sleeping pill, glance at his reflection in the mirror and bluntly ask himself, "Am I a gangster?"

It may have been a question that a quieter, more sedate Raft had difficulty reflecting upon, but for many others who knew him during his earlier years, the answer was hardly in doubt. If it is true that one's reputation is based on his affiliations, then George Raft truly was connected to the underworld.

Yet it has always been a matter of debate just how deep his involvement was.

Friend and future co-star James Cagney provided his insight. "He was of the underworld, yet not in the underworld. From Al Capone down, he knew them all. The worst hoods you could imagine."

Famed director John Huston offered his own trenchant, yet oddly vague, observation regarding Raft's "fascination" with gangland. "He was very much a Mafia type and liked to display it."

In a 1967 newspaper article, George Raft vehemently denied any direct association with the underworld, stating, "I'm not a member of any mob. I never was."

Yet, he'd clearly contradicted himself because just ten years earlier in a series of articles published in *The Saturday Evening Post*, he made the statement, "Sometimes I wish I had really been a top man in the gangs instead of a movie star. There would have been no misleading grays. Only black."

Raft biographer Lewis Yablonsky was another person who experienced George's contradictory stance when it came to the mob. As Yablonsky offered, one day Raft would deny any underworld affiliations, the next he would speak fondly about the hoods he had known.

Maybe George Raft did not want to become known as a gangster, particularly not onscreen after he had become a star. As he once explained in his refusal to play an underworld role, "It's not what you are that counts — but what people think you are." But the era made the man. Many of Raft's most notorious associations were formed during this period. Men with names like "Scarface" Al Capone, "Mad Dog" Vincent Coll, Charles "Lucky" Luciano, "Machine Gun" Jack McGurn and Benjamin "Bugsy" Siegel.

"I knew them all," George admitted in later years, at a time when the die had been cast and no further harm could be done to his reputation. "They were guys I looked up to. They were interesting company and when you talked to them, as I did, you learned a lot. Over dinner at a nightclub or restaurant, they were more fun and laughs than any businessman or studio head I ever met."

George's closest underworld tie would always be with his boyhood chum, Owney Madden. However, "Duke" Madden had been out of circulation since 1914, serving a 20-year manslaughter rap in Sing Sing for the killing of a hoodlum upstart named Patsy Doyle. But within the next few years Madden would be released from prison and become a major influence both on George's excursions into crime and his show business aspirations.

The decade started out miserably for George. Prohibition had closed the doors on most of the venues where he had made his living. Beer was always a more profitable draw than entertainment, so George's engagements became fewer once the selling of liquor became taboo.

George returned to entering dance competitions to make a few bucks. But he continually lost to a short, beefy contestant who wowed the judges with a dance called the Whirlwind, which George described as watching a "sawed-off silo spinning at about 500 r.p.m." This rotund marvel later proved that he did know about fancy footwork, because Al Weill, "The Whirlwind Man," would become the mastermind behind Rocky Marciano's undefeated heavyweight boxing career.

During this lean period, George went to work at the College Arms at Coney Island, a place he called "Siberia with bathing suits and popcorn." Here, he earned a measly twenty bucks a week for dancing eight shows a day. George finally quit the grueling schedule when he realized he could more easily steal twenty dollars a week.

Fortunately, the piano player at another Coney Island club, the College Inn, quickly offered George a job at his establishment. "Ragtime" Jimmy Durante was a most unlikely celebrity, possessed of a gravelly voice and pronounced proboscis, but he was a favorite with the Coney Island customers. Jimmy would hammer the piano keys as George broke into an energetic Charleston. Durante's popularity soon secured him backing to open his own nightclub on West 58th Street called the Club Durant, and he remembered George and offered him a dancing gig.

While Durante could not afford to put George on payroll, George made enough money off tips thrown at him following his specialty dances to more than cover his living expenses. Durante even went further and told George that if he was ever short of cash to help himself to a few bucks from the cash register. Once George took him up on his offer, and was rewarded by having the cash drawer slammed on his fingers by the uninformed cashier.

Eventually, the Club Durant became profitable enough for George to be hired as a regular act. George was thrilled because now he was considered a "member of the lodge."

Perhaps part of the reason for the Club Durant's success was its fronting for one of New York's largest floating crap games. These crap games were held in a small garage beneath the club that could only be accessed by a connecting staircase through a back room. It was here that George got to know many of the top names of the New York underworld, most notably a sharp Jewish gambler named Arnold Rothstein, a minor-league mobster whose reputation exceeded his talents, Waxey Gordon, and a ruthless bootlegger named Larry Fay. It was always presumed that "A.R." (Rothstein) bankrolled Durante's club. Another high roller who frequented the club was George McManus, who would later be tried and acquitted for the 1928 murder of Rothstein.

George was making okay money with his dance gigs, but he was awed by the thousands of dollars that exchanged hands at the basement-level crap table. Although George could never play in their league, he was often made present when cops would stage a "bogus" police raid. He was hired as a stand-in to cover for the big-roller boys who would exit out the rear once the raid warning was given. Raft would give a phony name when arrested and would always walk free when charges were dismissed. His work as a "pigeon" paid George $5 per pinch, and he felt generously rewarded.

George was looked upon as a "stand-up" guy by his gangster pals, who also genuinely appreciated his polished dancing skills, and as their bootleg clubs opened up throughout New York, they often asked George to perform a few numbers. Their motives were not entirely altruistic; George's dances were usually performed at such a swift, sweaty pace that patrons would anticipate his thirst and down their drinks faster, requiring immediate refills.

Perhaps the irony is that had George Raft's drinking habits been indicative of the nation, there never would have been the need for Prohibition. George detested alcohol. He disliked the taste, but more particularly the horrible toll drinking took on people during the so-called "dry years." He was witness to the violence that erupted not only through gang warfare, but even by the average speakeasy patron who would have "one too many" and then want to break up the joint. George also knew that some of the "cheap" bootleg suppliers would even add potentially poisonous ingredients into their brew just to profit from customer demand.

In a surprise and sudden move, George finally married in 1923. His bride was Grayce Mulrooney, an attractive social worker whose uncle would later become the New York City Police Commissioner under corrupt mayor Jimmy Walker. George and Grayce's union was doomed from the start, due to Grayce's ongoing affairs, which she admitted to George after their nuptials. But, apparently, George was willing to see if things could be worked out between them. He was playing an engagement in Philadelphia, and after the show, the couple went to a speakeasy where Grayce downed shots of booze like a champ while George ordered a soda. George's "soda" turned out to be home brew and he became temporarily blinded by the ingestion of bad liquor. His head swirling in a kaleidoscopic fog of contaminated alcohol and his wife's admissions, he made the decision then and there to end his so-called marriage, and was frustrated that his condition prevented him from beating the brains out of his smarmy server.

George Raft would eventually earn the reputation as one of Hollywood's most notorious ladies' men; his bedroom prowess legendary among starlets and hookers, his exploits eclipsing even that of Errol Flynn. Yet on the night of consummating his marriage, George Raft, the inveterate teetotaler, was literally blind drunk.

But that was not the worst of it. He was locked into a loveless marriage from which he could not escape. Not legally. Either out of vindictiveness or greed Grayce would not consent to a divorce, and, ironically, as a result, George Raft, the fabulous Broadway and later Hollywood playboy, would hold the record for one of Hollywood's longest marriages, lasting 47 years and ending only with Grayce's death in 1970.

To perhaps compensate for this mistake, George maintained a grueling work schedule. He continued to earn his living by dancing in clubs where the main trade was plying customers with booze, and where he was rubbing shoulders with some of the most notorious hoodlums of the era.

Under such conditions, it was difficult for George Raft to stay respectable. As he would later say: "If you were an entertainer on Broadway during those days you would have to be blind and lame not to associate with gangsters. Look, they owned the clubs."

Beyond his dancing chores he was often asked to perform special "favors" for his employers. His boyhood friend Owney Madden had finally been released from prison and went to work supplying liquor to the various nightclubs owned by gangster Larry Fay. Often, when Madden was short-handed, he would ask George to help on liquor runs and with other duties.

George maintained at least a semblance of legitimate employment when he was offered a $150 per week dancing gig at Larry Fay's El Fey Club, which was located at 107 West 45th Street. He was hired at the urging of Mary Cecilia "Texas" Guinan, a former Sunday school teacher who worked as the club's official hostess, and whose famous greeting to patrons was "Hello, suckers!"

By 1924, the El Fey Club was "the" nightspot for society swells and upper class hoodlums — and not a place that could afford to dispense inferior liquor to its clientele. Frequently, when the demand exceeded supply, Owney would be forced to hijack quality booze shipments. Again, he prevailed upon George to lend a hand.

One of Madden's and Fay's cronies was a hood named "Feets" Edson. It was "Feets" who taught George the intricacies of how to drive a car "gangland" style. These lessons would prove invaluable not only at the time in evading cops or rival gangsters, but many years later during the shooting of a film with Humphrey Bogart and Ann Sheridan.

George Raft the entertainer led a double life as George Raft the fringe gangster. Many nights after finishing his exhausting act, George, still in his tuxedo, would leave the club and lead a convoy of beer trucks from Owney Madden's 26th Street brewery to a specified location, where he would then turn the fleet over to Dutch Schultz or another Larry Fay associate.

The money George pocketed from these extra chores provided a nice supplement to his already-impressive dance income, but earning quick cash was not his sole reason for participating in these risky escapades. George felt an unbending loyalty to his friends in the rackets.

"To me, these men were not criminals," George would later say. "They were the only heroes we had to look up to in my neighborhood. And when they'd pat me on the back and tell me that I was an OK guy — it was like an orphan getting the nod from John D. Rockefeller."

Of course, George always retained a special fondness for Owney Madden. "I do not pretend that I would have sidestepped the more violent chores while working for Madden," he said. "I liked Madden and I owed him more than I could repay." In fact, everybody liked Owney: entertainers, newspapermen, even cops and politicians. Broadway columnist Ed Sullivan said, "It was like knowing the mayor to know Madden."

One of George's less-risky duties for Madden involved picking up the receipts of a popular Broadway show Owney had a large investment in called *Diamond Lil*. It was at the Royale that George first met the play's star, Mae West. Apparently, their business transactions quickly turned into passionate, if not romantic, interludes, which they fulfilled through rendezvous in West's dressing room, hotel suites, and even, on occasion, in the backseat of Owney's Packard.

George was exactly what Mae West wanted in a man: sleek, dark, graceful, slightly sinister, and she later said, "He was one guy I would have married … if I could have."

Mae was so smitten with George that she considered him for a part in a new play she was writing called *Sex*. But as she later said, George seemed nervous and unsure of himself as a serious actor.

Actor Jack LaRue was another of West's potential paramours during this time and, shortly before his death in 1984, spoke of Mae West's attraction to George Raft.

"I'd auditioned to play a Spaniard in *Diamond Lil*, and knowing nothing about the language, prepared for the audition by learning a few of the easier words. Between that and a passionate love scene we (Mae and I) virtually improvised, I got the part. Well, I'll tell you, our love scenes didn't stop on stage. It was a funny kind of reversal once George and Mae began their affair. Mae was the one who was more subdued in our relationship, but with George — and I know she really fell for the guy — she didn't care who knew it."

George admitted that he was attracted to the sultry Mae West, but given his marital status it wasn't surprising he did not want to publicize their affair. In those days, such infidelity could have cost him dearly, and George was just now starting to rebuild his career. He would, however, always consider Mae a cherished friend, and, in fact, would later prove instrumental in launching her on her legendary Hollywood career.

But, in the meantime, George continued his work at the El Fey Club, where between shows he often surrendered to envy when watching the big spenders. One night, after George was finishing his act, he was heckled by two overstuffed drunks sitting at a ringside table. George later followed one of them into the men's room where he lifted $500 from his pocket. Proud of his prize, George showed it to Texas Guinan, who told George that he'd just clipped one of the club's most valued patrons, Wilson Mizner, soon to be a top Hollywood screenwriter, who that night was in the company of James Rolph, Mayor of San Francisco.

Apologizing for his blunder, the next night George sheepishly attempted to return the money to Mizner, who instead handed the bills back to Raft, and with a hearty laugh said that anyone who could lift five hundred bucks from him deserved to keep it.

Mizner also dispensed a valuable piece of advice that George never forgot. "Remember, son — always say hello to everybody on the way up, because you'll meet the same people coming down."

George was relieved that in this instance things had turned out well, but it didn't discourage him from going after other tempting targets. "It was a poor week when I wasn't able to get my hands on $1000, one way of the other," he said. George's maneuvers were often bold, and he even had the audacity to clip the notorious Harry K. Thaw, the wealthy playboy whose 1906 murder of architect Stanford White became one of the most celebrated crimes of the early century, of $750 on a dare from Feets Edson.

This proved another mistake.

The following evening George was hustled into a corner by Big Frenchie DeMange, who accused him of taking the $750 from Thaw. George confessed and DeMange ordered him to return the money to Thaw immediately. George complied without protest.

George learned through experience never to argue with the big boys, but sometimes such acquiescence could have potentially dire consequences.

There was the night when George was having dinner after a late show in a Third Avenue speakeasy in the Bronx. Mobster Dutch Schultz and his entourage were seated at a table next to George's. Suddenly, the police raid buzzer sounded and Schultz calmly took his own gun and those from his three bodyguards and deposited them inside the pockets of George's overcoat, which Raft had placed over a chair next to him. When the cops frisked Schultz and his boys, they were surprised to find that each was clean.

Finally, the cops left and Schultz quickly collected the guns. Had George been discovered with the weapons, he would have had to stoically bear the consequences, which may have included jail time. Yet, Schultz never even gave George a thank you. Perhaps that was why out of all his gangster acquaintances, George never spoke too fondly about Dutch Schultz.

Or Larry Fay.

Fay had given George a well-paying dancing job at his club, but he was a man with psychotic tendencies whom one did not cross. Fay not only considered George his employee, but, indeed, his property. George vividly recalled the night when Fay told him that he would be going for a "boat ride." The purpose was to hijack a French freighter anchored in the harbor and strip the ship of its cargo, which happened to be five hundred cases of imported whisky, brandy and wine. George, along with the other gun-toting "pirates," was paid $10 for the job.

George knew he was risking a federal rap if caught, and he soon after began to ease off on his criminal sidelines. His reputation as a dancer was once more steadily on the rise. He was taking every booking he could handle, playing four venues in one day — from nightclubs to theaters.

"I saw too many shooting stars on Broadway," George explained. "Those who were big for a while and then just vanished. I was determined that wouldn't happen to me."

Although George was still married, he saw little of his wife. He paid her a small percentage of his earnings while he dated many of the most beautiful showgirls of the day. He frequently asked Grayce for a divorce, but she refused out of her so-called devout Catholicism — a claim that George never accepted.

An unhappy occurrence happened when George made one of his periodic visits to his mother. Depression and disappointment had finally taken their toll on Conrad Ranft and he was frequently not able to work. George quietly handed over money to Eva to keep the family coffers intact. But on one visit, the embarrassing truth was uncovered.

"I went to see her one evening and I was wearing a tight-fitting, velvet-collar overcoat which was popular among gangsters in those days. I was carrying a .38 police special in a sling under my arm, which she immediately noticed, I guess from the bulge. She questioned me, but what could I say? The jig was up. Then she told me that as long as I was doing 'that kind of dancing,' it'd be better if I didn't come over anymore. It was years before I saw her again."

When George did next see his mother, things had changed. He'd had a smash hit playing the role of George Spelvin in the Charles B. Dillingham production of *The City Chap*, which ran for seventy-two performances at the Liberty Theater on 42nd Street in 1925, and where George was even given a specialty number. Eva Ranft put aside her concerns and proudly embraced her son's Broadway success. As did Conrad Ranft. George's father would die in 1927, while his son was in Hollywood, but not before acknowledging with pride his son's marquee billing (even with the 'n' missing from the surname) at the Palace, an engagement that had been instrumented by George's old pool hall pal, Billy Rose.

George would later recall that from the time he left home at thirteen he maybe saw his father five times, and that they rarely spoke when they were together. Conrad was beyond arguing with his son by this point. He only offered the same words: "You're on your own in this world."

"We were like strangers," George said sadly.

Yet, in 1926, an ailing Conrad Ranft could point up to his son's name now prominently in lights along Broadway and boast to his co-workers or anyone else who happened by, "That's my son."

George admitted to "crying like a baby" when he received the news of his father's death.

CHAPTER THREE

"THOSE EARLY DAYS IN HOLLYWOOD WERE HEARTBREAKERS."

GEORGE RAFT

The death of his father was just one of the transitions occurring in George Raft's personal and professional life during the waning days of Prohibition. Another change soon to happen would elevate Broadway hoofer George Raft to the heights of Hollywood stardom. In George's whirlwind lifestyle it all seemed as though it had happened in an instant, but there were still a few hard roads yet to travel.

Around 1925, George was approached by a young fighter named Maxie Rosenbloom about maybe investing in his boxing career. George put up a few dollars but told the aspiring pugilist that he didn't look tough enough because his face was unmarred. Some weeks later, Maxie burst into George's apartment and proudly displayed a cauliflower ear. George was impressed, but was annoyed that Maxie had obviously been fighting without him in his corner. "You got me wrong, George," Maxie replied. "I ain't had any fights. I jus' kept hittin' it myself until it comes out like dis."

A professional high point occurred in 1926 when George embarked on a successful dance tour of Europe. During this trip he received an invitation to meet Edward, the Prince (later the Duke) of Wales. Although admittedly nervous at such a prestigious introduction, George was immediately put at ease by the Prince, whom he found to be a "regular guy," who encouraged George to tell him stories about his life in America, particularly the colorful gangsters and entertainers whom Raft knew or had an acquaintance. The two hit it off so well that the Prince even asked George to teach him how to dance, particularly the Charleston. George began visiting York House every day, guiding the Prince through various routines. As a token of appreciation, the Prince presented George with an engraved gold cigarette lighter that would remain one of Raft's most treasured possessions.

Back in New York in 1927, George was able to capitalize on his European success when he was asked by Owney Madden to dance with Texas Guinan at the Club Argonaut. This led to an even bigger opportunity when he appeared with Guinan at the Shubert Theater on Broadway in the revue *Padlocks of 1927*. During this time, Raft was happy to once more make the acquaintance of his old boxing sponsor, Maxie Greenberg (Mack Gray), who was still attempting to make inroads as a fight manager.

George was now a big name on Broadway, but he never played the part — especially when it came to old friends.

Despite, or perhaps because of, his celebrity, George continued to hobnob with big shots in the underworld. Part of the reason was his unwavering loyalty to his old pals. Another possibility may have been the changing climate of latter-day Prohibition New York.

Violence was spreading throughout the underworld as gangsters greedily attempted to add to their considerable profits and maintain tight control over their assets, which included popular club entertainers, some of whom were suddenly offered more lucrative opportunities elsewhere.

In Chicago, 1927, for example, singer Joe E. Lewis expressed his desire to move on from the Green Mill cabaret, a club partly owned by chief Capone trigger man, "Machine Gun" Jack McGurn. Lewis's career ambitions were frowned upon by McGurn, who, on the night of November 10, ordered three of his henchmen to burst into Lewis's hotel suite. The gangsters then proceeded to beat and knife-slash Lewis to the point of death. Miraculously, Lewis survived this vicious assault, though his gashed throat and other brutal injuries necessitated a long recovery. This violent act did not sit well with Al Capone, who was genuinely fond of entertainers and often welcomed them into the city by providing lavish dinner parties and presenting them with expensive gifts. Apparently, Capone even advanced Lewis $10,000 until he could recover sufficiently to resume his career.

McGurn did not stay in Capone's disfavor for long. He would later make amends with his boss in a big way by masterminding — if not participating in — gangland's greatest coup: The St. Valentine's Day Massacre.

George was wise enough never to deliberately look for trouble with the big shots – there were a lot of loose cannons like Dutch Schultz around — but he knew that if problems should arise, he could always depend on his friendship with Owney Madden to smooth the road.

Unfortunately, Madden was away on a trip when Larry Fay asked George to join both him and Texas Guinan on a train trip to Miami where they were planning to open a new nightspot.[3] George politely declined Fay's "invitation." He was committed to several Broadway shows and did not relish the thought of spending time away in Florida.

George remembered that Fay had a habit of fingering an ear while licking his lips when in a homicidal mood. He was animated in that gesture when he said to Raft: "Texas won't like it. But at least you'll see her off, yeah?" George agreed, he really had no choice, but he was apprehensive. The next morning when he went to Penn Station, he kissed Texas but as he put out his hand to shake Fay's, the gangster threw George an uppercut that put him out like a light.

George awoke and found himself shanghaied on a train bound for Florida. When the train pulled into North Philadelphia, George smashed the compartment window with a metal water bottle, climbed out through the broken glass and walked along the tracks until he could get out of the station and hail a cab that would take him back to New York.

George had played a dangerous move against a formidable adversary, and his only hope was to secure the protection of Owney Madden, who was possibly the only man in New York from whom Fay would back down.

The problem was … Madden still hadn't returned to the city.

Those were nervous days for George. He was afraid to go to sleep or unlock his hotel room door. When he'd drop in at Madden's office to check on his whereabouts, the young hoodlums would look away and refuse to speak to him.

He even began receiving telephone calls where an unidentified voice would whisper, "You'll get it."

George was dating an actress named Molly O'Day at the time. George was frightened for her safety, as well, and was glad when she was offered a job in California. Molly wanted George to see her off at the station, and though at first hesitant, he agreed to meet her at Grand Central Station. George escorted both Molly and her sister to their Pullman car, but as he kissed them goodbye, he noticed three men, hands buried deep in their overcoat pockets, walking toward him. George recognized two of the men – one, a thug named Brocco, was a paid killer.

George managed to move quickly, jumping onboard and slamming the door of the Pullman in their faces, and he rode along with the train until he exited at 125th Street. George disappeared from the city for the next two weeks. Then he called one of the people he knew he could trust, Big Frenchie DeMange, who told him that Owney was back and that he'd straightened things out.

Owney provided a novel solution to his pal's predicament. Texas Guinan had been contracted by Warner Brothers to appear in a movie loosely based on her life, to be called *Queen of the Night Clubs*. Owney suggested that George travel to Hollywood with her as a kind of companion/bodyguard.

George quickly agreed. He knew that Larry Fay was a man to bear a grudge and that the climate in New York was starting to become a little too unhealthy for him. Owney generously advanced George a substantial fee for his services and reputedly even asked Texas to find a part in the picture for George

It was in 1929 that George Raft made his screen debut. Although the future movie mobster first appeared before motion picture cameras performing a frenetic Charleston in Tex Malone's (Guinan) nightclub, the scene strangely never made it past the cutting room floor. Fortunately, George himself was not totally cut out of the final print and can be seen waving a baton before a nightclub orchestra.

Queen of the Night Clubs was an early talkie with a melodramatic storyline reminiscent of the durable *Madame X*. It caused no sensation at the box office, and neither did Raft. While in Hollywood, George managed to secure two further dance "bits," again for Warners in Roy Del Ruth's Technicolor *Gold Diggers of Broadway* and the uncredited role of Georgie Ames in RKO's *Side Street* (both 1929).

George returned to New York, but he quickly discovered that the Broadway he knew was rapidly disappearing, along with job offers. The rackets were changing and there was serious talk about the government repealing the Prohibition Act. Owney felt the time was right to have a long talk with George about his future. Since things were getting hot for him as well, especially with the psychopathic former Dutch Schultz lieutenant Vincent "Mad Dog" Coll running wild and brazenly challenging the city's mob leaders, Madden suggested that George join him on a car trip to Hollywood, with George handling the driving chores.[4] George had already had a very small taste of the movies, and enjoyed it, and Owney figured that with George's good looks and talent he could have a real shot at making it in the picture business. Madden so believed in his friend's potential that he even agreed to stake George while he attempted to break into pictures.

Prohibition was soon to pass into history, but a new cloud with even more devastating consequences was about to descend upon the American landscape when, on October 24, 1929, Wall Street collapsed, plunging the country into an era of economic despair known as the Great Depression. Initially, Hollywood was spared the effects of the Depression; indeed, the film community prospered as millions of people suddenly faced unemployment and looked to the movies as a way to escape a reality that was too frightening and uncertain to contemplate.

The Depression, however, had hit the Broadway Theater hard and so many performers who had previously thumbed their noses at motion pictures were now hastening to sign their names to lucrative movie contracts. The advent of sound provided many of these players with advantageous opportunities. Bette Davis, Clark Gable, Paul Muni, Edward G. Robinson, Spencer Tracy and a juvenile with a lisp named Humphrey Bogart were just a few of Hollywood's new acquisitions. Gable and Tracy both secured Hollywood contracts based on their strong individual interpretations of the convict "Killer" Mears in the hit John Wexley play *The Last Mile*. Paul Muni likewise was sought by studio executives after playing the stage role of gangster Benny Horowitz in *Four Walls*, as was Edward G. Robinson for an unforgettable performance as mobster Nick Scarsi in *The Racket*. All four men survived their options and began their journey into screen history.

Ironically, Humphrey Bogart, destined to play the most vicious movie mugs of them all, was signed up for pictures based on his role as bank clerk Roger Baldwin in a Broadway play called *It's a Wise Child*. Unfortunately, Bogart failed to make an impact on movie audiences, and after ten features he would return to New York to pick up the crumbs of a previously hardly-dynamic stage career.

Now George Raft sought a movie career, but unlike the others (including his New York pal James Cagney, just signed to Warner Brothers to reprise his Broadway role of Harry Delano in the film *Sinner's Holiday*, 1930) he hadn't proven his abilities as an actor with dramatic possibilities. He'd performed in a couple of well-received Broadway shows, but only as a dancer and, of course, his three cinematic ventures had also showcased him in the same role.

George took up residence in the modest Mark Twain Hotel on Wilcox Avenue, where his gambling, penchant for high living and expansive generosity quickly exhausted the sizeable bankroll provided him by Owney Madden.

Before long, George was again on the downside of his rags-to-riches-to-rags lifestyle. As he later stated with irony, "My so-called resemblance to Valentino wasn't causing any stampedes."

Part of George's problem was that he feared rejection, and, acutely aware of his limited education and lack of accepted social skills, he avoided putting himself in situations where he might face embarrassment.

"When it came to sports or dames or the names of the big shots running New York, I was all right," George later explained. "But as a Hell's Kitchen kid I was out of my league among polite social conversation in Hollywood. So I rarely opened my mouth unless I had to and kept away from parties, premieres, dinners and other places where I might be drawn into a conversation I couldn't handle. I hung around nightclubs, fights and the races where I could at least talk on my own level. People said that I was mysterious. In fact, I was lonely as hell."

Of course, possessed of such insecurity, it was difficult for him to adapt to the competitive nature of the movie business. He found the necessity of going on auditions both frustrating and humiliating. He always figured that the other actors lined up outside the casting director's office to read for a part were more capable than him, and he would often walk out before even giving himself a chance.

If George Raft's movie career was off to a slow start, his reputation as a man of questionable credentials was soon off and running.

Hollywood at the time was a small community where gossip was commonplace and, indeed, encouraged. In fact, gossip was the second major industry next to picture making, as proven by the popularity and proliferation of movie magazines and columns written by Hedda Hopper and Louella Parsons. A sharp newcomer like George, who frequently made the night scene, was instantly noticed and noted. It didn't take long for Hollywood insiders to discover that George had underworld connections, and in particular was a close friend of gangster Owney Madden. This actually made his presence appealing in some circles. But the local police also knew of his background, and almost from the moment he stepped off the train in California, George Raft's activities were closely monitored by the authorities.

On one occasion when George was short of cash, he sold one of his expensive suits for thirty dollars to a guy who also had a room at the Mark Twain. Just a couple of days later, George was collared in the lobby of the hotel by two tough-looking detectives who demanded to know if his name was Raft. George told them it was, at which point they frisked him and then questioned him about his whereabouts the night before. George told them that he had been sitting in the lobby all evening, which was later verified by the hotel clerks.

George discovered that the punk to whom he'd sold his suit was a professional stickup man who, when finally arrested, was wearing the suit, quickly identified because George liked all his clothing, from pajamas to tuxedos, to be personalized, and a label bearing his name "George Raft" was sewn into the inside pocket of the jacket.

George was off the hook, but the cops made it clear they didn't like "his kind" hanging around their city and that they'd be keeping a watch on him. They assumed that George's presence in Hollywood was to serve as a front for one of Owney Madden's illegal enterprises.

"I didn't have a job," George said, "and so to them it must have looked as if I was on some special assignment for the New York mob."

Actually, in a way, he was. Just a few days later, George got an urgent call from an East Coast mobster who said that one of the top underworld figures was trying to find his missing girlfriend, who supposedly was now in Hollywood and involved with an actor.

George was told the actor was Gary Cooper.

"Find her, Georgie," the hood said. "Or else this actor winds up on a slab." George agreed. He did some checking through his old friend Wilson Mizner, who gave George a lead to the girl's whereabouts. George rushed to the address, got the girl packed and hustled her aboard a train headed for Chicago.

George's ties to the underworld may have brought no end of negative repercussions to him, but in this instance and at least one other incident to be described later, his reputation very probably saved the life of a Hollywood superstar. George, however, later claimed that he never told Cooper about his "near miss," even after the two became good friends.

Such an experience probably provided George with some much-needed diversion. Still depressed about the way his so-called acting career was going, George took periodic trips back East to visit his mother and Owney Madden.

Apparently, Madden had spoken to a few people he knew in the industry about "giving his pal Georgie a break," but most bowed out with the explanation that, due to declining movie attendance, studios would soon be cutting back on more experienced personnel and that George Raft was still an unknown name.

At any rate, Owney Madden had his own troubles. His once-undisputed power in New York was waning with the emergence of a new breed of gangster: a triumvirate composed of "Lucky" Luciano, Meyer Lansky and "Bugsy" Siegel. These were ambitious characters possessed of vision (Luciano), brains (Lansky) and brawn (Siegel), who had formed a profitable allegiance during their back alley youth and excelled at their post-graduate underworld education, serving their most valuable practicum under the biggest shot of them all, Arnold Rothstein. Later, after Rothstein was killed, they went to work for Joe "the Boss" Masseria, whom Luciano suggested they double-cross to earn the favor of Masseria's bitter rival, Salvatore Maranzano, whom they also later killed in a clever coup. Owney Madden wasn't an Old World "Moustache Pete" as were Masseria and Maranzano, but he also represented the older breed of gangster whose policies were not conducive to the progress of the new national crime syndicate formulated by Luciano and his pals.

Madden had amassed a personal fortune from his various underworld enterprises and could well afford the "recommended" retirement in Hot Spring, Arkansas. He would live out a quiet, respectable life, unlike some of his contemporaries who would not knuckle under to Luciano and his newly-formed Commission. Case in point: Arthur Flegenheimer, the infamous Dutch Schultz. He managed to stay around a bit longer, but refused to accept the rulings of the new Syndicate. "Lucky" Luciano once said of the mercurial Schultz, "He's a bit of a loon. He can go from zero to psycho in seconds." When the Dutchman defied their order not to kill Special Prosecutor Thomas E. Dewey, who had indicted Schultz on various racketeering charges, Schultz was marked a liability, and on the evening of October 23, 1935, Dutch and three of his henchmen were ambushed by Syndicate gunmen at the Palace Chop House.

Larry Fay, George Raft's former boss, likewise met a similar fate. Fay, the one-time taxi driver, had fallen on hard times following the repeal of Prohibition. Ironically, he was forced to return to driving a hack until Owney Madden, ever sympathetic to a friend, set him up running a club called The Napoleon, situated in the old Woolworth Mansion on East 56th Street. Fay had hired a former cop as the club doorman, who, unbeknownst to him, hated gangsters, and on New Year's Day, 1933, the two got involved in a heated argument that resulted in the ex-cop pumping four bullets into Fay's back.

Larry Fay, the man whom George Raft had once feared, had even appealed to Raft during the actor's early days of Hollywood stardom to help him muscle into the city's taxicab business, a proposition that George firmly refused.[5]

Owney Madden had also reputedly asked George for a favor – a favor that Raft would later deny obliging.

One of Madden's post-Prohibition "enterprises" was managing fighters. His most promising discovery was a 6'6", 270-lb. Italian behemoth named

Primo Carnera. He had the fierce look of a devastating powerhouse; the only problem was he couldn't fight.

Madden shrewdly promoted Carnera, whose sheer physical presence quickly made him a crowd favorite, by arranging for his opponents (each of whom was more skilled and could have easily knocked the gentle giant into oblivion) to take a dive. However, a problem developed when an upcoming opponent, "Big Boy" Eddie Peterson, refused to forfeit the fight.

The story is that a few hours before the fight on January 24, 1930, George Raft visited Peterson in his suite at the Claridge Hotel with a bottle of cheap champagne and generously supplied him with a few calming drinks. By the time Peterson stepped into the ring he was groggy and awkward, and Carnera knocked him out in the first round.

The story of Primo Carnera is indicative of the crooked world of boxing at the time. After earning a reported $3 million dollars for Owney Madden and his associates, Carnera was let go and left the country with nary a nickel of his winnings after suffering a brutal beating at the hands of an honest fighter named Max Baer. This scandalous affair was later used as the basis for the 1956 Humphrey Bogart drama *The Harder They Fall*.

Whether or not George was involved in this scandal, he continued in his efforts to find work in pictures. Unable to afford even his modest lodgings at the Mark Twain Hotel, he was obliged to room with two old New York friends. One of whom was Ben Lieberman, formerly George's old New York partner in drugstore larceny, and now the co-owner along with his uncle of the Angelus Drugstore in downtown Los Angeles. Lieberman apparently had never forgot their previous thievery.

George recalled that even years later, after he had become a screen superstar, each time he walked into Lieberman's store, Ben would eye him suspiciously. George would joke, "It's okay, Ben. I've got all the perfume I need. I'll just lift a pack of cigarettes now and then."

Finally, it was Ben Lieberman who had fallen on hard times through his addiction to gambling, and at one point he appealed to George's well-known generosity to bail him out of a financial scrape. George, of course, complied, but Lieberman cheated him with some fancy financial maneuverings which, in fact, doubled George's original $2,500 loan, and before George could be repaid the $5,000 owed him, Lieberman put a bullet through his head.

The tide began to turn in George's favor during the summer of 1930. The afternoon following a night at the fights, George was sitting with some friends in the famous Brown Derby Restaurant, when director Rowland Brown approached his table. Brown, a former Detroit newspaperman who had once served jail time, was a friend of Owney Madden's and apparently had gone to the Derby specifically to meet Raft. Brown told George that he had seen him dance in vaudeville and might have a part for him in a picture he was planning to direct for Fox.

George admitted he didn't think the offer was serious. He said to Brown, "You'd better get someone to wake me. I sleep late and I sleep hard."

Fortunately, Brown was amused rather than offended by Raft's flippancy, and the next morning he had a film cutter named Barney Wolf waken Raft and drive him to the studio for his 8:00 A.M. appointment. He was being considered for the small role of Jimmy Kirk, Spencer Tracy's henchman in one of the era's earliest sound gangster dramas, *Quick Millions* (1931).

Raft remembered that the casting director, a man named Gardner, wanted to use a Fox contract player to play Jimmy Kirk and that it was Raft himself who settled the argument between Brown and Gardner by suggesting he test for the part. He recalled doing two scenes, in one of which he did a gangster bit, walking into a room crowded with tough guys and telling them that he was "taking over." The other test he performed with the future Mrs. Bing Crosby, Dixie Lee, and was used in the picture. It was a simple scene where Raft flirts with a secretary while Tracy is conducting "business" inside the office of a construction company. He says to her, "Say, honey, whaddaya do with your spare moments?" Miss Lee replies, "I go to wrestling shows." The test was a success and Raft was signed for his first important screen role.

Brown later admitted that his primary reason for casting George was that he knew of his New York background and that he would add "authenticity" to the movie.

Although coming up short in the early gangster movie sweepstakes, which included *Little Caesar, Doorway to Hell* (both 1930; the latter for which Rowland Brown had provided the story) and *The Public Enemy* (1931), *Quick Millions* is still a powerful story focusing on one ambitious man's ruthless climb to the top of the underworld. Daniel J. "Bugs" Raymond (Tracy) is a truck driver who admits that he's "too lazy to work and too nervous to steal." His credo is: "I do other people's thinking for them and make them like it." He organizes his own trucking association, demanding protection from his former fellow haulers, and later expands his empire to include extorting money from the city's building construction trade. Raymond attempts to become legitimate with his reluctant "partner" Kenneth Stone (John Wray), head of the construction firm his criminal tactics have infiltrated, and whose sister Dorothy (Marguerite Churchill) he has fallen for, this decision creating problems for his former associates. Dorothy, however, is engaged to marry another, and Raymond plans to thwart their wedding by kidnapping the bride. This rash decision provides Raymond's former associates the opportunity to eliminate their boss, who is assassinated en route to the church.

As Raymond's top hat rolls up the carpeted walkway, one gangster remarks, "Don't them society people have big weddings?"

To which his associate replies, "Yeah, but us hoodlums have the swell funerals."[6]

George Raft's role in the proceedings affords him plenty of screen time with the much-more accomplished Tracy, but he has little to do other than obediently carry out his boss's orders. Although initially loyal, Raft is lured into betraying Tracy by rival mobster Nails Markey (Warner Richmond), and this duplicity ultimately results in Raft's own death.

George is allowed two highlights in the film. He performs a quick cobra-like dance solo at an underworld party hosted by Tracy, and he commits the one graphic murder in the movie. Though his character is never seen pulling the trigger, the scene is effectively photographed from underneath a table, recording the gunshots and capturing the fall of the body.

While George's individual scenes are brief, within the film's 72-minute running time his Jimmy Kirk emerges as loyal, treacherous, ruthless, and ultimately cowardly.

George formed his first actor friendship with Spencer Tracy during the making of *Quick Millions*. But Tracy's insecurity in this new medium was also apparent, and a mutual wariness initially developed between the two film novices. According to Raft, Tracy lost his temper while the two actors were waiting to film a scene at the Lakeside Country Club. Raft had innocently carved the letters T and R in front of the A-C-Y already inscribed on the bench both were sitting on. The volatile Spencer thought George was carving his name and blew up at him. Raft responded in kind and Tracy soon backed down. The next day Tracy sheepishly approached George and told him that director Brown had said that Raft was going to get even with him for yelling at him by carving Tracy's name "on every shithouse in town." When George began to laugh, Tracy realized Brown had been kidding him and the two actors became good friends.

Critics were generous in their reviews of the film, with the National Board of Review calling *Quick Millions* "the most intelligent of the gangster films" and the *New York Times* praising the picture for being "exceedingly well directed and ably acted." George Raft's individual contribution, however, received no special notice, and in his next two movies under his two-picture contract deal with Fox, he descended even farther down the cast list.

He appeared uncredited as a pickpocket in a follow-up film with Tracy, the rarely-seen *Goldie*, which was also released in 1931. It seemed that whatever impression Raft had made upon producers and audiences with *Quick Millions* had yet to be fully realized.

Hush Money (1931) was another crime picture he made for Fox, and in this outing George appeared as Maxie, a small-time hood who, in his most impressive scene, sticks up a couple played by Joan Bennett and Hardie Albright in a park. About the only satisfaction George derived from this movie was the beginning of a long professional association and personal friendship with the lovely Miss Bennett, who would later recall Raft as the "most charming, most gentlemanly person I have ever had the pleasure of knowing."

Shortly after performing his bit in *Hush Money*, George was enjoying his favorite pastime, watching a ball game at Wrigley Field, when he was approached by Lieutenant Lefty James of the Los Angeles Police Department and asked to accompany him downtown.

Apparently, George's old girlfriend Molly O'Day had been robbed of all her money and jewels and George's shady background made him a prime suspect. The police chief called George a hood and advised him to be on the next train headed for New York. George replied that he was working in Hollywood as an actor, which was soon confirmed by Fox studio chief Winfield Sheehan.

However, this was the second time since arriving in Hollywood that George had been hauled in on "suspicion." As he later said, "I was off to a bad start with the local cops."

Fortunately, his film career continued, albeit in small roles. After *Hush Money*, George appeared in a somewhat larger part in an Eddie Cantor musical, *Palmy Days*, again playing … a gangster. Cantor was at the height of his popularity in 1931. He'd previously appeared in the two-strip Technicolor extravaganza *Whoopee!*, choreographed by Busby Berkeley. *Palmy Days* gave George a good showcase, even if his Joe the Frog is rather ineffectual. As one of crime boss Yolando's (Charles B. Middleton) henchmen, his major moments happen during the film's slapstick finale where his character is repeatedly knocked unconscious.

During the making of the film, George came to know two chorus girls, one of whom would later play an important role in his life.

The other was a beautiful young redhead whom George one day noticed was looking depressed. When George asked her what was the matter, the girl explained that she was flat broke, had no money for rent, and that her mother was coming out from New York for a visit. Without another word being said, George handed the girl a hundred dollars from his wallet and also insisted that she borrow his chauffeured limousine to pick up her mother at the train station.

Lucille Ball never forgot George's generosity and years later insisted on repaying George for the kindness he had since long forgotten.

George and Lucy even went out on a few dates together (she also later dated George's bodyguard/companion Mack Gray). But while a serious romance never blossomed between them, they always remained good friends.

However, the mutual attraction shared between George Raft and 16-year-old Betty Grable would in a few years blossom into one of Hollywood's most popular romances.

Thus far, George's movie roles had been restricted to minor hoodlum parts, and while he'd managed to earn screen credits, he knew these parts had demanded no special talent other than to look tough, and could have been played by any bit player on the studio roster.

A welcome change of pace occurred when George's old New York buddy James Cagney (who had just hit it big as gangster Tom Powers in *The Public Enemy*) requested George to play his dance rival in his latest Warner Brothers project, *Taxi!* (1932). The role of Willie Kenny was again just a bit, but showcased in a nice energetic scene that broke up the intensity of the central storyline concerning violent taxi wars. As Cagney remembered it, the dance hall competition required actors who could dance the Peabody. Cagney knew the steps well; the problem was finding someone who could match him and ultimately win the contest against him and partner Loretta Young. Fortunately, Cagney knew George was in Hollywood pursuing a movie career and suggested him to director Roy Del Ruth. As Cagney later said, the scene worked out "very well." Jimmy always considered George one of the finest dancers in the business, and was happy to give him a break.[7]

George enjoyed this brief reprieve from his criminal typecasting. But it would be his next role, which would again feature him as the familiar gangster, which would change his movie destiny and cement his stardom.

Howard Hawks had achieved the reputation as one of Hollywood's top directors with his work on *The Dawn Patrol* (1930) and *The Criminal Code* (1931). Now he was planning to capitalize on the success of mobster movies by preparing the genre's magnum opus: the gangster movie to end all gangster movies, to be produced independently by wealthy industrialist Howard Hughes and scripted by the famed playwright Ben Hecht.

The picture would be based on the book by the late Armitage Trail.[8] Its title ... *Scarface*.

CHAPTER FOUR

"ALL I KNOW IS THAT THEY ASKED ME A LOT OF QUESTIONS ABOUT CAPONE."

GEORGE RAFT

The machine-gunning years of Prohibition were over, but a new era of lawlessness was about to envelope the country as the ever-widening effects of the Great Depression took an economic toll on a once-prosperous America. The hardest hit areas were the Southern and Midwestern states, whose citizens not only saw their hard-earned monies dry up, but watched as once-fertile fields suffered a similar erosion. Banks and financiers were unsympathetic to their plight and were quick to foreclose on properties whose worth rarely exceeded the cost of the materials used in the building of ramshackle shelters. Forced off their land, many families headed to California, echoing the sentiments of those turn-of-the-century European immigrants who truly saw their journey taking them to the "land of milk and honey."

Some of these people were prompted in their decision to move west by their naïve belief in what they saw in Hollywood "picture shows," and by the glamorous photo spreads that appeared in movie magazines. Marble mansions and Olympic-sized swimming pools were totally beyond the comprehension of these dustbowl farmers. But as they trekked across the southern United States in vehicles often as beaten as their spirits, they struggled to maintain the optimism that if success beckoned for others, the same potential for opportunity may also exist for them.

These were the honest folk.

Then, there were others who uprooted in bitter pursuit of quick riches. The era of the Public Enemy had begun, and the dirt road criminal exploits of Charles Arthur "Pretty Boy" Floyd, the Ma Barker clan and Alvin "Old Creepy" Karpis became front page news to a nervous public. Soon their exploits would be further expanded upon by John Dillinger, "Baby Face" Nelson — and, most notoriously, Bonnie Parker and Clyde Barrow.

Not surprisingly, many of these outlaws were looked upon almost as heroes by a despairing and desperate American public. The movies took it from there.

Despite the protests of church and civic groups, who expressed concern at the moral value of such "entertainment" in the rise of a new national menace, crime movies were proving more popular than ever.

Of course, gangster movies had been around since the silent era. One of the first was D.W. Griffith's 17-minute *The Musketeers of Pig Alley* (1912), starring an actor named Elmer Booth who, as The Snapper Kid, prefigured the hoodlums made popular by James Cagney. Throughout the twenties, Hollywood produced such films as *Outside the Law* (1920), *While the City Sleeps* (1928), both of which proved that "grotesque-specialist" Lon Chaney had a knack for the genre; *The Racket* and *Underworld* (both 1927), with its intriguingly named Bull Weed (George Bancroft) as the "hero." Warner Brothers followed up their phenomenal success with *The Jazz Singer* (1927) by releasing their first "all talking" motion picture, *Lights of New York* (1928), a creaky effort that dealt with gangsters and speakeasies.

There was irony. While gangster pictures would become one of the financial staples of Warner Brothers, Jack L. Warner, youngest of the brothers and the studio's head of production, personally disliked such films and even forbid his son Jack Jr. to watch them.

His studio's *Little Caesar* and *The Public Enemy* had already been released to popular public reception, and their success prompted the studio to increase the output of hard-hitting, action-packed gangster movies. Films such as *Star Witness* and *The Finger Points* (both 1931) were on the agenda.

Even Louis B. Mayer capitalized on the gangster movie bonanza, with MGM releasing *The Big House* (1930) and *The Beast of the City* and *The Secret Six* in 1931.

What is interesting is that by the time *Scarface* was released in 1932, the sharp-suited Prohibition racketeers and the violent activities portrayed in the film seemed almost as far removed from contemporary consciousness as Billy the Kid. Still, the movie's bloodshed was intense and its impact on audiences far beyond anything that had been presented in previous gangster offerings. While its predecessors had been rather tame and often oblique in their depiction of mob violence, *Scarface* never shied away from the realities of gang warfare and as such benefited from a raw realism missing in both *Little Caesar* and *The Public Enemy*. The camera stayed bluntly focused on the bursts of machine gun fire and the victim dropping in agony under a barrage of lead.

In one particularly disturbing scene, a truck carrying a shipment of beer barrels is ambushed, and as it crashes one barrel breaks loose from its binding to roll through a basement apartment window. Seconds later, the audience hears a chilling female scream, and one is left only to imagine what terrible toll this random violence has taken upon the innocent.

Moments such as these provided *Scarface* with an uncompromising brutal authenticity. Had *Scarface* been produced under the auspices of a major Hollywood studio, it is almost certain that much of the film would have had to be radically altered, or perhaps the controversial production shelved altogether. But both director and producer remained bold, if not defiant, in their approach, refusing to sacrifice the honesty of their vision to the timidity of the censor. However, as it was, Hawks and Hughes finally capitulated to three demands to ensure the release of their film. They agreed to a silly title addendum: "Shame of a Nation," and they allowed an intrusive insertion wherein a pious civic official denounces gangsterism by demanding public cooperation and perhaps even the intervention of the army.

Finally, they submitted to filming an alternate ending where the gangster Tony Camonte is not mowed down under a spray of police machine gunfire, but instead is captured alive and brought to trial, where a judge is allowed to condemn his immoral actions before sentencing him to death on the gallows. This tacked-on legal coda so offended star Paul Muni that he refused to shoot the scenes and a faceless double was used in his place.[9]

Fortunately, audiences could not be patronized. They saw *Scarface* (*sans Shame of a Nation*) for the exciting story that it was. Hawks felt vindicated; he would always consider *Scarface* his favorite of the more than fifty movies he made, which included such impressive titles as *Twentieth Century* (1934), *Only Angels Have Wings* (1939), *Sergeant York* (1941), *To Have and Have Not* (1944) and *Red River* (1948).

When Hawks agreed to direct a movie based on Armitage Trail's book, he did two things. First, he tossed away the novel, which was burdened with a subplot featuring the gangster's policeman brother, and then he set out to meet with real-life gangsters and thugs from whom he hoped to collect insight into the workings of the underworld.

Hawks did his homework well. One night during production, while Hawks was viewing the day's rushes, he was visited by some tough-looking hoods apparently on Capone's payroll who had a few questions regarding his "research."

Hawks was not intimidated and even managed to convince the hoods to view the footage for themselves and comment on the realism of the action. They left the studio satisfied with the make-believe of the movie, but one guy, a little brighter than the others, paused at the doorway to the editing room to inquire, "So if this movie ain't about the big guy, why're yuh callin' it 'Scarface'?"

Hawks calmly replied, "Why not? Al's the most fascinating character of the twentieth century. Call the movie 'Scarface' and you're sure to make a box office killing. It's what we call showmanship."

The hood pondered for a moment, nodded, then told Hawks he'd pass on that explanation to Capone.

Hawks admitted that this wasn't the only time he'd been questioned by gangsters either in or out of Capone's employ, though each visit proved beneficial to the production.

"Some thug would come into the studio trying to muscle me for information," Hawks said, "and I'd tell him I was too busy and to come back tomorrow.

Then I'd hurriedly do a check on the guy, and when he came back the next day I'd throw some fake facts at him, which he'd counter with the real details of crimes he and his gang had committed, and that's how we got the realism."

Ben Hecht, the playwright who had earned an Oscar for his screenplay for the silent gangster movie *Underworld* (1927), was at first reluctant to commit to another gangster story, but Hawks talked him into accepting the assignment when he said his concept was to update the story of the Borgias to Prohibition-day Chicago. Hecht earned $20,000 for his screenplay, incorporating many of the details Hawks had been able to uncover.

Of course, the scripted realism had to be believably conveyed by the performances of the on-camera players.

A reluctant Paul Muni was persuaded by Hawks to accept the lead role of Tony "Scarface" Camonte, despite the actor's protestations that "I am just not that kind of man."

Born Meshilem Meier Weisenfreund, on September 22, 1895, to Austrian Jewish parents, Muni had achieved prominence as one of the leading players on the Broadway stage. In the late 1920s, he was offered an opportunity to appear in films, but had quickly become disillusioned with the whole Hollywood experience.

At the time Hawks pitched his gangster movie idea to Muni, the actor had just scored another Broadway success in Elmer Rice's *Counsellor-at-Law*.

Hawks's arguments regarding *Scarface* both intrigued and convinced him, and Muni began the intricate preparation that preceded each of his historical portrayals from Al Capone to Benito Juarez. His particular brand of Method acting often meant that he brought the character of Tony Camonte home with him at night, much to his wife Bella's consternation.

Hawks cast other prominent parts in the picture with such strong supporting players as Osgood Perkins (father of Anthony), who essayed the role of Camonte's boss and later would-be betrayer, Johnny Lovo; Ann Dvorak as Tony's sister Cesca; Karen Morley as the mistress, Poppy; C. Henry Gordon as the symbol of incorruptible justice, Lieutenant Ben Guarino; and an actor who had appeared as the convict Galloway in the director's previous film, *The Criminal Code*, and had just scored a "monster" hit as the creation in *Frankenstein*, Boris Karloff as Tony Camonte's "Bugs" Moran-inspired rival, Gaffney.

According to Jack LaRue, who by that point had accumulated more significant acting credentials than George Raft, it was he who was Howard Hawks' first choice to play Guino Rinaldo in *Scarface*. But when it was felt that he projected too much authority to be accepted as Paul Muni's "henchman," LaRue was dismissed — but not before suggesting his old Broadway friend George Raft as his replacement. Could this have happened? Possibly. Though it seems unlikely that an actor hungry for his own stardom would so graciously introduce his own competition.

In any event, George Raft's story of how he came to obtain his "break-through" role differs significantly from LaRue's version. Apparently, Howard Hawks had already seen George in *Quick Millions*, and when they later met at a prizefight during Hawks's preparation for the picture, the director asked George to drop by his office at the General Service Studio.

Raft was again becoming discouraged with his career and was planning to accept an offer from Owney Madden to tour with the Primo Carnera Boxing Carnival. Hawks immediately put a halt to that idea when he told George, "Starting today, you're on salary."[10]

Hawks' discerning eye was also shared by the picture's star. Celebrating his good news at a restaurant across the street, George was summoned to the table of Paul Muni, who also happened to be there and who told Raft that he would be ideal for a part in the Howard Hawks gangster picture he would be filming. When Raft replied that he'd already seen Hawks and had gotten the job, Muni was delighted.

The role of Rinaldo was considered a secondary part, certain to be over-shadowed by the ambitious nature and violent tirades of the title character. But since he would appear in many scenes with "Scarface," it was important that the co-player bring his own distinctive qualities to the part.

It was apparent to Hawks that George fit the bill. His slick, sleek and slightly sinister appearance perfectly epitomized the gunman Rinaldo. But George also offered another special contribution that Hawks was quick to utilize. Raft's association with the underworld afforded the director a reliable source for obtaining pertinent reference material.

In return, Hawks was patient in working with George on his role. Indeed, a lucky synchronicity occurred that would bring not only critical and public attention to George Raft — but to the overall production.

Hawks claimed credit for George's coin-flipping "piece of business" that became Raft's trademark and the most imitated gangster mannerism in cinema. The gesture was not motivated by artistic consideration. Hawks simply wanted to give the inexperienced actor something to do in his scenes with the flamboyant Muni and the other professional players. Raft practiced the trick for days until he became so proficient at it that he could flip the coin while never taking his eyes off his enemy.

However, Raft gave a later account of how the coin-flipping originated. He claimed that while standing on the set he noticed a lighting grip casually tossing a coin while listening to an argument. Raft thought the mannerism unique and, selecting a half-dollar as his tool, incorporated it into the next scene he filmed. According to George, Hawks immediately cut the scene and demanded to know what he was doing. When Raft explained the gimmick, Hawks told him it wasn't necessary and to stop trying to steal the scene, and an argument ensued. Raft remained stubborn, despite heated words and threats of being dismissed from the picture, and eventually Hawks

RAFT AS THE COIN-FLIPPING GUNMAN, GUINO RINALDO, IN *SCARFACE* (1932), THE MOVIE THAT MADE HIM A STAR.

permitted him to try the "business" in the scene. Raft said that it was only after viewing the day's rushes that Hawks saw how effective the trick was and allowed George to use it throughout the movie.

However it developed, the coin tossing and Hawks's coaching worked so well that George Raft emerged as the prime beneficiary of the picture. Even today it is sixth-billed George Raft who has become identified with the gangster menace of *Scarface*, more so than the movie's star. The *New York World-Telegram* reported: "George Raft plays Rinaldo as cold and repellent and deadly as a cobra."

George later explained his success in the role from his own perspective. "My movie hoodlums were always well-dressed, soft-spoken and underplayed. Some of my critics say that limited me as an actor — but I patterned these characters on people I really knew. The top gangsters were as quiet and efficient as bank presidents. The only loudmouths I remember were Dutch Schultz and Larry Fay."

George spoke little in the film, but his cool, controlled menace is apparent throughout. As is his sex appeal. An effective scene in the picture is Cesca's seductive little dance in front of Rinaldo. According to Hawks, the sequence originated from a real-life moment when Raft and Ann Dvorak were together at a party at the director's house and Dvorak, a little tipsy and dressed in a low-cut black silk gown, tried to entice George into dancing with her by performing an impromptu sexually-suggestive number — and succeeded. Hawks knew immediately that the scene had to be repeated for the motion picture cameras.

But the one scene that stands out most in *Scarface* is Guino Rinaldo's murder at the hands of his friend, Tony Camonte, whose incestuous attraction toward his own sister is thwarted when he discovers that Cesca is in love with Rinaldo and is, in fact, living with him, though unaware that the two have married. When Camonte knocks on the apartment door and Rinaldo opens it, elegantly attired in a silk robe flipping his trademark coin, with Cesca standing seductively in the background, Scarface loses all sense of reason and pumps bullets into his former comrade. Rinaldo misses his last catch of the coin as he slowly slides to the floor, the surprised look of death etched into his features.

It is a memorable moment in a film filled with many unforgettable scenes. But George claimed that this great bit of acting happened purely by accident. He recalled, "When Muni fired the pistol, my head reflexively flung back and hit the side of the door. I was slightly dazed and I guess that showed in my expression as my eyes rolled up as I fell to the floor. Everyone on the set said it was the greatest death scene they'd ever seen."

Despite Raft's being "murdered" by his co-star, George and the enigmatic Muni became friends on the picture, and George would later call Muni "the greatest actor I ever worked with." Indeed, Raft learned much about the craft of acting by observing Muni both on camera and in preparation, which included standing before a full-length mirror in his dressing room and reciting his lines into a Dictaphone, then playing back the dialogue and adding the appropriate gestures. George admitted that he found this kind of preparation extreme and said that if that was what it took to be an actor, he would rather quit.

Raft would also remain grateful to Howard Hawks for giving him his "break" in movies. Hawks would later remember that even after George achieved movie stardom, he would write him once a year offering to do any picture at any time, anywhere, for half his normal price.

As for producer Howard Hughes, Raft could not remember ever meeting the man. Apparently he never visited the set of *Scarface*, and this slight so insulted the temperamental Paul Muni that when Hughes later wanted to sign the actor to a personal contract, Muni politely reminded Hughes of the snub and refused to have any further dealings with him.

While Raft may not have personally met Hughes, the producer knew of the actor's reputation as a ladies' man and grew concerned when rumors began circulating that his "employee" was romancing actress Billie Dove, with whom Hughes was carrying on an affair. The promise of George Raft's acting career might have been abruptly halted had not Owney Madden encountered Hughes in the lobby of the Ambassador Hotel, where, in an upstairs suite, Raft and Billie were enjoying an afternoon tryst. Owney quickly called George's room and Raft said a hasty goodbye to Miss Dove before making his escape by way of the service elevator. "Hughes was the last man in the world I wanted to cross," George admitted.

Raft would later say of *Scarface*, "That was the big one. People remembered me. I was getting real mail — by the bushel basket — and even a dumb kid from Tenth Avenue could figure out how to translate that into money."

After completing his work in *Scarface*, George appeared in three quickie films, each made before the release of the Howard Hawks movie. For Universal, he was seen in the fascinating pre-Code *Night World* (1932), which, within its less than one-hour running time, managed to highlight a myriad number of plots, including club owner Happy MacDonald's (Boris Karloff) dealings with an unfaithful, ultimately treacherous wife, a wealthy playboy, Michael Rand (Lew Ayres), drinking himself into oblivion because of his mother's (Hedda Hopper) murderous betrayal of her husband, and a gambler Ed Powell (Raft) trying to move in on dancer Ruth Taylor (Mae Clarke), whose romantic desires are for Rand.

An interesting side note to the production and an incident that may have been a foreshadowing of later on-set Raft pugnaciousness occurred during the scene where the Ayres character is required to cuff Raft on the chin. While an action not called for in the script, the quick-tempered Raft responded by belting Ayres.

Raft was then summoned back to Warner Brothers to appear in *Love is a Racket* (1932), starring Douglas Fairbanks Jr., Lee Tracy and George's *Scarface* love interest, Ann Dvorak. Raft's minor underworld role as "Sneaky" (presumably one of Lyle Talbot's thugs) in this William Wellman-directed film was cut from the final print, a rather curious and humiliating experience after playing his great screen menace in *Scarface*.

Only a little less disappointing was George's bit as a jovial bandleader in *Winner Take All* (1932), starring James Cagney. Raft's blink-and-you'll-miss-him moment occurs in a flashback sequence near the beginning of the film (which also features a quick scene of Texas Guinan as herself), and was a clip culled from *Queen of the Night Clubs*.

Even before *Scarface* opened, George Raft was receiving studio contract offers. George chose to sign with Paramount, a studio that would seem the least likely to exploit his onscreen gangster image, while affording him the best financial terms, which really weren't that extraordinary, reportedly at under $200 per week.[11]

Paramount Pictures at the time was under the presidency of Adolph Zukor. Zukor, as with most studio chiefs, was not as interested in his talent as he was with keeping tight reins on the studio's finances. Yet even at this he may have been fallible. A classic Hollywood story has it that Zukor initially rejected a $75,000-per-film offer with the Marx Brothers, thinking the amount excessive, until a meeting was arranged between him and the wily Chico Marx, who managed to secure a $100,000-per-picture deal for the team!

In any event, Paramount, once the premiere studio of Hollywood, had fallen on hard economic times. Box office receipts were down due to the Depression, and the studio was forced to cut back on salaries and even terminate many of its high-priced executives. George had scored a hit with *Scarface*, but he was still a virtual unknown in pictures and would require careful studio buildup to be accepted as a "star" by the public.

After completing the first movie under his Paramount contract, George was asked to go on a personal appearance tour to help promote *Scarface*.

Among *Scarface's* many admirers was the film's inspiration, Al Capone himself. George remembered that when he was first offered the picture he asked Owney Madden's opinion, and that Madden told him he was sure Capone wouldn't mind. But after *Scarface* opened and Raft found himself in Chicago, he heard rumors that Capone wasn't too happy with the movie. One night after finishing his act at the Oriental Theater, George was accosted by a young hood who said, "Raft, the big guy wants to see you." Raft had no choice but to go along, and he followed the hood into a black limousine that took them to Capone's headquarters in the Lexington Hotel on South Michigan Avenue. George was escorted through checkpoints upstairs to Capone's private office, where the "big guy" (who was actually four years younger than Raft) was seated behind a mahogany desk, surrounded by the many eccentric showpieces of his success.

George and Capone were not exactly strangers to one another. Raft had met Capone many times in New York where Capone (then calling himself "Al Brown") played craps in the back room of the El Fey Club. According to Raft, their talk was more of a Capone interrogation.

"Georgie, I hear you been playin' my bodyguard, Frankie Rio, in this *Scarface* picture," Capone said.

"Yes, I did, Al," Raft replied, trying not to sound nervous. "But it's nothing personal. Actors do what they're told."

"Well, you tell them Hollywood guys that no one's bumpin' off Al Capone while he's runnin' Chicago."

After a bit more conversation, Raft got up to leave. Capone called after him.

"Georgie, I see you tossin' a coin all through the picture. A four-bit piece, yeah?"

"No, it was a nickel."

"That's worse. You tell 'em if any of my boys are tossin' coins, they'll be twenty-dollar gold pieces."

George promised to convey the message to Hollywood, then he asked a question of his own. "Did you like the picture, Al?"

"Yeah, I liked it," Capone replied, fingering the long vertical scar on his face. "And even if I didn't I couldn't stop 'em from makin' it. They've blamed me for everything except the Chicago fire."

During his Chicago stay, Capone offered George the protection of "Machine Gun" Jack McGurn, who a few years earlier had almost killed entertainer Joe E. Lewis. In another note of irony, McGurn would be murdered on February 13, 1936 in a Chicago bowling alley in a scene eerily reminiscent of Boris Karloff's demise in *Scarface*. Had McGurn's assassins been inspired by the famous movie scene?

After his Chicago experience, Raft was happy to return to the sunshine of Hollywood, where his first Paramount feature had opened to good reviews.

While not a gangster drama per se, *Dancers in the Dark* explored a world familiar to the pre-Hollywood George Raft, set primarily in the claustrophobic atmosphere of a Prohibition nightclub, replete with taxi dancers and racketeers.

Jack Oakie, a popular star of the time (who, unbeknownst to movie fans, suffered from an almost total hearing loss), played the candy-striped-jacketed bandleader, Duke Taylor, whose affections for Gloria Bishop (Miriam Hopkins) are compromised by gangster Louie Brooks (Raft), even after Duke has engineered the hasty exit from town of Gloria's true love Floyd Stevens (William Collier, Jr.).

Raft's Louie Brooks is every bit as unwholesome a character as Jimmy Kirk or Guino Rinaldo. He is an unregenerate, unrepentant bad guy who kills (off-camera) the owner of a jewelry store during a holdup, then later attempts to kill Duke. At the climax, Louie's fondness for the song "St. Louis Blues" alerts the police to his presence in the club and results in his plunging to his death while trying to escape out a window.

Raft later claimed that he was actually required to climb out onto the five-story window ledge for this final scene by the film's director, David Burton. Naturally, he was hesitant, and certainly would have refused such a potentially dangerous action had Burton ordered him. However, when the director merely reassured him with the words, "That's nothin', George. You can do it," Raft felt confident and did the scene as required.

The picture, written by future *Citizen Kane* scenarist Herman J. Mankiewicz, was a melodramatic hodgepodge, but it afforded Raft his first good, strong role since *Scarface*, and allowed for a favorable review from Mordaunt Hall of *The New York Times*, who wrote that "[Raft] gives an excellent account of himself."

Unfortunately, during the making of the film, Raft's temper once again got the better of him when he and co-star Miriam Hopkins got into an off-screen quarrel that escalated to the point where Raft gave her a painful pinch on her behind. As he often was after such blow-ups, George was remorseful, but glad that he hadn't followed through on his original threat to punch Miss Hopkins in the nose. Especially since prior to the making of *Dancers in the Dark*, the two were occasionally seen together socially.

Yet perhaps in this instance his action was justified. Even the cultured Edward G. Robinson would later respond to Miss Hopkins' prima donna attitude in a less than gentlemanly manner by slapping her with a bit more emphasis than what was required in the script of *Barbary Coast* (1935).

After finishing *Dancers in the Dark*, Raft was rushed into another small role, as a gangster, in *Madame Racketeer* (1932), starring that quintessential scene-stealer of the early talkies, Alison Skipworth.

In this offering, George was Chicago racketeer Jack Houston, whose romance with ex-con Skipworth's daughter Patsy (Gertrude Messinger) prompts self-sacrificing Skipworth to join up with his gang in an attempt to expose his nefarious dealings. Interestingly, *Madame Racketeer* was nominated as one of the ten best films of the year by the National Film Board.

By this time, apparently even the press was wondering about the misuse of George Raft in such lesser fare. In their review of the film, *The New York American* wrote "… it appears an error to put George Raft, a potential star, in a walk-on bit, which any studio kid might have played with equal distinction."

Raft himself was experiencing and, indeed, expressing, his own dissatisfaction with the way his career was going — if not starting to question his abilities as an actor. During one particularly frustrating take alongside Miss Skipworth, Raft's jealousy at his co-star's easy talent prompted him to smash his fist through one of the scenery sets.

Positive box office and critical notice of Raft finally decided Paramount to headline George Raft in a film of his own. George, however, was initially reluctant to accept the starring role in a movie tentatively titled *Number 99*, based on the Louis Bromfield novel *Single Night*. Raft may have become discouraged playing his familiar gangster support in film after film, but he was indeed nervous about taking on the lead in a movie. His reasoning was "Suppose they promote me as the star and no one comes to see the picture?"

Finally, however, George accepted the challenge and was cast in the almost semi-autobiographical role of ex-boxer-turned-Prohibition gangster-turned-

GEORGE RAFT IN HIS FIRST STARRING ROLE: AS NIGHTCLUB OWNER JOE ANTON IN *NIGHT AFTER NIGHT* (1932). WITH HIM IS CONSTANCE CUMMINGS, WHOM RAFT BRIEFLY DATED

nightclub owner Joe Anton in the retitled *Night After Night* (1932). Raft soon learned that Texas Guinan was being considered for the role of Maudie Triplett, his character's former girlfriend. Raft knew Texas would be good in the role and he wanted to reciprocate the break she had previously given him, but he knew that there was really only one actress who could bring the character to life.

"I know a woman who would be sensational," George told director Archie Mayo — and on George Raft's recommendation, the one-time "Queen of the Night Clubs" Texas Guinan faded into obscurity and Mae West emerged as the biggest, brassiest film star of the 1930s. For her screen debut, Miss West was reportedly paid $5,000 per week. Miss Skipworth received a weekly salary of $500. George, though top-billed, was low man at his weekly contract rate of around $200.

Despite his misgivings about headlining the picture, the filming of *Night After Night* proved a pleasant experience for George. He knew the nightclub setting well, and he enjoyed his first attempt at playing (subdued) comedy. Alison Skipworth was again on hand, this time playing the matronly Mabel Jellyman, who teaches Joe Anton elocution lessons, with Raft's love interest played by the lovely Constance Cummings, with whom Raft was also seen socially. But it was Mae West who walked away with the picture. "She stole everything but the camera," was a classic comment attributed to George. And indeed, how could she not make an impression with her famous screen entrance, slinking into the club dripping with expensive jewelry, prompting the club's hatcheck girl to remark, "Goodness, what beautiful jewels," to which West replies, "Goodness had nothing to do with it, dearie."

Mae West was destined for cinematic stardom after making such a stunning debut. Raft, despite his warm feelings toward West, was wise enough to know that no co-star could match her onscreen presence and a couple of years later refused the opportunity to act with her in *Belle of the Nineties* (1934). He would not, in fact, appear with her in a movie until the end of both their careers.

In truth, *Night After Night* is a pretty dull offering — except for those moments when Miss West is onscreen. Raft also could not have been pleased by the mostly negative reviews he received for his first starring role. *The New York Times* wrote: "Mr. Raft's eyes and sleek hair cause him to remind one of the late Rudolph Valentino."

Raft did have one bad experience on the set with director Archie Mayo. During one scene Mayo was growing impatient with how slow Raft was removing a shirt from a drawer. While Raft was still basically a screen novice with no formal acting training, directors such as Rowland Brown and Howard Hawks recognized his limitations and worked with them. Archie Mayo, on the other hand, was a studio "workhorse" hired to bring in product within budget under a pre-union time clock that did not recognize a five o'clock quitting time, and in exasperation, in front of the crew, he shouted, "Just pick up the shirt, you sonofabitch."

George held onto the reins of his temper. But early the next morning, before anyone else had arrived on the set, Raft collared Mayo and told him in a language they both understood that if he ever yelled at him again in front of the cast and crew, he would punch him out.

**AN EARLY PARAMOUNT PUBLICITY PHOTO OF RAFT HIGHLIGHTS HIS
GANGSTER IMAGE**

The remainder of production proceeded without incident.

With the box office success of *Night After Night*, George Raft's stock had risen considerably. In his next film he was onscreen for about ten minutes, but received second billing to Gary Cooper, in *If I Had a Million*, (1932).

In the picture, George plays Eddie Jackson, a gambler, who along with the rest of the leading characters in the photoplay, including W.C Fields and Charles Laughton, receives a $1,000,000 check from an unknown benefi-ciary, played by Richard Bennett. For each, this windfall brings interesting and ironic consequences. In Eddie's case, his gangster reputation prevents him from cashing the check. In desperation he tries to sell off the check in decreasing increments until he finally hands over the check to the proprietor of a flophouse for a night's ten-cent lodging, who then calls the police before casually lighting his cigar with the "worthless paper."

The major criticism leveled against Raft in the movie was that he tended to shout his lines when trying to display emotion. This would become a common complaint in many of Raft's future films.

Despite Paramount's promise to not showcase George wholly in gangster or hoodlum roles, each of the movies in which he had performed for the studio up to this point had him playing at least a variation of the underworld character.

When George requested to be put on the right side of the law for a change, the studio obliged, but they still found a way to capitalize on his most marketable image.

Under-Cover Man (1932) cast George as Nick Darrow, a man of questionable character who volunteers to go undercover for the police after his father has been murdered by gangsters. The law agrees to his proposal, but on the understanding that if he is discovered, they cannot intercede. Paramount obviously did not want to stray too far from Raft's popular gangster image. In the course of the film, Darrow assumes the identity of Ollie Snell, a big-shot racketeer from Toledo, and the plot develops from there. His female co-star was Nancy Carroll, who, as Lora Madigan, assists Darrow in capturing the criminals who had also killed her brother. Roscoe Karns and Gregory Ratoff as the leader of the crooks filled out the bill.

"The Most Talked-About Man in Motion Pictures" the studio ads for the picture hyped, as George Raft was ballyhooed across the country in Paramount theaters.

About this time, George was interviewed by journalists in his hotel suite and was asked about his resemblance to his late friend Rudolph Valentino and the so-called "Valentino Curse" that might limit his career. Somewhat annoyed, Raft replied: "What if I do look like Valentino? People have always said that. But my picture career is no part of *that*. I'm strictly on my own, and will play any part they give me, from gorilla to romantic lead. They might as well lay off the Rudy stuff. I'll make my own way, looking very much like George Raft."

George was originally intended to co-star with Carole Lombard in *No Man of Her Own* (1932), a screwball comedy where Raft was to play a tough card cheat named Babe Stewart. However, Raft was substituted in the role by Clark Gable, resulting in screen fireworks that would later transcend into Gable and Miss Lombard's personal lives.

In the first year of his Paramount contract, George Raft had completed five films for the studio, for a total of nine features in release. He had enjoyed

AN EARLY PARAMOUNT PUBLICITY SHOT

a phenomenally successful year for a virtual screen newcomer, rising from his uncredited dancing bit in *Taxi!* to two starring roles.

Naturally, Paramount wanted to continue promoting their new star, and George Raft was frequently required to appear at premieres where he would be asked to say a few words on microphone for radio audiences. During these early years of his career, George was never at ease speaking spontaneously, and newsreel cameras at the time recorded a noticeably nervous man whose eyes rarely lifted from the microphone.

Raft admitted his insecurity was based on his lack of formal education. While he would later achieve distinction as one of the most urbane, if not sophisticated, men in Hollywood, Raft, during the 1930s, was still a raw specimen, possessed of a street fighter mentality and acutely sensitive to real or perceived criticism. His engaging man-about-town image was frequently compromised by violent episodes that stamped him with bad press personally, while heightening his cinematic tough guy appeal.

In fairness, George was rarely the instigator of these incidents. He remembered many times when his gangster image would follow him into a restaurant or nightclub, and he would be challenged by a drunk trying to impress his pals or girlfriend, and where George would be forced to rely on his street fighting skills to cool the guy off. Of course, if the press or paparazzi were present, as was frequently the case, it was movie tough guy George Raft who would receive the bad publicity.

Raft did later admit that he rarely fought fair. "I had a reputation for a fast left and Hollywood is full of people who went down or out when I clipped them. But I suppose I was a fraud. I usually hit them without warning, and by the time they got up bystanders were keeping us apart. It was a trick I learned in New York from Owney Madden. He told me that if guys start to get tough, hit 'em fast before they get their hands up."

Raft was also known to employ other brutal techniques to subdue an aggressive enemy. One of his most violent was to kick a downed opponent's head against a curb to prevent retaliation. In later years, George refused to elaborate on these altercations except to say that he was confused, angry and quick to take offense.

The flip side of the coin was that George was also becoming known as "the softest touch in Hollywood." As his success increased, so did his generosity. George was always quick to give a buck to anyone who appeared that they might really need it. His tips to valets, hatcheck girls and waiters were legendary. George was starting to earn big money, but it just as quickly slipped through his fingers. He later estimated that he probably loaned or gave away close to a million dollars. He added that very few of his loans were ever paid back.

George's generosity was not limited to cash handouts, either. He was known to take the tailor-made suit jacket right off his back and present it to an admiring fan. And that also went for shirts, hats ... and even pants! Not that George had to worry about depleting his expensive wardrobe. Shortly after he achieved screen stardom, he moved into the penthouse of the ritzy El Royale Apartments, where he tore down a wall to create more closet space for his sartorial extravagances. It was important for George to look sharp, even if in these early days, his "natty" style of dress was more relevant to Broadway than to Hollywood.

For a kid who'd grown up poor, uneducated and virtually friendless on the mean streets of New York, George found himself overwhelmed by his sudden wealth and celebrity. He was mobbed at personal appearances and even a simple pleasure such as enjoying a baseball game (where he could consume his two favorite treats: hot dogs and root beer) was compromised by the intrusion of eager fans. But George knew that the reason he was successful was because audiences liked him, and so was always gracious and obliging to admirers and autograph seekers — even if his penmanship was limited to his standard signing: "Sincerely yours, George Raft."

Where George did not have patience was with figures from his past who tried to put the bite on him through blackmail. Unfortunately, George's background made him a prime candidate for such shakedown tactics, and he was often forced to deal with these erstwhile blackmailers in a less than diplomatic fashion.

In one instance, George was on a personal appearance tour in New York when there was a knock on the door of his suite at the Waldorf-Astoria. George opened the door to discover a creepy little guy who immediately reminded George of a long-forgotten incident regarding an illegal shipment of booze confiscated from Raft's car. He asked George for $500 to have a lapse of memory. George immediately grabbed the guy by his coat and tossed him out into the hallway. He'd come a long way since Prohibition and believed he was beyond the point where he should fear having his past exposed.

"Some of these chiselers were real big shots back in the old days," George remembered. "Guys who wouldn't give me a second look. Now they had no other way to make a buck so they came after me."

On the other hand, George was always willing to lend a hand to old Broadway pals who had fallen on hard times, and often this help took the form of finding them bit or extra work in his movies.

In particular, George always tried to see to it that Mack Gray was given a part in each of his pictures. George and Gray had resumed their friendship during Raft's early days in Hollywood, when the two had met at the Friday night fights at the Hollywood Legion Stadium. Gray was having a difficult time with his career managing second-rate boxers and George, ever sympathetic, offered him work as his assistant. But Gray's duties far exceeded that of a mere gofer. He became George's closest companion, since the two shared many similar interests — primarily women and sports — and "spoke the same language." Gray accompanied George virtually every day that Raft was shooting a film, going over lines with him in the back of the limo as they rode to the studio. Directors usually acceded to Raft's request to write in a small role for Gray, knowing that by doing so they would prevent George from becoming difficult during production.

This was no small concession. Before the Screen Actors Guild was established to lessen the contract player's workload, long hot hours on the soundstage coupled with tight, rushed filming schedules often shortened the fuses of cast and crew alike. Raft, impatient and still unsure of his abilities as an actor, was frequently frustrated by the demands of moviemaking, just as he took quick offense at the temperamental or condescending behavior of some of his co-stars. Mack Gray's presence on the set provided a steadying influence for George.

LOOKING AS IF THEY JUST POSTED BAIL: RAFT AND HIS CLOSE PALS, BROTHERS MACK AND JOE GRAY. JOE'S STRONG RESEMBLANCE TO DEAN MARTIN LED TO HIS DOUBLING FOR THE ACTOR/SINGER IN MANY OF HIS MOVIES
PHOTO COURTESY OF THE JOE GRAY ESTATE

George's quick temper would have further negative repercussions as he became more embraced by his celebrity. But for the moment, he continued cranking out movies for Paramount, who were pleased with the steady box office returns from his pictures.

In early 1933 George returned to Hollywood from a successful personal appearance tour in New York, where the actor had been hyped by Paramount: "George Raft, The Strong Arm Man, will do his Strong Arm Stuff at the Brooklyn Paramount." It had been an extremely gratifying trip for the former street kid/hustler. He was delighted to be recognized by old friends and new fans as a bona fide star. Now the studio had scheduled a busy workload for him. However, of the four films Paramount proposed, only two actually went before the cameras — and one without Raft.

The titles *Fly On* and *Police Surgeon* were never filmed. But George took over from Gary Cooper for his first film of 1933, *Pick- Up*, after Cooper was delayed on assignment at MGM. Although the picture had crime elements inherent in the story line, with top-billed Sylvia Sidney playing a character nicknamed "Baby Face" Mary, Raft's role featured him as Harry Glynn, a tough-edged but honest cab driver who eventually falls in love with Mary and helps to clear her when she is accused of being an accomplice in the prison escape of her husband, portrayed by William Harrigan.

Miss Sidney would later appear with George in two further pictures and would always retain warm feelings toward him. As she once commented, "Whatever George Raft lacked in talent, he more than made up for in charm."

Raft's change-of-pace role garnered him mostly positive reviews, though the *New York Herald-Tribune* regarded his good guy playing with mixed sentiments: "Mr. Raft, whose underacting has its good points, continues to be an interesting and vivid screen type even though he is more effective in sinister roles."

George must have bristled at such reviews. While he understood that it was his effective portrayal of criminals that had established him as a popular screen player, he also knew that to continue playing such parts could eventually type him. Therefore, he was outraged when Paramount next presented him with a script based on the controversial William Faulkner novel *Sanctuary*, to be filmed under the title *The Story of Temple Drake* (1933).

The role offered to him was based on a repellent character called "Popeye" in the book. As portrayed in Faulkner's pages, Popeye is a psychopath who rapes the heroine with a corncob (he had been castrated for a previous crime) and then kills the retarded handyman who tries to rescue her.

Raft found the part so distasteful that he resolutely refused to do the picture, his stance garnering the support of church and civic groups who found the novel obscene. He considered the role "career suicide," though he did offer a compromise to Paramount president Adolph Zukor. He would agree to do the movie on the condition that the studio put two million dollars in his bank account, so sure was he that the picture would finish him as an actor.

Raft gave several interviews to the press in which he defended his position, stating that while another actor might get away with doing the part, Raft's audiences, used to seeing him in unsavory roles, would think that he himself was like Popeye. What's more, he desperately wanted to move away from hoodlum and gangster parts and believed that Paramount, by assigning him to the picture, had lied in their promise that he would no longer have to do unsympathetic parts.

"It's not that I mind being the guy on the wrong side of the law," Raft said at the time. "But I won't take a role that's a pure heel. The character has to have some ray of warmth, some redeeming quality — or it just isn't real … "

Or, as he more succinctly put it, "You've got to grow or you've got to go … "

Of course, such atrocities as depicted in the novel were significantly watered down for the movie, as was the character of Popeye himself. The "symbol of moral decadence" became "Trigger" and emerged onscreen as a

RAFT LOOKING SLEEK AND MYSTERIOUS IN *THE MIDNIGHT CLUB* (1934)

traditional 1930s movie gangster at large in the South. His key scene, the famous rape sequence, was achieved through suggestion that still, however, had the power to shock audiences of the day.

If Jack LaRue's account of how George Raft landed the role of Guino Rinaldo in *Scarface* was true, Raft inadvertently reciprocated the favor when his refusal of the part led to Paramount casting LaRue as Trigger. It would be LaRue's most important screen role to date. Unfortunately, it also proved to be one of his last major film parts. Controversy continued to plague the movie into its release and it was banned in both Pennsylvania and Ohio. Once the Production Code came into effect in 1934, Joe Breen ordered that the film never again be re-released. The film's star, Miriam Hopkins, emerged unscathed from the backlash and enjoyed many more years of screen stardom. But the adverse publicity ultimately crippled LaRue's starring role future as audiences too closely identified the villainous character with the sinister-visaged actor.

LaRue (born Gaspar Biondolillo), who in real life was a kind and gentle man, at the time of our interview living in comfortable retirement with his sister, would, with few exceptions (his roles as a priest in both *A Farewell to Arms*, 1932, and *Captains Courageous*, 1937), thereafter be typecast as a supporting bad guy in B movies. (Fortunately, he was able to supplement his meager film salaries with the profits he earned from his popular Sunset Boulevard restaurant.)

George could consider himself lucky that he escaped a similar fate. Although he was briefly placed on suspension for his refusal of the part, he quickly resumed the momentum of his leading man career. *The Midnight Club* (1933) featured Raft as American detective Nick Mason, assigned by Scotland Yard to round up a British jewelry theft ring led by the debonair Colin Grant (Clive Brook). Of course, during his investigation, he falls in love with one of the crooks, Iris Whitney (Helen Vinson), and the denouement finds Colin Grant performing a noble beau geste to ensure Iris's freedom and her romantic future with Nick. The 67-minute film was a rather forgettable exercise (though it does offer the comedic potential of rough-edged American Raft trying to cope with the polite and proper British way of life), its main interest being that it provided George with another opportunity to break typecasting and that he was once again co-starred with Alison Skipworth.

Critical comments regarding George's performance were generally favorable. *The New York Herald-Tribune* said of him: "Mr. Raft continues to be more a type than actor, but he is, save in his romantic scenes, of considerable help to the photoplay." Interestingly, while touted as a great romantic off screen, George's awkwardness in on-camera love scenes would become a standard complaint leveled against him by reviewers.

His next picture was another step in the right direction. Producer Darryl F. Zanuck had left Warner Brothers to form a new film company, to be called Twentieth Century Corporation, and the first movie on the production agenda was to be a rowdy and boisterous recreation of the Gay '90s titled *The Bowery* (1933). Zanuck hired Raoul Walsh to direct and set as his stars the popular team of Wallace Beery and Jackie Cooper, who had scored a hit with *The Champ* (1931). Fay Wray, fresh from the clutches of *King Kong* (1933), was assigned the role of the romantic interest, and Beery's adversary Steve Brodie was initially intended for Clark Gable, whose box office (he was rated #7) was superior to Raft's. Fortunately for George, Raoul Walsh interceded, insisting that the New York-bred Raft was better suited to the role than former Ohio coal miner Gable, and Raft was borrowed from Paramount to do the part.

From the moment the jaunty, sartorially resplendent Steve Brodie makes his first entrance inside Beery's saloon, Raft embodies a character completely different from the dour and deadly criminals he had mostly been playing. He is engaged in a constant game of one-upmanship with Beery's Chuck

RAOUL WALSH (RIGHT) DIRECTING A SNAPPILY-ATTIRED RAFT ON THE SET OF
***THE BOWERY* (1933)**

Connors, from pitting John L. Sullivan against Connor's lesser fighter to rushing his volunteer fire brigade to the scene of a blaze ahead of Connor's squad. But he finally gets in over his head when he persuades Connors to wager his saloon against his boast to leap from the Brooklyn Bridge, a dare that he doesn't plan to honor, substituting a dummy, but which circumstances force him to undertake. The rivalry between Brodie and Connors culminates in brutal fisticuffs aboard a barge, but the "happy" climax sees the two becoming pals and marching off to war in Cuba, with little Swipes McGurk (Cooper) in tow.

While the film is fun to watch, filled with many memorable vignettes perfectly capturing the era, the production itself was often difficult. During the volunteer fireman scene, Raft's and Beery's men were supposed to clash in a free-for-all brawl and Walsh wanted realism. He craftily planted seeds of dissention between both sides and when it came time for filming, pandemonium broke out on the set, much to Walsh's delight, though many extras wound up in the hospital.

There was trouble brewing between George and Wallace Beery, as well. Part of the problem may have stemmed from Beery's dissatisfaction at Raft's taking over the role from Gable, whom Beery genuinely liked and with whom he'd previously worked with in *The Secret Six* (1931) and *Hell Divers*

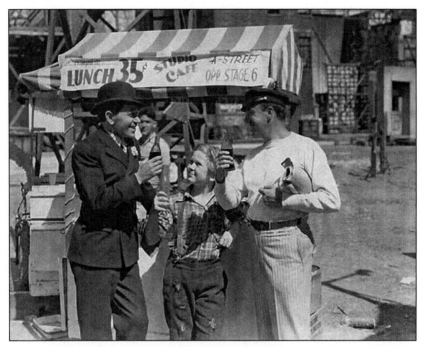

ENJOYING A SODA AT THE STUDIO FOOD CART ON THE FOX LOT WITH AN ADMIRING JACKIE COOPER AND DIRECTOR WALSH WHILE MAKING *THE BOWERY* (1933)

(1932). But in his 1981 autobiography, *Please Don't Shoot My Dog*, Jackie Cooper may have provided another clue. He writes about George Raft with affection, remembering him as "warm and friendly." Beery, on the other hand, was cold and aloof and in their previous screen pairings, the actor rudely ignored the boy off-camera. During the making of *The Bowery*, however, perhaps a bit jealous of Cooper's admiration for Raft, Beery began planting his own seeds of suspicion, telling young Jackie that Raft was a gangster and manufacturing other sordid details about his past, which Cooper promptly relayed to Raft.

"Directing Raft and Beery, I found out, was like trying to keep the peace between a lion and a tiger," commented Raoul Walsh years later in his autobiography.

Before the two eventually became friends, however, tensions between the two escalated until it came time to shoot the climactic fight scene aboard the barge. Beery threw the first punch and instead of pulling back, let go with all his considerable might, knocking George out for several minutes. When Raft revived and collected himself he quickly retaliated, charging Beery and delivering several hard shots into his ample belly. The crew jumped in and separated the two before either man could be seriously hurt. Needless to say, George and Beery were at odds after that.

George also became the victim of a Walsh practical joke during the filming of the picture. For the scene where the Steve Brodie character is to jump from the Brooklyn Bridge, a dummy was going to be used. Walsh never told Raft this and, in fact, hid the dummy. Instead, almost at the last minute, Walsh approached George, who was seated beside Mack Gray in his limo, and told him the stand-in he had hired had gotten nervous and taken a powder and that Raft would have to do the jump himself. Raft, who could not swim, was terrified and Walsh's taunts regarding his "toughness" and arguments guaranteeing his safety did nothing to assure him. Walsh even promised that Twentieth Century would provide him with a fine funeral should he not survive the stunt. Surprisingly, George got out of the limo, steadied himself and climbed over the railing onto a girder. At that point, Walsh saw that George really would have done the stunt, and finally had the prop boy bring out the dummy, revealing the gag. Walsh had to admit that George Raft was every bit as brave as his image. George, however, told Walsh that, toughness aside, he had peed his pants.

On the plus side, the movie required plenty of extras and George was able to provide many of his New York expatriate friends with jobs (including a role for Mack Gray, the first of twenty-one bits he would play in Raft films). Though in one instance his generosity backfired when two hoodlum acquaintances left the set on lunch break and never came back — having been gunned down by gangsters in a nearby restaurant.

Raft had performed in only three films in 1933, but happily none presented him as a criminal and one, *The Bowery*, was an unqualified hit, its success providing a strong launching pad for the soon-to-be Twentieth Century-Fox.

For his next movie, George went back to Paramount and returned to, at least the fringes of, the underworld.

Despite the talents of Fredric March and Miriam Hopkins, *All of Me* (1934), adapted from the unsuccessful 1932 Broadway play *Chrysalis*, which had featured Humphrey Bogart, is an insufferably dreary drama until the introduction of George Raft as the incongruously-named minor criminal Honey Rogers and Helen Mack as his pregnant "moll," Eve. At that point the pace of the picture picks up considerably. Don Ellis (March) and Lydia Darrow (Hopkins) go "slumming" in a speakeasy, where they overhear the conversation between Honey and his girl. Their hard-luck story, which culminates both in Honey's swiping Lydia's purse and his later arrest, inspires Lydia to reconsider her own reservations about Dan's offer for her to join him while he works on the Boulder Dam project — a proposition far removed from the life of luxury Lydia desires. Improbably, her romantic "awakening" leads her to assist Honey in a prison break that results in the killing of a guard, and Honey's freeing of Eve from a woman's halfway house. The two enjoy a brief respite in the company of Lydia before the police corner them in a hotel room. Rather than again be separated, the fugitive lovers choose suicide and Eve follows Honey in his death leap from the hotel window. Lydia is arrested as an accessory, but Dan is there to stand beside her.

Raft might have been displeased at playing another criminal — and a murderer to boot! — but he probably accepted the part of Honey Rogers because of the character's overriding sympathetic qualities. Another incentive was that Carole Lombard, of whom Raft was very fond, was originally announced as the female lead, only to be replaced by George's old adversary Miriam Hopkins.

As for critical comments regarding Raft's "return to form," *Variety* said only that Raft's performance was "plausible."

Even if George was hoping to break away from playing gangsters on screen, he certainly had no qualms about associating with them off the set. Case in point: Owney Madden, Raft's pal and indeed benefactor, who had come to California around this time and was often seen in Raft's company until he was arrested by a vigilant police officer for a suspected parole violation. When a jailed Madden became hungry later that night, George paid two detectives $150 to bring Owney a couple of sandwiches. Madden was eventually returned to Sing Sing to serve out his original sentence, and upon his release he retired to Hot Springs, Arkansas, where he lived quietly.

But Raft didn't need his association with gangsters to bring him trouble. During this period he found himself involved in a number of unpleasant episodes, owing to his extreme sensitivity and hot temper. In one incident in August of that year, he and Mack Gray were emerging from the Brown Derby after lunch when a man named Sam Satz began making insulting remarks at them. George had recently undergone plastic surgery to remove the scar on his left ear from his long-ago knife fight with Sammy Schwartz, and was still wearing a bandage, as was Mack Gray, who had accompanied Raft to the hospital for a nose job. George tried to ignore Satz's rude comments about his being a "pretty boy," but Satz kept at it until finally Raft became incensed and began slugging. Naturally, Mack Gray stepped in to assist and, in the melee, a female onlooker was accidentally struck by one of Raft's wild punches. A traffic cop, who had to be summoned from his station at Hollywood and Vine, finally broke up the battle. Although George had been provoked into the fight, it was he — the movie tough guy — who received the resulting bad press. Newspaper reports of the incident mentioned Mack Gray's involvement and also that George was a former prizefighter.

Nineteen-thirty-four proved a personally troublesome year for George. On another occasion, he was sitting at the Chez Paris while on a publicity tour in Chicago when a man approached his table and insisted that George dance with his wife. George politely declined since he didn't want to appear as a showoff on the dance floor. Later, as Raft was leaving the restaurant, the man, now drunk, became belligerent and another fight ensued. Once again, George was not the instigator but the next day's newspaper headlines read: RAFT IN BRAWL IN CHICAGO NIGHTCLUB.

In what proved to be an embarrassing incident for Raft, he got into a fight with actor Gene Raymond at the Brown Derby when he took offense to a remark made by Raymond. Unfortunately, before this confrontation could be broken up, Raft found himself on the floor.

While his dates found George charming and a gentleman, on occasion Raft's short fuse even created problems in his romantic involvements. Raft had been dating an actress named Marjorie King. One night while the two were in New York and staying at the Waldorf, they got into a quarrel and Miss King began insulting George's manners, calling him "crude" and saying he had no education. Raft managed to control his temper, but at three in the morning he flew into a rage and, together with Mack Gray, ran up two flights of stairs, bursting into Miss King's hotel room. He then began destroying all the clothing he'd bought her that day with a pair of scissors. Of course, the next morning, George deeply regretted his actions and sent her an apologetic note along with $1,500 in cash to replace her wardrobe. At first Miss King refused his gesture and stormed up to George's room, throwing the money into his face. Mack Gray carefully retrieved the cash from the floor and returned it to Miss King, who counted the bills, only to scream at Gray, "You louse! I'm a hundred dollars short!"

Even Mack Gray wasn't immune to his friend's unpredictable temper. One night they got into an argument in their penthouse suite at the El Royale Apartments and Raft took what he supposed was an unloaded gun and aimed it at Gray's feet while urging him to dance — as was a common scene in old Westerns. Gray complied, but George fired the gun anyway and the bullet plowed through the floor and crashed into the bedroom wall of the apartment below, which, fortunately, wasn't occupied, but that happened to be the suite of Mrs. Jack Warner. Raft later said that incident was a foreshadowing of troubles to come with Warner Brothers.

Raft was well aware that his temper was interfering with his enjoying the pleasures of his success. Hollywood director Gregory LaCava was a good friend of George's and suggested that he consult a psychiatrist to deal with his explosive temper, compulsion to steal and other conflicts that were making life miserable for him and others. Raft reluctantly agreed and scheduled an appointment, but never showed up because he was afraid of revealing his insecurities.

Raft explained, "I was afraid. I was always afraid that people might discover that George Raft was mysterious and stayed away from Hollywood parties only because he was ignorant and could barely write his own name. Ridicule was and is a popular Hollywood weapon, and I thought that alongside me anyone with a high school diploma would sound like Professor Einstein himself."

CHAPTER FIVE

"I DON'T THINK ANYONE WILL COME TO SEE GEORGE RAFT ALONE IN ANY PICTURE."

GEORGE RAFT

The truth is that George Raft always fared best on screen when he was cast alongside a strong male co-star. His work with Spencer Tracy, Paul Muni, Fredric March and even Wallace Beery stood as proof of that. As Raft's film career progressed into the mid-to-late 1930s, his most memorable movies would see him teamed with some of Hollywood's top talent; professional associations from which Raft would definitely benefit.

After the underworld dramatics of *All of Me*, George again appealed to Paramount to put him in a picture where he didn't have to "run from the cops." Unknown to Raft, the studio had the perfect movie in mind for him. Not only would he not play a criminal, he would be given the opportunity to showcase his dancing. To add frosting to the cake, his co-star would be the vivacious Carole Lombard, with whom he was to have played opposite in *No Man of Her Own*.

George was enthusiastic — until he read the script for *Bolero* (1934). His part, as written, was his most unsympathetic since his role in *Dancers in the Dark*. Raoul DeBaere was certainly not a gangster, but the character was possessed of those same self-serving qualities that Raft knew would not endear him to audiences.

But what really angered George was a scene in the script where, as a publicity stunt, the ambitious Raoul suggests to his press agent that he should have some photographs taken beside his mother's grave.

Raft knew that his character was unappealing enough as is, but the inclusion of such repellent dialogue as "I'll take an oath on my dead mother's grave" would really make him look like a "heel" (not to mention that George's real mother was still alive and he idolized her). He firmly told associate producer Benjamin Glazer (who, as the associate producer on *The Story of Temple Drake* had already had a run-in with Raft) that he would not speak the lines. Glazer tried to exercise his authority by telling George that he was expected to do exactly as he was told — and Raft responded by hauling off and decking the producer and walking off the set.

Raft's action, which was tantamount to hitting Adolph Zukor himself, could have had severe professional repercussions for the actor. Fortunately, the two men managed to iron out their differences, and Glazer even agreed to cut

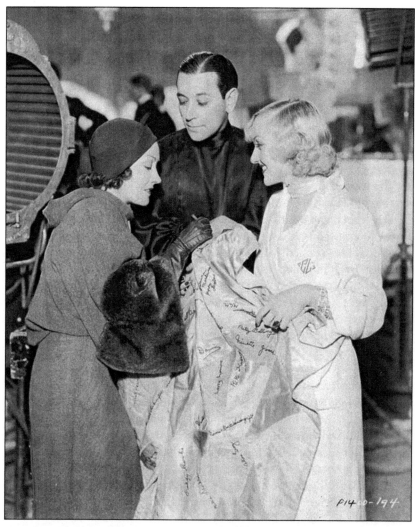

ON-SET PHOTO FROM *BOLERO*. WITH VISITOR GLORIA SWANSON AND CO-STAR CAROLE LOMBARD

the speech from the film. Actor Ray Milland, who appeared as Lord Robert Coray in the film, was on the set during the blowup and also later remembered seeing Raft and Glazer together at a Christmas Eve party on the set with their arms around each other and swearing eternal friendship. Milland thought they were drunk — until he remembered that Raft didn't drink.

Bolero proved popular with audiences, but outside of the dance numbers (some of which were doubled by the professional dance team of Veloz and Yolanda) and his enjoyment at working with Carole Lombard, the picture was never one of George's favorites. But, then, as with virtually all of his movies, he never watched *Bolero* to give it a fair appraisal. When Carole later had a showing of the film at her Malibu beach house, George's fondness for her prompted him to accept her invitation to attend, but once the picture started, he and Mack Grey slipped outside and walked along the beach until he was sure the movie was over.

Critical reviews for Raft's performance were mixed. *The New York American* reported that Raft offered "a pale mask and monotone delivery of lines." A left-handed compliment appeared in the *Los Angeles Times'* review of the film: "Raft, light on his feet but heavy on his lines, makes an ideal type pictorially for the role." The most positive review came from a reviewer for the *London Times*, who wrote, "Mr. Raft and Miss Lombard act extremely well together."

One point that many of the critics noted was that in the film the story takes place during World War I, but the Maurice Ravel composition did not premiere until 1928!

Reportedly, George and Carole Lombard's romance transcended their on-camera playing. While George would later admit that he truly loved the free-spirited and straight-shooting Carole, the shadow of his estranged wife Grayce would hinder the potential of their affair as it would all of George's later serious relationships.

Grayce publicly claimed that she would not divorce George because of her devout Catholicism. Raft believed her reasons were not religious but purely financial. He had agreed to sign over ten percent of his earnings to her, and with his stardom now assured, she shrewdly saw that it was more profitable over the long run to stay married to him than to accept a cash settlement.

There was apparently some acrimony in the dissolution of the Raft-Lombard romance. At a later date when Lombard and Clark Gable became hot Hollywood copy, Gable jokingly presented Carole with a shrunken head as a surprise gift, which Lombard promptly buried in a drawer with the disgusted explanation, "It reminds me of George Raft."

Later, the no-holds-barred Lombard commented on George's virtually insatiable sexual appetite, stating that he required sex sometimes as much as three times a day. That was a daily demand that few men in Hollywood could equal (or that few females could endure), including such notorious bedroom athletes as John Barrymore and Errol Flynn. It was speculated, though never confirmed, that this was another reason why the Raft/Lombard romance never went as far as it could.[12]

Carole Lombard was one of early Hollywood's most notorious purveyors of practical jokes. Her main targets were those stars whose egos were matched only by their press agents' hyperbole. While George was one of the more modest and self-effacing stars, Carole still couldn't resist teasing with him when she decorated his dressing room and toilet with little tin stars. She later had a big package delivered to George that upon unwrapping revealed an economy-sized ham with a handsome studio glossy of Raft pasted on it. While never known for his sense of humor, George appreciated her jokes.

As did Mack Gray, whom Lombard playfully christened "Killer" from the Yiddish word killa, meaning hernia, an operation for which Gray had just undergone. Gray remembered that Carole compounded her joke by always asking the receptionist to see "the Killer" each time she visited him at the

BEHIND-THE-SCENES SHOT OF RAFT AND HIS FAVORITE LEADING LADY CAROLE LOMBARD IN THE FIRST OF THEIR TWO TEAMINGS: *BOLERO* (1934). DIRECTOR WESLEY RUGGLES IS UNDER THE CAMERA BOOM WITH WHITE HANKERCHIEF IN HIS BREAST POCKET

hospital, and even posted guards around Gray's room armed with toy pistols, explaining to the worried hospital staff that the mob had a contract out on Gray. Knowing that Gray worked for George Raft certainly didn't lessen their apprehensions — until Carole explained that it was all a gag.

Hoping to again capitalize on the slight Valentino comparison evident in *Bolero*, Paramount next cast Raft as a Mexican bullfighter in a very thin reworking of the classic 1920 film *Blood and Sand*, called *The Trumpet Blows* (1934).

Unfortunately, George was totally out of his element in the role of Manuel Montes, an American-educated aspiring matador who is discouraged in his ambition by his retired bandit brother Pancho (played by an equally miscast Adolphe Menjou). The lovely, doe-eyed Frances Drake (who had also appeared as one of Raft's dance partners in *Bolero*) essayed the role of love interest Chulita, while the only other performer of note was a pre-Charlie Chan Sidney Toler, also cast against all believability as a Mexican. During the 1930s Hollywood casting occasionally defied all logic.

Although Raft was coached in the art of bullfighting by the real-life matador Jose Ortiz, he looked uncomfortable decked out in full bullfighter regalia practicing his moves against the charging beast. Not surprisingly, the reviews for his performance were merciless. *The New York Sun* said, "The expressionless performances of Mr. Raft and Miss Drake as the pseudo-romantic lovers may have had a good deal to do with the general flatness of *The Trumpet Blows*." Another review cruelly noted that the only institution from which the supposedly educated Raft character could have believably emerged was a detention center for juvenile delinquents.

George and co-star Adolphe Menjou's paths had briefly crossed during the 1920s, when Raft was appearing in clubs and was literally called from bed one night to come downtown to perform a specialty dance for Menjou, who was then a major star in silent movies. After completing his number, George was disappointed not to receive a special gratuity for his work, which was the usual custom. It was during the making of *The Trumpet Blows* that George reminded Menjou that he still owed him. Perhaps that was the reason when a scene in the film called for Menjou to belt Raft, the urbane actor failed to pull his punch, splitting George's lip in the process.

After (wisely) passing on the opportunity to again appear with the scene-stealing Mae West in *Belle of the Nineties* (he was replaced by Roger Pryor), George avoided suspension at the studio by (unwisely) taking on the role of the half-caste Chinese silk smuggler Harry Young in 1934's *Limehouse Blues* (later reissued for television as *East End Chant*). Once again he proved absurd in an ethnic role, though at least he was in more familiar — if not necessarily comfortable — territory, playing a racketeer. In the film Harry Young is a silk smuggler operating in the Limehouse district of London. Though he has a mistress, Tu Tuan (Anna May Wong), Harry is attracted to Caucasian Toni (Jean Parker), who is in love with pet shop owner Eric Benton (Kent Taylor). At the climax, the jealous Tu Tuan informs Scotland Yard of Harry's illegal dealings before committing suicide. Although Harry has arranged to have Eric killed to make the way clear for him and Toni, he has a change of heart and sacrifices his life in a police trap to save him. The final scene shows Raft dying before a statue of Buddha.

Raft's impersonation of an Asian received the expected critical scathing. Perhaps the most generous review was reported in the *New York Times*: "Though equipped with a pair of artificially slanted eyebrows, Mr. Raft is not convincing as a Chinaman."

The potential of a brief on-camera dance with Miss Wong, unfortunately, also emerged as ludicrous, as Raft performs the scene in a full and flowing Oriental gown.

Although George and Carole Lombard's footwork posed no threat to the on-screen dancing skills of Fred Astaire and Ginger Rogers, their movie *Bolero* had proved successful enough for Paramount to cast them in a follow-up. While *Bolero* may not have been a superior motion picture, *Rumba* (1935) was even worse. The slight storyline presented George in yet another ethnic role as the half-Cuban Joe Martin, an ambitious dancer performing his act in Havana, who witnesses a young girl Carmelita (Margo) dancing the rumba ("It's our native dance of love," she explains), which prompts Joe to highlight the number in his nightclub. A gangster subplot is revealed to be the publicity ploy of Joe's manager, Flash, played by Lynne Overman, which does, however, succeed in reuniting Joe and his lover Diane Harrison (Lombard) and sees them (actually their doubles, Veloz and Yolanda) dancing the title number.

The film received very few favorable reviews and even the dance sequences did not particularly impress critics. "... to show him [Raft] as a dancer is to ensure a certain amount of boredom for all those not especially interested in a dance which, as shown on the screen, lacks all grace and beauty," *The London Daily Telegraph* concluded their review.

Though the film lacked punch, there remained a definite chemistry between George and Carole Lombard. But *Rumba* would prove to be the last of their on-screen partnerships.

While George had become a "star," it appeared that the momentum of his career was beginning to slow. Very few of his post-*Scarface* pictures could be considered hits, although some, such as *Night After Night* and *Bolero*, had done respectable business. It seemed as if Paramount was unsure of what to do with him. So, for his next offering, the studio decided to cast George in a movie that contained the two elements best associated with Raft and also favored by movie audiences of the time: music and crime. The result was *Stolen Harmony* (1935).

Co-star Lloyd Nolan remembered, "I went under contract to Paramount soon after I appeared with Cagney in *"G" Men*, which I made for Warners in about '35. I got to know George right from the start, and though I'd heard all the stories about how troublesome he could be on the set, when I worked with him in *Stolen Harmony*, I can't remember there being any difficulties during production."

While entertaining, *Stolen Harmony* does suffer from its schizophrenic nature, as the two genres blend uneasily, culminating in one of the most violent cops-and-robbers shootouts this side of *Scarface*.

George plays Ray Angelo (alias Ray Ferraro), a saxophone-playing convict, who, upon his release from prison, is hired by Jack Conrad (Ben Bernie) to tour cross-country with his band. All goes well until Ray is falsely accused of robbing the band's receipts and he is ostracized by the group, including his romantic interest Jean Loring (Grace Bradley), only to redeem himself when he and the others are kidnapped by gangsters led by the Dillinger-like

Chesty Burrage (Nolan). Of course, the romantic fadeout finds the wounded but exonerated Ray back in the arms of Loring.

Besides good playing by Lloyd Nolan, in his first underworld role, *Stolen Harmony* also features one of the few film appearances of James Cagney's lookalike brother, William, who, as Schoolboy Howe, performs a "dance of death" at the movie's end, similar to his brother's climactic gutter scene from *The Public Enemy*. Apparently, George suggested Bill Cagney for the small role as a way to repay Jimmy for helping him get the dance bit in *Taxi!* Perhaps it was all for naught as William Cagney soon retired from acting to become his brother's business manager and later a film producer.

George's next film was a good one. A straight crime drama based on a book by the popular mystery writer Dashiell Hammett, creator of *The Thin Man*, which had been made into an enormously popular movie the previous year. Unfortunately, *The Glass Key* (1935) had a rather ridiculous publicity campaign that highlighted the toughness of the picture's star. Audiences were presented with such exaggerated copy as "The kind of a fighter who'd stand toe to toe and slug with Max Baer." Or worse: "The kind of lover who'd tell Mae West to go out and get herself a reputation." Despite the corniness of the advertising, *The Glass Key* managed to stand on its own merits as a tough, absorbing thriller.

In the Frank Tuttle-directed film, Raft was the mysterious good guy Ed (rechristened from the novel's "Ned") Beaumont, lieutenant to crooked politician Paul Madvig (Edward Arnold), who is attempting to go straight and merge with Senator Henry (Charles Richman), who is seeking re-election. When Madvig closes down a crooked gambling casino, its underworld owner Shad O'Rory (Robert Gleckler) retaliates by murdering the senator's son, Taylor (Ray Milland), and pinning the crime on Madvig. It is left to loyal Ed Beaumont to clear his boss and expose the real culprit.

Among the highlights of *The Glass Key* is one of the most graphically brutal beatings ever displayed on the screen up to that point, delivered with sadistic delight by O'Rory's punch-drunk henchman, Jeff (Guinn "Big Boy" Williams), with Beaumont the victim of his abuse. It is a scene that, even today, more than seventy years later, remains excruciating to watch. (Incidentally, the bit part of the nurse who later tends to Beaumont's injuries was played by Ann Sheridan.)

For once, George was awarded mostly positive reviews for his performance. In fact, some critics went so far as to say that *The Glass Key* provided Raft with his best film performance since *Scarface*. The *New York World-Telegram* wrote, "Mr. Raft, though not exactly as Mr. Hammett visualized Ed Beaumont, is in every way superb." John Scott, writing for the *Los Angeles Times*, was likewise enthusiastic: "Raft's role does him justice in this instance. He is more at ease in the characterization — which makes for a harmonious production." Even the *London Times* praised Raft: "It is a part well-suited to Mr. Raft's imperturbable calm. He moves through the story immaculate

A 1930s PORTRAIT OF AN ULTRA-SUAVE RAFT LIGHTING UP A LUCKY STRIKE

and almost expressionless, that most beloved of film characters, a 'tough guy' with a heart of gold."

The Glass Key was successful enough for Paramount to remake it under the same title in 1942, with Alan Ladd reprising the Beaumont role, Brian Donlevy as Medvig and burly William Bendix as the brutal Jeff.

Raft met Hammett on the set and said of the author: "He was really a very distinguished man. He'd read all these different books. Me, I was never much for reading — and I didn't have a lot to say to him."

George was finally enjoying well-deserved critical accolades, which made

1935 a professionally satisfying year. George's personal life also took a positive turn when he met and fell in love with wealthy socialite Virginia Pine, separated from Edward Lehman, Jr., a wealthy Chicago department store owner, and the mother of a two-year-old daughter Joanie.

Raft's "wife" Grayce had already filed a suit for separation, claiming cruelty, non-payment and abandonment, and seeking a reported $1,200 per week alimony. She also said in her suit that her husband had been "attentive" to other women, a raging understatement considering that George was not shy about being seen around town with the likes of Virginia Cherrill (later Mrs. Cary Grant), Constance Cummings, Billie Dove, Miriam Hopkins, Marjorie King and Molly O'Day, among numerous other starlets.

George's enormous sexual appetite became the basis of Tinseltown rumors that he may, in fact, have been bisexual. Friend and fellow actor Cesar Romero once remarked: "George Raft may or may not have gone both ways, but he was very sensitive to what they said about him, and it was one factor why he decided to play all those gangsters in the movies."

However, Raft biographer Lewis Yablonsky strongly disputes this possibility, maintaining that Raft's sexual preference was exclusively female.

Yet none of these were serious romances. After all, George was still legally married and, besides, he was busy building his career. With Virginia Pine, however, George fell madly in love. He was taken by her striking good looks and sophistication, so foreign to the rough world he knew.

The fact that she had a child posed no problem since George was immensely fond of children. Thirties child actress Sybil Jason recalls a later event that demonstrated the affection he had for children: "Although I never worked with George Raft, I was extremely fond of him because he was a genuinely nice man and was very fond of kids. One lovely summer day in the thirties he opened up his beautiful home with the fantastic swimming pool to all the kids from *Our Gang* and also to me, one of the only kids who wasn't connected to *Our Gang*. We had a delightful full day of swimming … all kinds of foods that kids love, like hot dogs and hamburgers … a showing of cartoons, and there was no adult around to put the kibosh on our fun! He had an extensive property and we were all allowed to roam or run free around it. This was the time span when he was so very much in love with Betty Grable. I had seen his Warner movies and he was soooo very unlike what he portrayed on the screen. He was gentle and generous. The perfect gentleman! I had seen him on the Warners lot, but, except for that invitation that was extended to me at that party, I had never met him before."

Although George enjoyed the single life and his ladies' man reputation, he also yearned for the stability of a family. He was as attentive as a real father to little Joanie and enjoyed surprising her with gifts and spending hours playing with her. George and Virginia had a relationship that was both loving and caring. Although refined and sophisticated, Virginia had no qualms about accompanying George to nightclubs or various sporting events. For his part, George frequently took Virginia on expensive shopping trips in Beverly Hills. He also benefited from his romance with Virginia in that she helped teach him class and respectability, and improved his social skills to the point where he was no longer uncomfortable in a social setting. She even altered his flashy New York wardrobe to the more fashionably acceptable dress of Beverly Hills that quickly had him featured on best-dressed lists and led to an appearance in the 1935 short subject *The Fashion Side of Hollywood*. An eager and willing pupil, George completely surrendered to Virginia's tutelage.

As George became more polished, he found that he was not so badgered by his tough-guy reputation, Previously, his off-screen image so worked against him that more than one director backed out of a film when learning that George Raft was to appear in it. They would comment, "Raft's a knuckleduster and I'm not going to have him work me over."

Raft would still endure some quick temper moments, but, with Virginia's persistent and patient help, he was also gaining the desired reputation as a suave gentleman. And, of course, George continued to be an easy touch, even if he was learning to be more careful with his money. Yet he would always remain generous to those truly in need. He paid the rent for a studio stenographer who was injured in an accident and was especially kind and thoughtful to a Paramount contract actress who was hospitalized for a year. At one point he even offered to adopt a boy who was having behavioral problems, but the plans fell through when the boy's natural parents intervened. Stories of George's generosity are legion, even if he once said to a reporter, "Sure, I know a lot of people are taking me. But can I let that stop me from helping someone who really needs a buck? I couldn't sleep at night if I thought I turned someone down who was really hungry or had rent to pay."

Mack Gray agreed. He was quoted as saying, "He takes care of more broken-down bums than the midnight mission, and he's a sucker for a sad tale. He grew up in New York's Hell Kitchen and he's never forgotten its characters."

There was little question that George wanted to marry Virginia and adopt Joanie as his own. However, he still had to face the obstacle that he was a married man, and that Grayce was not willing to grant him a divorce. Each time George would plead with her to divorce him she'd refuse and up her demand for more money.

His movie work continued with another musical, *Every Night at Eight* (1935). The film was a mediocre endeavor centering on radio amateur hours, a popular entertainment of the time. Raft appears as an orchestra bandleader named Tops Cardona who encourages the singing career of the Swanee Sisters (Alice Faye, Patsy Kelly and Frances Langford). Raft's big moments come when he enthusiastically, if unconvincingly, waves his baton (as he did for those few seconds in *Winner Take All*). Although hyped by Paramount

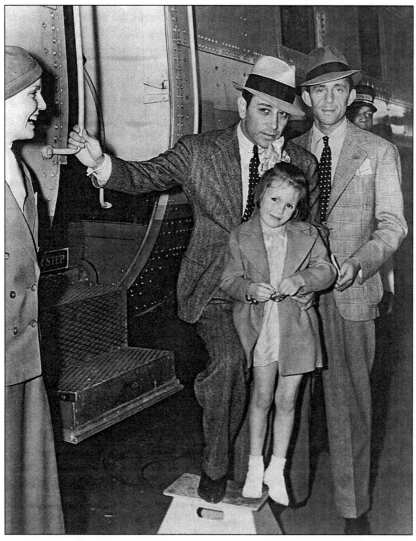

A CANDID SHOT TAKEN DURING THE LATE 1930'S WITH VIRGINA PINE (LEFT) AND HER DAUGHTER JOANIE, SAYING GOODBYE AS RAFT AND MACK GRAY PREPARE TO TAKE A TRAIN TO NEW YORK ON A PUBLICITY TOUR

PHOTO COURTESY OF THE MACK GRAY ESTATE

as "The busiest musical picture you ever saw," about the film's only virtues are that it was directed by an unlikely Raoul Walsh (who reportedly specifically asked for George for the film) and that it introduced the songs "I Feel a Song Comin' On" and "I'm in the Mood for Love."

The late Frances Langford played Raft's love interest in this film and wrote to this author that although she remembered little of the movie, she did recall that Raft "was very pleasant."

Raft went on loanout to Harry Cohn's Columbia Pictures for his next movie, a society comedy called *She Couldn't Take It* (1935). This was one of Raft's better films where he gives a good account of himself in a familiar role, Spot Ricardi, a jailed bootlegger, who is made guardian of the family of his wealthy cellmate Mr. Van Dyke (Walter Connolly) just before the latter succumbs to a heart attack. This proves no easy task as the Van Dyke clan is both undisciplined and eccentric. Spot has a particularly difficult time with the spoiled and independent-minded Carol (Joan Bennett), who resents the interference of the ex-con and attempts to get even by arranging her own fake kidnapping. The hoods, led by Tex (Lloyd Nolan), decide to really kidnap Carol, and it is up to Spot to rescue her after a wild car chase and punch-out with the villains. Sobered by the experience, Carol realizes that she is in love with Spot.

While certainly not on a par with Columbia's screwball classic *It Happened One Night* (1934), *She Couldn't Take It* is fast-paced entertainment that provided Raft with one of his best roles of the '30s, where he was finally given the chance to flirt with comedy, under the able direction of Tay Garnett. The *New York Herald-Tribune* wrote that his role was "his most ingratiating characterization since the days when he was playing minor villains." *Liberty* magazine went so far as to say that "Raft and Joan Bennett are excellent as the battling lovers" and that Raft "emerges with his best performance since *Scarface*."

As an indication of George Raft's present status in motion pictures, just four years earlier, he was way down the cast list of the Joan Bennett-starrer *Hush Money*, and now was receiving top billing over Miss Bennett.

His new prominence notwithstanding, George had a terrible incident that he would always regret. A lifelong baseball fan (he'd had it written into his Paramount contract that he would be free to attend all World Series games), he headed East in October to be in the stands for the 1935 Detroit-Chicago World Series. The exciting game ended when Goose Goslin won the Series for Detroit with a ninth-inning single. As pandemonium reigned on the field, Goose approached George's box and presented him with the bat that had won the game.

George admitted, "I am sentimental and easily moved, and that prize was just as valuable as an Oscar."

Raft was in a rush to get back to California and after thanking Goose profusely for his gift he hopped into a taxi and told the driver to get him to the train station in a hurry, offering an extra ten-spot as an incentive.

George only had about twenty minutes to make the train, and the taxi driver was fighting the traffic around the stadium. Suddenly, a truck cut in front, causing them to miss a green light. Enraged, George leaned out the window and yelled at the truck driver, "I oughta beat your brains out. If you've got any." The driver, who, according to Raft, was "as big as King

Kong," accepted the challenge. "OK, wise guy. Pull over past the light and you can try."

George said later that he knew it would have been suicide to physically take on the guy, so instead he had the cabbie pull alongside the truck at the next set of lights, rolled down the window, and fired his prized bat like a torpedo at the trucker's head. The lights changed to green and the taxi peeled rubber. George never found out how bad he had hurt the guy. But, worse for him, was that his temper had caused him to lose a prized memento. The next time George saw Goose Goslin, he lied and said that he still had the bat.

After refusing the role of a hood in the Paramount football yarn *Hold 'Em Yale* (1935), Raft was loaned to the newly-formed Twentieth Century-Fox. In *It Had to Happen* (1936), Raft was teamed with Rosalind Russell. The film was another comedy/drama, directed by Roy Del Ruth, in which George played an Italian immigrant named Enrico Scaffa, who rises to become a political force in New York. Problems arise when Enrico is accused of bribery and has to clear himself. Naturally, he develops a romantic attraction to Miss Russell's character and their affair is allowed to blossom once he redeems himself. Apparently, both Raft and Miss Russell were ill throughout much of the production, with George suffering from a case of laryngitis that necessitated his later dubbing of many of his lines on the soundtrack, yet that did not stop Raft or Russell from giving performances that were highly complimented by the press. *Liberty* magazine reported: "The surprising and most gratifying thing about the picture, though, is that it shows that Raft can handle a comedy scene when given the chance." The tone of the *New York Herald-Tribune's* review was almost an apology for Raft's past movie performances: "It is not a suave, subtle piece of work. But it has more depth and reality than his earlier rumba roles had, and he gets certain shadings in the part which indicate material for a good and varied character actor."

With two of his 1936 film appearances made at other studios, Raft returned to Paramount to close out the year with *Yours for the Asking*. Here, he was back in the familiar milieu of gambling house operator Johnny Lamb. The film, which co-starred Dolores Costello (ex-wife of John Barrymore) and the young Ida Lupino, was basically a rehash of the earlier and more successful *Night After Night*, and reviewers made note of that fact, while noting the absence of Mae West, whose presence certainly would have given the proceedings a much-needed boost. However, Raft's patented tough guy rated a special nod from the *Brooklyn Daily Eagle*: "The acting is generally on a farce-comedy level, ably assisted by the first-rate performance of George Raft."

A reunion film with Carole Lombard was offered to George with *The Princess Comes Across* (1936), but Raft, though personally and professionally fond of Carole, turned down the assignment, reportedly because he felt that cameraman Ted Tetzlaff would give Carole preferential treatment, as Raft

RAFT IN A CASUAL POSE FOR A PARAMOUNT PUBLICITY PHOTO

believed he had in *Rumba*. Rising Paramount star Fred MacMurray was brought in to replace George.

Ninety-thirty-six was also the year George Raft first achieved a distinctive kind of cinematic immortality — as an animated figure, in the Warner Brothers cartoon *The CooCoo Nut Grove*. Later, his cartoon likeness would be seen in *Malibu Beach Party* (1941) and, together with Humphrey Bogart, James Cagney and Edward G. Robinson, in *Hollywood Steps Out* (1941). He also "appeared" as a spy character named "Tattle-Tale Grey" in the Warner

Brothers Porky Pig cartoon *Ali Baba Bound* (1940). This character of Tattle-Tale Grey was modeled after his *Scarface* character, Guino Rinaldo, and in the cartoon Tattle Tale Grey flips a coin with his feet.[13]

George also began doing a fair amount of radio, as both a guest and dramatic star, on such popular programs as *The Kraft Music Hall* (his radio debut, appearing with host Bing Crosby[14]), *Lux Radio Theater*, *Standard Brands Hour* and the *Campbell Soup Playhouse*, among others.

Around this time George traveled to New York to attend the premiere of *Every Night at Eight*, and he brought along his proud mother as his escort. Unbeknownst to her, the studio had also provided a police escort for her son and when Eva Ranft saw the two uniformed officers stepping up to join them upon entering the theater lobby, she misunderstood and began to panic.

"Run, Georgie, run! Don't let the cops get you!"

Apparently, she had become similarly confused while watching one of George's crime films where he was being pursued by the police, and she started shouting at the screen for her son to run faster.

Was George Raft such a convincing movie gangster that even his own mother had a difficult time distinguishing the reel from the real?

Fortunately, in his next film for Paramount, Raft's character, though introduced as a mate on a slave ship, emerges as likeable, romantic and, ultimately, heroic.

Souls at Sea (1937) was a picture George had initially refused to do. Although he welcomed the chance to work with his good friend Gary Cooper (the two had appeared in *If I Had a Million*, but in different episodes), George regarded the role of Powdah as a secondary part — and, worse from Raft's standpoint, the character died at the end. Even though Powdah's going down with the ship was motivated by romanticism and a sacrifice to ensure the survival of friend and government agent Nuggin Taylor (Cooper), Raft apparently could not grasp the sympathetic qualities of the character and prepared to go on suspension again. Both Lloyd Nolan and newcomer Anthony Quinn were considered as replacements, though Nolan was quickly rejected because it was thought he too closely resembled Cooper. Fearing competition and forfeiture of his reported $4,500 per week salary, Raft finally changed his mind and accepted the part.

As a result, the Henry Hathaway-directed *Souls at Sea* turned out to be George's best picture since *Scarface*. His colorful role allowed him the opportunity to really act — by displaying a variety of emotions — from extreme terror at the prospect of drowning at sea, to a teasing humor while he and Nuggin try to impress their romantic interests (Frances Dee and Olympe Bradna), to a heartbreaking despair as he discovers his dead love (Bradna) on the sinking ship and tenderly removes his earring to place on the girl's lifeless finger, as if it were a wedding band. Even his appearance was altered for the film. His hair was not glossy and slicked back by a pound of Vaseline, and instead was allowed to look full and natural, if also slightly curled.

The making of the picture (much of it shot off Catalina Island) went smoothly. Henry Hathaway was a true man's man director who had the reputation of being tough on his actors, but he behaved well toward George and Gary Cooper (with whom he had worked previously in the classic *The*

GARY COOPER, RICHARD ARLEN, DIRECTOR HENRY HATHAWAY AND RAFT ON THE
***SOULS AT SEA* SET**

Lives of a Bengal Lancer, 1935). The only problems Raft encountered were in having to wear "lifts" to make his 5'10" self appear taller next to the 6'3" Cooper, and later in a scene where his character was required to throw a rock at Miss Dee. Raft refused to do the scene since he felt it would make his character appear unsympathetic (plus the fact Miss Dee had those proper ladylike qualities that reminded George of Virginia Pine). Raft remained so adamant in his stance that he even threatened to walk off the picture. The problem was finally resolved when star Gary Cooper sided with George and the scene remained unfilmed.

It was during the filming of *Souls at Sea* that George's underworld past again caught up with him when he was interviewed by FBI agents in connection with an investigation looking into the whereabouts of New York mobster and notorious head of Murder Incorporated, Louis "Lepke" Buchalter. Raft couldn't provide any information, other than admitting to having an acquain-

STUDIO PORTRAIT OF RAFT AS THE HEROIC SAILOR POWDAH IN PARAMOUNT'S 1937 NAUTICAL EPIC *SOULS AT SEA*

tance with someone who knew Lepke and his partner Jacob "Gurrah" Shapiro. Perhaps not quite satisfied, the agents visited the *Souls at Sea* set and questioned Cooper and Frances Dee about Raft's mobster ties. All Cooper was able to provide was that George was a man who lived somewhat beyond his financial means, and that he had a distorted sense of loyalty to his old New York associates, who were not always of the best character.

Some years later, Miss Dee spoke succinctly about this experience and her co-star, "Everyone knew he [Raft] was a gangster."

It has been erroneously reported that Raft was nominated for a Best Supporting Oscar for his work in *Souls at Sea*. While this was not the case, his uncharacteristic performance was indeed worthy of an award, and even Gary Cooper admitted that George stole the film.

Critics were not short on praise, either. *Variety* said, "Raft is a bit of a surprise as a sympathetic player who meets his dramatic opportunities more than half way."

George himself would call *Souls at Sea*, "A helluva good adventure movie."

The movie opened in New York, where Paramount charged ticket buyers an unusually steep two-dollar admission. Nevertheless, *Souls at Sea* proved a spectacular hit with audiences.

Unfortunately, after completing this success, Raft was suspended by Paramount for refusing two pictures: a film to be called *Caviar for His Excellency* and a movie to be directed by Norman Krasna.

Still, riding high on his success, George purchased property in Coldwater Canyon and began building a quarter of a million-dollar estate that he planned to move into with Virginia Pine and her daughter Joanie. He still hoped to marry Virginia and, ever the gentleman, maintained his residence at the El Royale until that legal union could be arranged.

However, the Raft-Pine romance became one of a number of Hollywood unions that soon garnered unwanted publicity when *Photoplay* magazine published an article entitled "Hollywood's Unmarried Husbands and Wives". Included in the scandal were Robert Taylor and Barbara Stanwyck, Charles Chaplin and Paulette Goddard, Constance Bennett and Gilbert Roland, and Clark Gable and Carole Lombard. The month following the article's publication, studio pressure prompted *Photoplay* to print a public apology.

Sadly, Raft's happy year was marred by the death of his mother. She'd suffered from respiratory problems for many years — the same condition her son had begun to develop from his four-pack-a-day Lucky Strike habit, and possibly heredity — and when George visited her for the final time, she could no longer speak.

Eva Ranft had always been her son's biggest booster. George recalled that she used to wander around her New York neighborhood, trading photographs of her son and making sure that every store or shop she entered had at least two or three pictures prominently displayed.

When Eva passed away, George made the funeral arrangements and was extremely touched to find Owney Madden and Big Frenchie DeMange sitting inside the funeral parlor on Broadway. He remembered Owney saying to him, "Georgie, Frenchie and I figured you might need someone around." While none of Raft's Hollywood friends attended the service, Owney had made a gallant gesture since he had been warned by rival gangsters to stay out of New York. Indeed, he had risked his life to pay his final respects to Mrs. Ranft.[15]

George recalled that the day after the funeral, he and Mack Gray had gone to an uptown bank to sign papers for his mother's estate. Because he didn't want to be bothered at that sensitive time by fans or autograph seekers, he and Gray had dressed in long trench coats with sunglasses and hats pulled down low. The moment they entered the bank, buzzers began going off and suddenly four cops burst in with their guns drawn. They ordered

AN AERIAL VIEW OF RAFT'S COLDWATER CANYON ESTATE, CIRCA 1938-1939 WHEN IT WAS FIRST BUILT PHOTO COURTESYOF THE MACK GRAY ESTATE

George and Gray to put their hands up. Once the cops discovered, with surprise, that these suspicious characters were George Raft and his pal, they were embarrassed and apologetic. George, however, was not so easily mollified. It was left to the bank manager to explain that "You walked in here looking like a gangster and we rang the holdup alarm." Raft had to admit that he'd made similar sinister entrances so many times on the silver screen that it had become a habit.

When George returned to California, he began to have frequent arguments with Virginia regarding their future together. Virginia loved George deeply, but she wanted the marriage that Raft, despite all his efforts, was unable to provide. Because Virginia harbored ambitions to be an actress, George tried to smooth their rough patches by attempting to find her work in one of his pictures, but to no avail. Finally, George discovered that Virginia had begun seeing other men — and once again his temper flared. One afternoon he learned that she had been lunching with Joseph Schenck, an executive with Twentieth Century-Fox. He followed the two from the restaurant to Schenck's house and when no one answered the ringing of the bell, he broke down the door.

Fortunately, further violence was avoided as George regained his composure and, without speaking a word to the couple, simply turned and walked away. But Raft knew that their relationship was over. Virginia soon moved out of 1218 Coldwater Canyon and went to New York. George and Mack Gray then packed up their belongings from the El Royale and moved into the house — as bachelors. Still adoring of little Joanie, George would continue to send her presents after the breakup. In 1942 Virginia Pine married the noted war correspondent Quentin Reynolds.

"NOBODY LIKES ME ON SIGHT. THERE MUST BE SOMETHING ABOUT THE TONE OF MY VOICE, OR THIS ARROGANT FACE — SOMETHING THAT ANTAGONIZES EVERYBODY."

HUMPHREY BOGART

By 1937, George Raft's "lifetime contract" with Paramount was earning him the enormous yearly salary of $202,666. He was second only to Warner Baxter ("The Cisco Kid") and Gary Cooper in actors' annual income. Yet, as Cooper had pointed out, George had a difficult time holding onto his money. He was a lavish spender, with a penchant for women and the ponies, and had begun to spend a lot of time on suspension at the studio for refusing roles he thought unsuitable.

While on his latest suspension, George was asked to be borrowed from Paramount to play the role of slum-bred gangster "Baby Face" Martin in the Samuel Goldwyn production of the hit Broadway play *Dead End* (1937).[16] The problem was: Raft didn't want to do the part.

Not only was Martin an ambitious, amoral killer, who would die at the hands of the hero at the film's end, the character also had further scenes in the photoplay that disturbed Raft. The film introduced to movie audiences the Dead End Kids (Billy Halop, Leo Gorcey, Huntz Hall, Gabriel Dell, Bobby Jordan and Bernard Punsley), six young New York actors who had appeared in the original stage version that ran for 687 performances. Later, the Dead End Kids would evolve into the East Side Kids and the Bowery Boys and become on-camera delinquent comedians, but their playing in *Dead End* was deadly serious. They were to be tutored in the art of "crime does pay" by the gangster Martin — himself on the run from the law. George just could not bring himself to do that. He wanted to play his scenes with them differently. Instead of encouraging them, he wanted his character to discourage the young ruffians from following his life course. Of course, that would have destroyed the whole point of the picture — and while Raft would have been a major asset to the production, neither Goldwyn nor director William Wyler would compromise on the story. George also strongly objected to the scene where Martin's mother (Marjorie Main) berates him for being a criminal. George

HUMPHREY BOGART AS "BABY FACE" MARTIN IN DEAD END (1937), THE FIRST OF MANY SUCCESSFUL ROLES HE INHERITED FROM GEORGE RAFT

saw too much connection with his own mother, who had worried about him as a reckless young man but lived to see him become a huge success. He suggested that the scene be altered to showing him with a tear in his eye after his mother slaps him and condemns his way of life, to let the audience know she is right and that he regrets his criminal path. Again, Goldwyn and Wyler were not listening. "Baby Face" Martin had to be presented as thoroughly ruthless, without a thread of sympathy. Even though producer and director pleaded with Raft to "do it our way," Raft walked away from the assignment.

James Cagney had been the original choice for Martin, but he, too, was trying to disengage himself from gangster parts, and, besides, he was involved in another contract dispute with Warner Brothers, which precluded his working elsewhere. Edward G. Robinson never would have never been believable as a character dubbed "Baby Face," and so the only other tough guy of note to consider was Humphrey Bogart, who'd scored a hit as the Dillinger-like Duke Mantee both in the stage and film versions of *The Petrified Forest* (1936), but had since been playing a parade of supporting movie mobsters at Warner Brothers, tagged with such nicknames as "Bugs" and "Turkey." Bogart was shrewd when it came to his career. He had the perspective of past failures and, while he would spend much of his early career griping about the quality of his roles, he certainly recognized both the artistic and commercial considerations of *Dead End*.[17]

And his interpretation of "Baby Face" Martin was brilliant. Even though billed below Sylvia Sidney and Joel McCrea (one wonders how the billing would have read had Raft decided to accept the part), he was the one audiences left the theater talking about (along with the Dead End Kids, of course, but they were of a different category). In short, it was Bogie's best film role since *The Petrified Forest* and would remain so until *High Sierra* (1941).

Humphrey DeForest Bogart, destined to become the most prolific and deadly of the early "Big 4" movie gangsters, was born on January 23, 1899, into a posh setting on New York's Upper West Side, geographically less than a mile away, but culturally a continent apart from George Raft's Hell's Kitchen environment.

Young Humphrey was not lacking in financial privileges, but his was not a happy home. While Humphrey loved and respected his father, Dr. Belmont DeForest Bogart, a prominent surgeon, he felt less close to his mother, Maude, a respected and highly successful artist, but a cold and unaffectionate woman. Despite his well-to-do upbringing, Humphrey, from an early age, displayed a rebellious independence. He disappointed his parents by dropping out of (or being asked to leave) Phillips Academy at Andover, Massachusetts, where he had enrolled in preparation for medical studies at Yale. After a short, undistinguished stint in the Navy, young Humphrey returned to New York, where for the next two years he worked at odd jobs, such as a runner for a Wall Street investment firm. But Humphrey was restless and unsure of what direction to take in life. Soon, he drifted into the theatre and began appearing in various plays, usually cast as the colorless juvenile. Eventually, he was called to Hollywood, but his early work in pictures was mainly undistinguished (except, perhaps significantly, for his role as a gangster in *Three on a Match*, 1932) and, discouraged, he returned to New York and the stage. Fortune shone on Humphrey when he was cast as escaped killer Duke Mantee in the Broadway production of *The Petrified Forest*, starring Leslie Howard. Not counting *Three on a Match* and the film *Midnight*

(1934), where he played another gangster, it was a role unlike any Humphrey had ever played before — and he was a smash!

The success of the play (running for 197 performances) resulted in Warner Brothers purchasing the film rights. Leslie Howard was, naturally, retained as the star, the doomed intellectual poet Alan Squier — and Edward G. Robinson, whose career was beginning to slip but was still under a high-priced contract, was considered for the role of Mantee. Fortunately for Bogart, Leslie Howard intervened on his behalf and firmly told Warners that he would not appear in the movie version of *The Petrified Forest* unless Humphrey was allowed to play the character of Duke Mantee. Apparently, this gallant gesture was motivated not only by friendship, but by Howard's dramatic smarts of how well the two had complemented each other onstage.

And how could Bogart not be noticed when he made his first major appearance in the picture. Flanked by his hoods, Duke Mantee walks stiffly into the desert café, head slightly cocked, *sans* traditional gangster fedora, arms bent at the elbow with his hands hanging out in front of him, as if still bound by handcuffs. Then the famous introductory line spoken by actor Joe Sawyer: "This is Duke Mantee, folks, the world-famous killer. And he's hungry." No other movie gangster up to that point had enjoyed such a dramatic entrance.

After the success of the motion picture, *The Petrified Forest*, Humphrey was immediately placed under contract to Warners, at a modest $550 per week ($200 less than he received for *The Petrified Forest*, based on his minimum artists' agreement), and began his long apprenticeship, primarily in "B" picture underworld roles, waiting for lightning to strike again. The first bolt came with *Dead End*.

As for his benefactor, George Raft, unlike some of his later famous movie rejects, he maintained his posture regarding *Dead End* and never voiced regret at turning it down.

Besides, his career was still going strong, and on his return to Paramount he was offered another strong role in a film again to be directed by Henry Hathaway, *Spawn of the North* (1938).

A rugged adventure epic, the story dealt with attempts by Russian pirates to infiltrate the Alaskan salmon industry. George played Tyler Dawson, the good/bad guy who aligns himself with the pirates, but redeems himself at the picture's end by crashing his vessel into a mass of icebergs, killing both himself and the lead villain, Red Skain, portrayed by the versatile Akim Tamiroff. Paramount rounded out the supporting cast with such exceptional talent as Henry Fonda, Dorothy Lamour, John Barrymore and Lynne Overman. But perhaps the true star of the movie was the scene-stealing Slicker the seal.

George received the expected fine reviews for his characterization. *The New York Times* wrote that Raft gave a "surprisingly sympathetic performance." *The Herald-Tribune* concurred: "Mr. Raft never has been better and seldom has been so good."

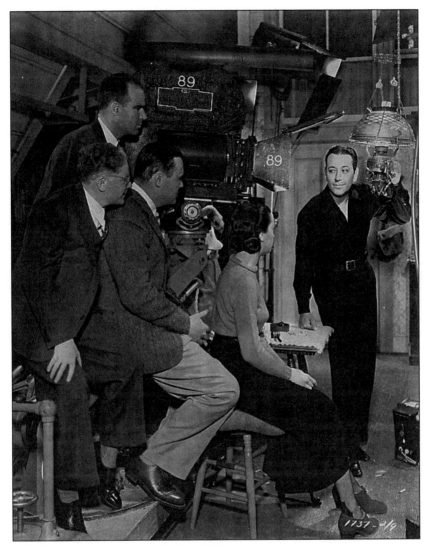

SETTING UP A SHOT WITH DIRECTOR HENRY HATHAWAY AND DOROTHY LAMOUR FOR THE ACTION-PACKED *SPAWN OF THE NORTH* (1938)

Spawn of the North was another box office success and was awarded a special Academy Award for its outstanding special photographic and sound effects. Much of this footage was later used in the 1954 remake, *Alaska Seas*, starring Robert Ryan in the Raft part.

Also in 1938, Raft was once more teamed with Sylvia Sidney in an odd comedy/drama/fantasy produced and directed by Fritz Lang from a story by Norman Krasna, *You and Me*. Raft played ex-con Joe Dennis, working as a department store sales clerk alongside Helen (Sidney), who, unbeknownst to Joe, is also on parole. The two fall in love and marry, but when Joe discovers the truth about Helen, he becomes disillusioned and decides to throw in with the other ex-convicts employed at the store to rob it. Together with the sympathetic store owner Mr. Morris (Harry Carey), Helen manages to prevent Joe and the others from carrying through with the plan, bringing down the principal heavy Mickey (Barton MacLane) in the process.

RAFT IN ONE OF HIS FINAL FILMS FOR PARAMOUNT: *YOU AND ME* **(1938), WITH (FROM LEFT) BARTON MACLANE, ROBERT CUMMINGS, WARREN HYMER AND GEORGE E. STONE**

It was well known in the industry how Lang could become dictatorial, if not an outright tyrant, on the sets of his pictures. According to Miss Sidney, Lang tried to create dissention between her and Raft during the making of the picture, as he had with Sidney and Fonda in *You Only Live Once* (1937). George, however, quickly caught on and put Lang straight.

Miss Sidney would say of Raft, "George was a tough pussycat, very much like his screen image. Of all the actors I worked with, he was the greatest gentleman." Considering that during her lengthy career Sylvia Sidney worked with the likes of Humphrey Bogart, Gary Cooper, Henry Fonda, Joel McCrea and Spencer Tracy, this was quite a compliment indeed.

You and Me did not prove successful with audiences, who perhaps saw it as too offbeat, which it was, with strange musical interludes thrown into the mix, such as the "Stick with the Mob" number. Fortunately, both Raft and Miss Sidney were spared much of the criticism. *Variety* approved of a "softer

Raft," adding that "more will like him this way." *The New York Times* said in their review, "George Raft and Sylvia sustain interest in a disjointed drama through their doggedly honest performances."

Nineteen-thirty-eight was the year that George Raft began to get restless at Paramount. He rejected a number of film roles, including *Stolen Heaven, Argentina Love, The Magnificent Fraud* and *St. Louis Blues* (the latter two

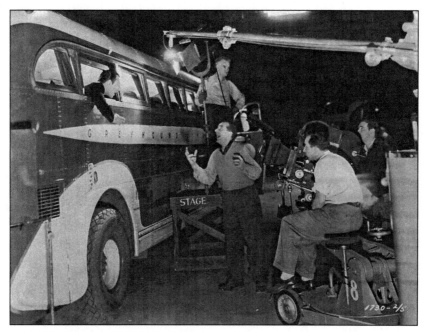

BEING DIRECTED BY THE GREAT BUT DEMANDING FRITZ LANG IN *YOU AND ME*

were taken over by Lloyd Nolan). Reportedly, he was even offered another adventure blockbuster, Paramount's remake of *Beau Geste* (1939), but he had no interest.

Instead, Raft agreed to do *The Lady's from Kentucky* (1939), with Ellen Drew, an affair so forgettable that it was relegated to the lower half of the double bill — a curious fate for a film starring a player as important as Raft. One can only speculate that the reason Raft decided to do this unimportant picture was because of his great passion for horse racing.

Still, while the film didn't generate excitement at the box office, George received complimentary reviews. As if overlooking some of Raft's recent successes, *The New York World-Telegram* said, "… for the first time in a long while he has an ideal part. He stalks through the film with an unconcern that is a pleasure to watch."

The lackluster returns from George's last two pictures led to a mutual decision by George and Paramount to terminate Raft's quarter-of-a-million-dollar-a-year contract with the studio, which became official on January 22, 1939. He had been at Paramount for nearly eight years and had appeared in twenty-one pictures on the lot. He'd also entered the studio record books for an unprecedented twenty-two suspensions. Raft was now, temporarily at least, a free agent.

Surprisingly, given many of his rows with Paramount, the first film role he accepted was as a circumstantially-created criminal in Universal's *I Stole a Million* (1939), directed by Frank Tuttle and co-starring Claire Trevor. George played Joe Laurik, a cab driver, who is swindled by a disreputable finance company and soon after finds himself on the run after being made the "fall guy" by a gang of bank robbers. Joe meets and marries Laura Benson (Trevor) and tries to go legitimate by opening a garage, but his identity is discovered and he is forced to resort to a series of robberies. At the film's conclusion he is finally persuaded by Laura to surrender to the authorities with the promise that she will be waiting for him.

It is curious why Raft chose this particular project for his first freelance feature. While his role is basically sympathetic, his character still emerges as an outlaw who must ultimately pay for his crimes. Perhaps the consolation for George was that this was one of his very few criminal roles where he was not required to die at the end. (Though *Variety's* favorable review of the film erroneously states that his character "retaliates for initial injustice against himself in a succession of lawless ventures which ends in his own death — a sacrifice to make life easier for his wife and child.")

Raft often told the story of how during the making of the movie he refused to play the scene of his character robbing a post office, explaining to director Tuttle, "As a kid I learned that no gunman in his right mind fools around with Uncle Sam." Tuttle then supposedly compromised by changing the setting to a tourist bureau. However, on viewing the film, Raft's character does indeed stick up a post office. Was the scene originally shot as George had insisted, substituting a tourist bureau, then later changed back to a post office? Since it was known that George never watched his own films, perhaps Tuttle figured he would have no way of discovering the switch.

In any event, Raft, to his dismay, was about to begin his career in cinema crime in earnest. And at the one Hollywood studio where he should have known his most profitable screen image would be exploited to the fullest: Warner Brothers.

CHAPTER SEVEN

"WARNERS WAS LIKE ALCATRAZ."

GEORGE RAFT

It should have been the perfect match. That is, if George Raft had accepted — or at least been more tolerant of his on-screen association with gangster types. Just as Universal specialized in horror movies and MGM lavish musicals, Jack L. Warner's studio had built much of its reputation on gritty urban crime dramas that were stark and dark and relentless in their violence. The major stars of these movies could best be termed antiheroes — defiant and challenging of the system — though the word had not yet been invented. So, instead, Warners' stable of tough guys was referred to as Murderer's Row. The list was exclusive and included just three names: James Cagney, Edward G. Robinson and Humphrey Bogart (later John Garfield would be added as a fringe member). The studio, of course, had lesser hoodlum types on its payroll: faces, if not names, familiar to film fans: Abner Biberman, Joseph Downing, Paul Kelly, Marc Lawrence, Barton MacLane and Edward Pawley. But these men were mere utility heavies, whose main purpose was to play in support of one of the "Big 3," either as a gang member or rival, and it was a sure bet they would not very often survive to the end credits.

Despite his personal dislike for gangster movies, Jack Warner wanted to keep his Murderer's Row intact — indeed, he wanted to add to it, should Cagney decide to take another powder or Eddie Robinson or Bogie decide to sit out a suspension rather than commit to another hoodlum role. Therefore, Warner must have been delighted to learn that George Raft was at liberty. He had a crackerjack prison script ready to go with Cagney in the good guy lead ... and now it looked as if he had found Jimmy his ideal bad guy co-star.

According to producer David Lewis, it was his idea to cast George Raft in *Each Dawn I Die* (1939). "I thought he would add a lot of name value against Cagney, but Warners balked at paying his $5,000 fee. With the help of Charlie Einfeld, who was in charge of publicity, I convinced them to take him. Later, they signed him to a long-term contract."

The irony is that, right up until almost the start of production of *Each Dawn I Die*, Humphrey Bogart had been slated for the role of Judson "Hood" Stacey, the big-shot gangster serving a 199-year stretch at Rocky Point Prison. Cagney and Bogie had already worked together in *Angels with Dirty Faces* (1938) and *The Oklahoma Kid* (1939), and had proved an effective pairing. The problem was that Bogart, as talented as he was, was not considered a star.

WITH GOOD FRIEND AND CO-STAR JAMES CAGNEY, REVIEWING THE SCRIPT OF
***EACH DAWN I DIE.* NOTE RAFT'S SHOES. HE LOVED THOSE SHOES AND EVEN WORE**
THEM AT POOLSIDE IN HIS BATHING SUIT

George Raft was a star. Paramount contractee Fred MacMurray was also a name bandied around for the co-starring role opposite Cagney.

David Lewis says it was he who nixed Bogart's casting. "Raft had a kind of thing in the audience's eyes that made him right to cast against Cagney. When I started [on the picture], I knew I had Cagney and that I could have had Humphrey Bogart, who strangely enough, would not have been as positive a force as Raft. Bogie had a tendency to sleep through the things he wasn't much interested in. Raft, on the other hand, had just been let go by Paramount and had something to prove."

Jack Warner offered Raft the role. George, again exercising his contradictory judgment over appearing in gangster roles, accepted. Perhaps the incentive was less the role than the opportunity to again work with his pal Cagney.

But the part was a goodie. Stacey may have been a gangster, but he was a heroic hood who sacrifices (if improbably) both his freedom and his life to help clear newspaper reporter Frank Ross (Cagney) of a manslaughter frame-up. Bogart could play the good guy (quite well) and he could play the bad guy (very well), but rarely had his film characters combined both qualities. Raft, on the other hand, had just successfully played a role similar to Stacey in *Spawn of the North* and, of course, had also gallantly sacrificed his life in *Souls at Sea*. Add to that George's still-sturdy box office appeal and the enticing and exciting co-star teaming of Cagney and Raft, and Warners saw themselves with a potential hit on their hands.

Raft arrived at the Warner Brothers studio in March to begin filming *Each Dawn I Die*, under the direction of William Keighley (who had also helmed Cagney's popular *"G" Men*, 1935). What the studio had hoped for was proven true with the finished film. *Each Dawn I Die* was dynamite entertainment!

Frank Ross is sentenced to one to twenty years at Rocky Point after being framed by local shysters for attempting to expose their crooked political dealings. In prison, Frank meets "Hood" Stacey, racketeer, and at first the two share a mutual animosity. Later, though, after Frank saves Stacey from an attempted assassination at the hands of the treacherous Limpy Julien (Joseph Downing), the two men form a friendship and Ross is admitted into the prison elite, which includes the gentle simpleton Fargo Red (Maxie Rosenbloom, Raft's former boxing protégé), the half-crazed Mueller (Stanley Ridges), the hardened Dale (Edward Pawley) and nice-guy Joe Lassiter (Louis Jean Heydt). After Limpy is knifed in the prison theater, Stacey sees the perfect opportunity to plan a break and asks Frank to inform on him — even though he is innocent — promising that he will work on the outside to uncover the men who framed him. Reluctantly, Frank agrees and Stacey makes good his escape when he is transferred to the courthouse for trial. Frank is implicated in the break and is placed in solitary confinement, where he is tormented by the guards and becomes embittered and hardened, threatening to get out if he has to kill "every screw in the hole." Stacey, while at first refusing to make good on his promise, thinking that Ross almost messed up his escape by crowding the courtroom with newspapermen, has discovered the identity of the finger man in Frank's frame, Polecat Carlisle (Alan Baxter), who, it turns out, is serving a term at Rocky Point. Stacey realizes that the only way he can keep his promise to Frank is by turning himself in to Warden Armstrong (George Bancroft) and "persuading" Polecat to confess. This he does, in the presence of the warden, during a bloody prison break, in which most of the escapees are shot down by National Guard troops.

Stacey and Polecat are also killed by a grenade tossed by one of the guardsmen. Frank is freed and leaves prison with his girl Joyce (Jane Bryan).

Although Cagney gives his usual magnificent performance (and has a particularly effective scene where he tearfully breaks down before the parole board), George Raft provides the movie with its backbone. He delivers such a strong, authoritative presence that he dominates virtually every scene he's in,

RAFT CALLING THE SHOTS IN *EACH DAWN I DIE* (1939), WITH JANE BRYAN AND CLAY CLEMENT

leading his co-star to later remark, "… I didn't mind at all that George stole the picture from me." Perhaps even more than Guino Rinaldo in *Scarface*, Raft creates the quintessential movie hood — tough, brave, possessed of his own code that includes a fierce loyalty. Unusual for the time, Stacey even comments on the societal hypocrisy that prompted his entry into a life of crime.

In their onscreen matching, Cagney and Raft perfectly complemented each other's personalities. Of course, their real-life friendship was also a valuable asset to the movie. The studio's original casting probably would not have worked as well. Cagney and Bogart were never that chummy off-camera (which was why, perhaps, they worked so well as onscreen adversaries), and it is doubtful that the same chemistry would have existed between them.

Each Dawn I Die was a rewarding experience for George. However, during its making, there was a behind-the-scenes tension on the set that could have had potentially fatal consequences. It concerned James Cagney (then president of the Screen Actors Guild) and a ruthless union racketeer named Willie Bioff. Together with his partner George Browne, Bioff controlled the International Alliance of Theatrical Stage Employees. IATSE was extorting vast sums of money from producers, actors and other important industry people by threatening strikes and walkouts. Their threats were taken seriously because they were backed up by thugs imported from Chicago.

EDWARD PAWLEY, RAFT, GEORGE BANCROFT AND WILLARD ROBERTSON IN A TENSE SCENE FROM *EACH DAWN I DIE*

George remembered: "Willie showed up on our set several times and watched Cagney with obvious dislike. I saw Willie often staring at the big [klieg] lights overhead and exchanging looks with some of his goons, but nothing happened."

After *Each Dawn I Die* opened and was a box office smash, George happened to run into Willie Bioff in New York. Bioff made a strange comment to Raft. "You did pretty good with *Each Dawn I Die*," he said, adding, "You can thank me for that."

George was puzzled and asked him to explain.

"I was going to take care of Cagney," Bioff replied. "We were all set to drop a lamp on him. But I got word to lay off because you were in the picture."

George immediately saw red. "Why, you sonofabitch," he snapped. "It's a good thing nothing happened to Cagney. Jimmy's one of the greatest guys in Hollywood, and if you had hurt him, you would have hurt me."

Jimmy Cagney himself became aware of this incident and later said simply, "He [Raft] may have saved my life."

Raft claimed he never knew why Bioff wanted to hurt Cagney. But Bioff was later tried for extortion and he "sang like a canary" against the Chicago mobsters. Bioff was convicted, sent to prison, and was later paroled. He moved to Phoenix, Arizona, where he lived under an alias, William Nelson,

STUDIO PUBLICITY SHOT OF RAFT AND CO-STAR JAMES CAGNEY,
EACH DAWN I DIE **(1939)**

still fearful of reprisals from his Chicago "friends." He had good reason to be looking over his shoulder.

Newspaperwoman Florabel Muir wrote: "If the old Capone gang never gets Willie, they'll worry him to death by just living in the same world with him." But it's a truism that the mob never forgets and eventually "they" did get him. On the morning of November 4, 1955, "Mr. Nelson" turned over the ignition on his truck, and was blown into oblivion.

Raft was later to say, "I don't like to see men killed, even when they're cheap blackmailers, but in this case I knew that no one would weep for Willie. I could say to myself: Here's one racketeer who won't be coming back to Hollywood to make trouble for my friends."

Bioff's comment to George that he "did pretty good with *Each Dawn I Die*" proved to be an understatement. "Cagney meets a Raft of Trouble" the posters for the film announced. Critics were unanimous in their praise. In its review of the picture, the *New York Daily Mirror* said Jimmy and George "never have been better." *The New York Sun* wrote: "The little toughie [Cagney] is put in his place this time by the quieter and far more effective performance of George Raft." And, of course, Raft was also singled out for special merit. *Variety* called his "a fiery, wholly persuasive and telling enactment." Harold Barnes of the *New York Herald-Tribune* said of Raft: "... he recaptures much of the sinister power which made his make-believe in *Scarface* so memorable." Finally, the *New York Journal American* concluded their review of the film by saying, "In such parts as these Mr. Raft literally shines, the sinister shadow of his playing dominating every scene in which he appears, and most of the rest in which he is not seen at all. If that isn't picture stealing, then I don't know what is."

With the success of *Each Dawn I Die*, Warner Brothers exercised its option for a second picture with Raft. Perhaps not wanting to mess with a surefire formula, the studio returned George to prison (albeit temporarily), and paired him with another player recruited from Murderer's Row. The picture was *Invisible Stripes* (1939). George Raft's fourth-billed co-star: Humphrey Bogart.

Upon their release from Sing Sing, convicts Cliff Taylor (Raft) and Chuck Martin (Bogart) choose separate paths. Cliff feels he has been rehabilitated and expresses his desire for an honest, law-abiding life to the warden (Moroni Olsen). Chuck, however, remains embittered and is determined to avenge himself on society for the years taken away from him while in prison. On the train trip back into Manhattan, Chuck tells parolee Cliff that he is in for a hard ride because for the next year he will be wearing "invisible stripes." It appears that Chuck may be right, for Cliff's attempts at resuming an honest life quickly meet with discouragement. First, his girl Sue (Margot Stevenson) rejects him because she can never marry an ex-con. Then Cliff quickly loses his old mechanic's job because as a parolee he is not allowed to drive and his boss will not trust him alone with the cash register. He later secures labor as a loader, but is harassed by burly co-worker Schranke (William Haade) to the point where he is provoked into a fight, and is again fired. A potentially promising job opportunity turns out to be a front as a "labor stoolie," and Cliff hotly rejects the offer by socking this employer on the jaw. Meanwhile, Chuck Martin has returned wholly to his criminal lifestyle. He is welcomed back into Ed Kruger's (Paul Kelly) gang, even if that means teaming up with the treacherous Lefty Sloane (Marc Lawrence).

Further complicating Cliff's situation is that his younger brother Tim (William Holden) is frustrated in his own attempts to marry sweetheart Peggy (Jane Bryan) and is veering toward a criminal path.

Cliff finally lands a menial job as a stock boy, and he is eventually promoted to a clerk. However, when the store is robbed during an employee dance, Cliff is hauled in on suspicion, and even though he is later found innocent, he is let go from his job. Tim has become so resentful by his own situation and Cliff's perpetual harassment that he rolls a drunk for six bucks. Cliff and Tim come to blows over this rash action, and then Cliff decides to help Tim out the only way he knows how — by joining up with Chuck and his gang in a series of bank robberies. After he has accumulated enough cash to buy his brother a garage, Cliff quits the gang, alienating all except for Chuck.

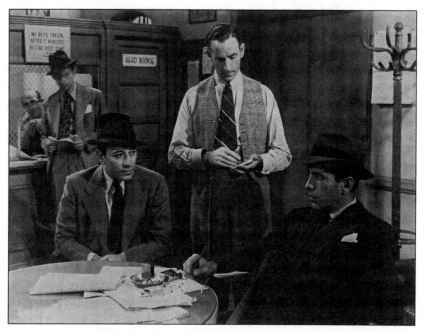

MACK GRAY, RAFT, RAYMOND BAILEY AND HUMPHREY BOGART IN THE FIRST OF BOGIE'S TWO TEAMINGS WITH RAFT: *INVISIBLE STRIPES* (1939)

Tim and Peggy marry, but problems arise when Chuck's gang pull another robbery that results in a couple of killings and the criminals are forced to rely on Tim's garage for temporary cover. Chuck, who was wounded in the get-away, tells Tim that Cliff hadn't been working as a tractor salesman as he'd claimed, and had really been a part of the gang. Tim agrees to help Chuck get to his girl, Molly (Lee Patrick), but once he returns to the garage, he is arrested as an accessory. Molly calls Cliff to come help Chuck, who explains the situation and says that if Tim doesn't talk, he will get only a short prison term and then will be looked after by the gang. Although Cliff feels he owes Chuck, he won't let his brother take the rap for the other gangsters and convinces Tim to identify them. Cliff then returns to Chuck's apartment to help him get away before the police arrive. The other gangsters have tailed him, and, suspecting Cliff of informing, shoot down Chuck, and then Lefty plugs Cliff before the police finish off Lefty and Ed. Cliff dies, content that at least he won't be returning to prison. The final scene has Tim showing Peggy his newly-renovated Taylor Brothers garage and explaining to a curious beat cop that Cliff is a silent partner.

Invisible Stripes came on the heels of Warner Brothers 1930s gangster bonanza and was not as critically or commercially regarded as some of the studio's past underworld efforts. Released in Hollywood's "glory year" of

INVISIBLE STRIPES. RAFT AND THE WARNERS TOUGH GUY ELITE: JOSEPH DOWNING, HUMPHREY BOGART, PAUL KELLY AND MARC LAWRENCE

1939, it was virtually ignored in the competition of such cinema classics as *Goodbye Mr. Chips, Gunga Din, Stagecoach, The Wizard of Oz* and *Gone with the Wind.* Which is unfortunate as *Invisible Stripes* is a surprisingly effective gangster entry that stands alongside Warner Brothers' best. The film offers crisp direction, a taut, suspenseful storyline, exciting gun-blazing action and solid performances from Bogart and Raft. Wanda Hale was particularly positive in her *New York Daily News* review: "George Raft makes his Cliff Taylor so sympathetic and real that you hate to think of what is obviously coming to him."

Poster art for *Invisible Stripes* was misleading, with the copy boldly proclaiming: "George Raft: Tougher than in *Each Dawn I Die.*" Although Raft gives a fine account of an ex-con trying to go straight only to be thwarted by his prison record, his Cliff Taylor is nowhere in the hard-edged league of Hood Stacey. In certain instances, in fact, his character comes across as almost too earnest and just as overly sentimental in his approach to his devoted mother. If truth be told, it is really Bogart's bitter and cynical crook who steals the show. Although a comparatively small role, his gangster dominates much of the proceedings just as Raft's convict had in *Each Dawn I Die*. From his opening swaggering moments in the warden's office and on the train where he rejects any notion of going straight, to his final scene, where, as he lay dying, he mutters, "What do I care. You can't live forever," Chuck Martin is a true hardboiled specimen and a memorable addition to Bogart's "rogue gallery."

William Holden (formerly Bill Beedle of Pasadena) was just 21 when he appeared in *Invisible Stripes*. It was only his second film following his screen debut as Joe Bonaparte in Columbia Pictures' *Golden Boy* (1939). When he walked onto on the Burbank set, he experienced more than a little apprehension. Not only was Warners a new studio, but Holden would be co-starring with two of the toughest men in pictures. In addition, he knew that he was not director Lloyd Bacon's first choice for the role. Initially, a new studio acquisition, 25-year-old John Garfield, formerly of New York's Group Theater, was considered for the part of the hot-headed Tim Taylor.

Garfield had captivated audiences with his dynamic screen debut as the cynical pianist Mickey Borden in Michael Curtiz's *Four Daughters* (1938). Because of his sudden popularity, Jack Warner removed Garfield from further discussion regarding *Invisible Stripes*. Tim Taylor was a secondary part, not worthy of the talents of the studio's hot new star. Garfield would soon achieve his own reputation as a screen hoodlum, but appearing in *Invisible Stripes* would not be on his agenda.

With Garfield out of the running, director Bacon preferred contract player Wayne Morris. Morris had made a promising appearance as the bellhop-turned-boxer in *Kid Galahad* (1937), co-starring with Edward G. Robinson, Bette Davis and Bogart. But within just a couple of years, his potential had slipped and he was relegated to B-pictures, such as *Men are Such Fools* (1937) and *The Return of Dr. X* (1939), both of which featured Bogart. Paramount/Columbia contract player William Holden, on the other hand, was riding high on the publicity surrounding *Golden Boy*.

Bacon, however, was not convinced that young Holden possessed the maturity to play opposite Raft. To show that he could hold his own against the established screen actor, Holden, according to his biographer Bob Thomas, played a bit opposite Raft in *Each Dawn I Die*, though keen-eyed observers have had a hard time spotting him in the movie.

Reportedly, the filming of *Invisible Stripes* was far from tranquil. Bogart wasn't overly fond of Holden (who, after all, had received higher billing than Bogart in only his second movie — and at Bogie's home studio!), and Raft apparently annoyed both co-stars with his demands to have his dialogue changed so that his character would appear less hard-bitten, and by his repetitious way of playing a scene.

Bogart was to later report, "He reads every line the same way. One two three pause. One two three pause. How do you compete against that?" Such grumbling from Bogie the Beefer could hardly have endeared George to his co-star.

Another problem had to do with the physical heights of Raft and Bogart. Bogie stood 5'10½. George was just a half-inch shorter. During the prison shower scene that opens the picture, George instructed Mack Gray to get him the "lifts" he had worn in *Souls at Sea*, so that he would appear taller than Bogart.

Jack Warner was hearing frequent complaints from director Bacon about Raft's behavior on the set and at one point devised a way to kill off Raft's character prematurely: By having one of the hoodlums in the staircase scene knock Raft down a flight of stairs. In his autobiography, *My First Hundred Years in Hollywood*, Warner wrote that the scene was shot, with Moroni Olsen (who could not be the actor Warner meant since he played the sympathetic warden, not a gangster) really belting Raft down the stairs. Of course, that ending is not in the movie and likely was never filmed. It is more probable that Warner made the threat and that Raft behaved from then on.

If William Holden had grievances against Raft, they were forgiven and forgotten. Many years later in an appearance on *The Tonight Show* with Johnny Carson, Holden, seated next to Raft, had only generous words for his old co-star.

"George was really my big brother onscreen and off. When it came time in the movie for us to throw a few punches at each other, I really hit him and cut open his eye. Instead of hitting me back, which I'd heard was George's trademark, he was as nice as could be. He also was supportive in the problems I was having with Lloyd Bacon, who was a tough man."

Two other *Invisible Stripes* co-stars shared their recollections of George Raft for this book.

The late Marc Lawrence, probably the Hollywood actor with the most gangster roles to his credit, said that in the scene where Raft was supposed to throw a punch at his character, "Lefty," Raft really let go and socked him right in the windpipe, leaving Lawrence unable to speak for twenty minutes. He further went on to say that of all the movie toughs he knew or worked with, George Raft was by far the most convincing, explaining, "Because he was a gangster. Raft was never that good an actor unless he was playing a heavy."

The late Frankie Thomas, a well-known youth actor of the day, who had appeared with Spencer Tracy in *Boy's Town* (1938), among many other roles, played two scenes (as Tommy the sympathetic stock boy) with Raft in the picture. He retained a subtle remembrance of Raft.

"I remember Raft as a very quiet man. But I do remember that there were these two guys wearing dark suits that stood off to the side of the stage when

RAFT, IN A GANGSTER POSE, FOR A WARNER BROTHERS PUBLICITY SHOT

we were filming our scenes, and after the director called 'cut,' Raft would walk over to them and engage in some very quiet conversation. I recall that they very definitely looked like underworld types."

While *Invisible Stripes* was not as successful as *Each Dawn I Die*, Warners was impressed enough with the film and Raft's onscreen work to offer him a long-term contract, calling for three pictures a year. The deal, which reportedly paid Raft $5,000 per week, was signed on July 15, 1939. George had known Jack Warner socially for many years and considered him a friend. Therefore, he took Warner at his word when the mogul assured him that he would be given a variety of parts and not be cast exclusively in hoodlum roles. He was also promised a letter from Jack Warner confirming that he would not be asked to play "out and out heavies."

George's personal life also took another positive turn in 1939 when he began his second serious Hollywood romance, with Norma Shearer, the glamorous MGM star and the widow of the boy genius Irving Thalberg. George had first met Norma at a party at Jack Warner's house, but did not begin dating her until after he accepted an invitation to accompany Charles Boyer and his wife Pat to the World's Fair in New York (where Raft was promoting the release of *Each Dawn I Die*), and discovered that the Boyers had asked Norma to join them. Later, the two couples visited the New York night spots and even began planning a European trip together.

On August 1, George and Norma joined a group of celebrities, including the Boyers, Mr. and Mrs. Edward G. Robinson, Bob Hope and Mrs. Eleanor Roosevelt for a voyage on the luxury liner *Normandie*. According to newspaper coverage of the event, Raft stood out among all the luminaries as the number one attraction among the fans who gathered about the pier. The same attention and adulation continued in Europe, where George was often mobbed by fans.

During their travels in London, Paris and the south of France, George and Norma grew close, though publicly denying there was any romance between them. Later, after both returned separately to Hollywood, they resumed their affair. By this time Louella Parsons had leaked out through her popular column that George and Norma had indeed fallen in love.

Thanks to his period with Virginia Pine, George had refined his manners and was a welcome and popular guest at almost any formal function. This was important in his new relationship because this was the world to which the Canadian-born Norma had become accustomed during her marriage to Thalberg. Norma expanded George's limited knowledge of culture and the arts by having him escort her to various museums, art galleries and even libraries. She reciprocated by accompanying George to his favorite entertainment haunts: nightclubs, ballgames, the race track and prizefights. This was a far cry from the elegant, if perhaps somewhat stifling, environment she had shared with Thalberg, but apparently she enjoyed the excitement of these new experiences.

As Mack Gray offered, "She was like a kid, playing hookey from school."

As with Virginia Pine, Norma was also a mother. She had two young children from Thalberg, a son, Irving, Jr., and daughter, Katherine. Once again George's strong paternal instincts were aroused and he showered both kids with gifts and affection. It was not unusual for George to stop by Norma's Malibu beach house and build sand castles with Katherine, and to take Irving Junior to ballgames. Norma and her children provided George with the family he desperately wanted.

**MGM STUDIO SHOT OF NORMA SHEARER, RAFT'S SECOND SERIOUS
HOLLYWOOD ROMANCE**

But there were problems. Many of Norma's friends disapproved of their relationship. Raft's tough-guy image and occasional bad press was part of the concern. As, of course, was the fact that George was a married man. Louis B. Mayer was particularly unhappy over their romance. He took a paternal interest in all of his studio's stars. Although he had loved Irving Thalberg like a son, he'd cautioned Norma against marrying him because he was destined to have a short life. George Raft was a completely different matter. He voiced his dissatisfaction thusly: "A nice Jewish girl like Norma shouldn't go with a roughneck like that."

Shearer went so far as to suggest that she and Raft co-star together, in Warners' remake of *One Way Passage*, to be titled '*Til We Meet Again*. Producer David Lewis claims he talked her out of it, although he thought the teaming would have the same spark that an earlier Shearer/Gable teaming had in *A Free Soul*. Nevertheless, "... There had been a good deal of gossip about Norma and Raft, not too favorable," Lewis remarked, "and I thought too much of Norma to allow it." The roles were recast with Merle Oberon and George Brent.

Facing such pressure and naturally wanting stability for her children, Norma decided to end her affair with George. Fortunately, she and George would remain friends, even after she married a much younger man, ski instructor Martin Arrouge, in 1942.[18]

But for the moment, George was left heartbroken. His only consolation was that he was kept busy with film offers. But already there was trouble brewing with Warner Brothers. A number of pictures were proposed for George, including a re-teaming with James Cagney in a property called *Two Sons*. Raft refused the role that was originally intended for Pat O'Brien, and the film was never produced.

Raft had earned his first suspension at his new studio.

In July of 1940, George's agent mentioned to Jack Warner's assistant Roy Obringer that the letter Warner had promised Raft regarding the studio's guarantee not to ask him to play a "dirty heavy" had never been received. This had now become a matter of extreme importance to George as the studio had him lined up for the lead in a movie to be called *King of the Roaring Nineties* — in which he was expected to play ... a "dirty heavy."

Raft responded to his boss's "oversight" — or was it deliberate neglect? — by having a memo delivered to Jack Warner, ensconced in his suite at the Waldorf Astoria in New York, in which he also took a shot at Humphrey Bogart (perhaps in retaliation against those remarks made about him by Bogie). "I was afraid the studio would put me into parts that Humphrey Bogart should play, and you told me I would never have to play a Humphrey Bogart part." The writing of this memo makes it particularly curious why George Raft next did what he did.

After refusing *King of the Roaring Nineties*, Raft received an offer from United Artists to appear in the crime drama *The House Across the Bay* (1940). Although the part was that of a criminal who dies at the end, George desperately wanted the role. Hal Wallis, who was the producer on *Invisible Stripes*, was both shocked and annoyed. Raft had only made two movies on his three-picture-a-year deal and was already asking to go on loanout to play the exact same kind of part he didn't want Warners to hand him! Raft even went so far as to say that if he wasn't allowed to do the picture, his future would be ruined and that he had begun to develop digestive troubles. Finally, Warners approved the loan to United Artists and Raft started work on the picture opposite Joan Bennett, Walter Pidgeon and Lloyd Nolan.

The film featured Raft as nightclub owner Steve Larwitt, who falls for Brenda "Lucky" Bentley, an Indiana farm girl who gets a job singing at his club. The two soon marry, but their happiness is almost cut short following a gangland assassination attempt against Steve. Desperate to protect her husband, Brenda turns him in for income tax fraud, only to

RAFT AND MACK GRAY IN *THE HOUSE ACROSS THE BAY* (1940)

have Steve's lawyer Slant Kolma (Nolan), who has his own designs on Brenda, undermine Steve's courtroom defense, with Steve being convicted and sentenced to ten years in Alcatraz. Brenda moves to San Francisco to be near her husband, where she meets airplane manufacturer Tim Nolan (Pidgeon), who is interested in Brenda, but whose gentlemanly advances she discourages. Steve soon learns of Slant's double-cross and escapes from Alcatraz, swimming across the Bay. He kills Slant and then prepares to do the same to Brenda, after he's learned from Kolma that it was she who had turned him in. But Steve comes to his senses and instead decides to return to prison. He never makes it, as he is shot by police as he again swims across the Bay.

According to Miss Bennett, George had a rift with director Archie Mayo over the role and even walked off the set for a few days. Both she and Lloyd Nolan later claimed that Alfred Hitchcock was called in to reshoot the final scenes of the movie, which may explain why the climax appears rushed.

Far from the glowing reviews George received for his two Warners crime dramas, his performance in *The House Across the Bay* did not receive critical accolades. *Variety* reported that the "picture will not help the popularity of either Raft or Miss Bennett."

Reviews aside, Raft had reached the height of his popularity, which was confirmed Hollywood-style when his handprints and signature ("To My Pal Sid") were immortalized in cement at the forecourt of Grauman's Chinese Theater in Ceremony #53 on March 25, 1940.[19]

Raft returned to Warners, where he was announced for two films: *Torrid Zone* and *City for Conquest* (both 1940). Although both movies were produced, with James Cagney in the lead, George's reported roles never materialized in either. The latter production would have featured him in the rather smallish part of the slick dancer Murray Burns. However, the studio must have realized how insignificant the role was and instead tested Cesar Romero before casting Anthony Quinn. Elia Kazan, who played the part of the gangster Googie in *City for Conquest*, later made an interesting observation concerning both Arthur Kennedy (who played Cagney's violinist brother) and himself: "Warners plan was to have me replace George Raft when he got too old, and Arthur was going to be the next Cagney." Of course, Kazan was proven wrong on both counts.

Raft next rejected two other projects: *South of Suez* (George Brent replaced him) and the role of gangster-on-the-lam Chips Maguire (alias "Mr. Grasselli") in Warners sentimental comedy-drama *It All Came True* (both 1940). While Maguire is at first presented as a bad guy, killing a rival mobster and attempting to pin the crime on his friend, played by Jeffrey Lynn, he redeems himself at the end by confessing to the police … and even setting things right among the eccentric residents of the boarding house where he has been hiding out. The part had those sympathetic qualities George demanded in his characters, but in this case he perceived Chips Maguire as a little too rough-edged and too much a "Humphrey Bogart" part and walked away. And, of course, Bogart was given the role.

When Raft next appeared before the Warners cameras it was in *They Drive by Night* (1940), directed by Raoul Walsh, co-starring with (again, fourth-billed) Humphrey Bogart (whose salary for the picture was $11,200 against Raft's $60,000) as truck driving brothers, Joe and Paul Fabrini.[20] Together, they battle unscrupulous bosses, exhaustion on the long hauls and the murderous intentions of Lana Carlsen (Ida Lupino, in a memorable performance). The movie offered George exactly the type of part he was looking for: tough, brave and romantic (with Ann Sheridan's "Cassie Hartley"). The role presented him as a "hardworking man of the people" — to which George aspired, onscreen and off. He even managed to have a line inserted into the dialogue which expressed his dislike for alcohol ("He never touches the stuff," says Lupino at one point). Another memorable piece of dialogue could have served as the catch phrase for the picture (if not, indeed, for George Raft's whole Hollywood career): "We're tougher than any truck ever come off any assembly line."

Just how tough was demonstrated in a scene where Raft's character is driving the truck down a long hill with Bogie and Miss Sheridan as his passengers, and the brakes suddenly failed. George managed to avoid a terrible

RAFT AND TRUCKER BROTHER HUMPHREY BOGART WITH ADMIRING WAITRESS ANN SHERIDAN. *THEY DRIVE BY NIGHT* (1940)

accident by utilizing the superior driving skills he had mastered during his New York bootlegging days, and maneuvered the truck up an embankment on the other side of the road.

George recalled how shaken they all were after the incident, though Bogart found the breath to say, "Thanks, pal." Raft was unable to speak, but replied in thought, "Don't thank me. Write a letter to Owney Madden or Feets Edson."

They Drive by Night proved an enormous success and many people consider it Raft's best Warners film. Yet it is really Bogart who emerges with the most memorable part in the movie. Tired of the road but unwilling to walk out on his brother, Paul Fabrini ultimately loses his arm in an accident and becomes embittered, venting his anger and frustration at being a cripple dependent on what he perceives as his brother's charity in a brief yet compelling scene. Raft, on the other hand, plays Joe as the tough but cool-headed fellow, and is not afforded a single scene to match the dramatic intensity of his co-star, not even in his later sequences with the psychotic Lana. Perhaps Raft's shining moment comes in the usual way when he engages in a vigorous fistfight with another trucker, in which he gets to display a series of quick rights.

George recalled that shortly after completing the movie he was intending to go to Europe for a vacation. Mark Hellinger (who was the associate

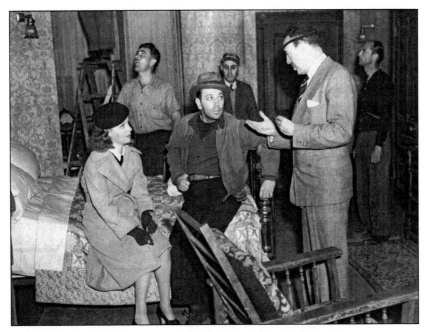

RAFT AND ANN SHERIDAN LISTEN ATTENTIVELY TO RAOUL WALSH'S DIRECTION DURING THE FILMING OF *THEY DRIVE BY NIGHT*

producer on the film) hosted a bon voyage party for George at the Cotton Club, and while there urged George to have a glass of beer. George agreed and found that he didn't mind it.

"So this is the stuff all the shooting was about during Prohibition," he said to Hellinger. "I used to convoy beer trucks for Owney Madden."

Hellinger replied, "Well, 'convoy' some more of it. Good for what ails you."

Raft had a second glass and then accommodated the audience by taking to the stage to dance his signature number, "Sweet Georgia Brown." Raft claimed he didn't remember a thing after that — only that the liner, *Ile de France,* sailed to Europe with his trunks onboard while he was sleeping it off in his hotel room. Later, George discovered that his "pal" Hellinger had spiked his beer with brandy. George swore he never again touched alcohol afterwards.

Pleased with Raft's heroic turn in *They Drive by Night*, Warners and Hal Wallis sought George for their upcoming production of Jack London's classic *The Sea Wolf* (1941). Edward G. Robinson was lined up to play the brutal though intellectual captain of *The Ghost*, Wolf Larsen, and the studio thought it would be inspired casting to have George play his nemesis, the honest but rebellious seaman, George Leach.

The part seemed perfect for Raft — with not a suggestion of the underworld attached to it. But George said no. His reasoning was that the role "was just a little bit better than a bit." Hal Wallis tried to reason with Raft by writing him that George Leach "was a great role in a great script, and should be one of the most important pictures of the year, and you should be in it. It is the kind of part you have been wanting to play, namely the romantic lead in a good, gutsy picture. You are not a heavy, and you get the girl."

Despite Wallis's convincing arguments, Raft still did not feel the part was important enough and refused it. He was replaced by the younger John Garfield, whose participation in the prestigious production helped to further cement his stardom.

Warner Brothers was having its difficulties with Raft, certainly, even though he still had his champions at the studio. Steve Trilling, Warners head of casting, was particularly enthusiastic when it came to Raft's talent, going so far as to say that George Raft could act on the screen better than anyone else. "He's a guy who's got acting for films down cold," Trilling said.

Most of Raft's critics would (generously) call Trilling's comment an exaggeration. But George's pictures were moneymakers, and not even the Brothers Warner were going to argue with positive box office. They were in the business to make money. Hiring actors who were popular with the public was their major way of drawing patrons into the theater. As was audience acceptance of the character the actor would be called upon to play. It was important that the player fit the part — and George Raft did have his limitations. One would be hard-pressed to picture him as Rhett Butler, for instance, even though Clark Gable likewise began his film career playing gangsters and heavies in such films as *Dance, Fools, Dance, The Finger Points* and *A Free Soul* (1931).

Therefore, when Warners purchased the rights to the latest book by the celebrated crime novelist William Riley (W.R.) Burnett (author of *Little Caesar*), they felt the title character, an aging and weary bank bandit named Roy Earldon, would be the ideal role for their leading screen gangster, George Raft.

Actually, Raft was not the studio's first choice. For a while it looked as if Paul Muni might take the part. He was still regarded as one of Warners' top (and highest paid) stars, even if his last couple of pictures for the studio, *Juarez* and *We Are Not Alone* (both 1939), were not commercial successes. Muni had just returned from an eight-month national theater tour of Maxwell Anderson's *Key Largo*, and was hoping to do as his next film a biography of Beethoven. Although Jack Warner had tentatively agreed to the Beethoven film, he cited the less-than-spectacular box office returns of *Juarez* as a reason to postpone, if not completely abandon, the project. He also reportedly quoted the famous line, "Nobody wants to see a movie about a blind composer." With the world in turmoil and America itself at the brink of war, "People want escapism," Warner argued.

Warners tried to make the deal as attractive as possible to Muni — including a script written by the book's author (along with John Huston, to whom Muni was not particularly close). But eventually Muni refused and, in a dramatic gesture worthy of his theatrical temperament, literally tore up his contract with the studio. Humphrey Bogart had coveted the role of (the now-shortened) Roy Earle, but remained aware of his lesser position on the studio's Murderer's Row roster.

A story, probably apocryphal, has Hal Wallis once explaining to Bogart, "Look, you want Raft's roles, Raft wants Eddie Robinson's roles, Robinson wants Muni's roles." To which Bogart replied, "All I do is bump off Muni, and we all move up a step."

Muni had successfully eliminated himself from studio competition. Still, Bogie wasn't immediately called up to fill the vacancy, even though he wrote the following to Hal Wallis: "You told me once to let you know when I found a part I wanted. A few weeks ago I left a note for you concerning *High Sierra*. I never received an answer so I'm bringing it up again as I understand there is some doubt about Muni doing it."

Bogart had served an impressive criminal apprenticeship at the studio, appearing in such films as *Bullets or Ballots* (1936), *Kid Galahad* (1937), *Racket Busters* (1938), *King of the Underworld* and *You Can't Get Away with Murder* (both 1939), among others. But he was not the most liked person on the Warners lot. Jack Warner called him an "apple polisher" and said that his success came from "licking assholes." Even Cagney, who respected Raft so much for his raw toughness, said of Bogart: "A lot of people disliked him, and he knew it. He said, 'I beat 'em to it … I don't like 'em first.' He hated just about everyone, but that was his aim — to hate them first. When it came to fighting, he was about as tough as Shirley Temple."

Still, if only for his talent, Bogart had his champions who felt he was worthy of better material (such as *High Sierra*). But, acting skills aside, he wasn't considered the potent box office of George Raft.

But Raft was not interested. Here was another role as a gangster who gets killed at the end. Despite the fact that he'd recently played similar characters who met the same fate in *Each Dawn I Die*, *Invisible Stripes* and *The House Across the Bay*, he resolutely refused to have anything to do with the certainly more prestigious *High Sierra*.

Jack Warner finally sent director Raoul Walsh to talk over the matter with Raft. They conversed for two hours, but Walsh could not budge the stubborn actor from his determined position not to die in another picture.

However, turning down the part of "Mad Dog" (a sobriquet Raft must have particularly disliked) Roy Earle may not have entirely been George's decision. According to W.R. Burnett, the devious Bogie had talked Raft out of the role by pointing out that George was too big a star to play a gangster who both loses the girl and dies at the end. He added that Raft's doing the film was just a studio ploy to get his name out to the public to sell tickets. Whether or not Bogie's tactics decided Raft, George told Jack Warner through Raoul Walsh that he would not do the picture. To wit: "Tell Jack Warner to shove it."

Instead, he received permission from Warners to go to New York on a personal appearance tour for the release of *They Drive by Night*. After Cagney, Edward G. Robinson and even the youngish John Garfield were considered for the role of Roy Earle, the studio settled on a delighted Humphrey Bogart, who subsequently delivered his third great screen characterization — two of which, of course, were courtesy of George Raft.

High Sierra was a hit with moviegoers seeking the "escapism" Warner had predicted, and Bogie received excellent notices for his tough, yet sensitive portrayal as a last remnant of the Dillinger Gang who has outlived his past. Harold Barnes in the *New York Herald-Tribune* wrote: "Humphrey Bogart was a perfect choice to play the role. Always a fine actor, he is particularly splendid as a farm boy turned outlaw, who is shocked and hurt when newspapers refer to him as a mad dog. His steady portrayal is what makes the melodrama something more than merely exciting." The *Times* added, "Mr. Bogart plays the leading role with a perfection of hard-boiled vitality ... " Unfortunately, even though he was clearly recognized as the picture's star, casting intrigue still worked against him as he was given second billing beneath Ida Lupino, still riding high on her laurels after her success as the murderess in *They Drive by Night*. But Warners must have realized they'd made the right choice in casting Humphrey Bogart. "Duke Mantee" Bogart possessed the requisite rustic qualities of the grassroots bandit that certainly would have been lacking in "Guino Rinaldo" Raft.

One way that George managed to supplement his income while on suspension at the studio, was by continuing to perform in radio programs. He'd done a number of dramas based on films in which he'd appeared, such as *Spawn of the North* (with Fred MacMurray replacing Henry Fonda), *Each Dawn I Die* (Franchot Tone miscast in the Cagney role) and most recently *They Drive by Night* (with Lana Turner and Lucille Ball). He even attempted the radio role of the famed British sleuth Bulldog Drummond, though he was not convincing trying to deliver an English accent.

It was also reported in 1941 that Raft was involved in a business venture with The Frolics Club in Miami. The Club was in the process of being remodeled with a proposed gambling casino, and, if licensing was approved, it was intended that George would oversee the operations of the casino, including the entertainment. However, nothing came of this deal, most likely owing to Raft's film commitments.

When Raft returned to Warner Brothers, the studio half-heartedly offered him the lead in *Carnival*, which was a remake of *Kid Galahad*, though set in a circus milieu rather than the boxing arena. To no one's surprise, Raft rejected the "B" assignment, utilizing the clause in his contract that stated he could refuse remakes. Once again Bogart stepped into the movie, now titled *The Wagons Roll at Night* (1941) and performed as well as could be expected in this undistinguished effort.

Raft also turned down the role of vicious waterfront gangster Harold Goff in *Out of the Fog* (1941), based on Irwin Shaw's 1939 play *The Gentle People*. The part was not at all sympathetic in that the character bullies and belittles everyone in his own self-serving interests. It was a role that was as distasteful to George as had been "Trigger" and "Baby Face" Martin. Reportedly, James Cagney also refused the part. Humphrey Bogart, on the other hand, lobbied for it, going so far as to write Jack Warner: "It seems to me that I am the logical person on the lot to play in *The Gentle People*. I would be very disappointed if I didn't get it. I would like very much to talk to you about it." But on this occasion Bogie didn't get a Raft reject. Ida Lupino was assigned as the movie's star and, the story goes, she refused Bogart because of his supposed mistreatment of her on *High Sierra*. Miss Lupino would later deny this, claiming that the studio was trying to keep some of its stars at odds, namely Bogart, Errol Flynn and herself. In any event, John Garfield stepped into the role and delivered a dynamic performance.

Bogart's disappointment at losing the role was somewhat eased when he was announced as George Raft's co-star in another "workingman" drama to be called *Manpower* (1941). Marlene Dietrich was borrowed from Universal to complete the romantic triangle. The film was a remake of two earlier Warners films: *Slim* (1937), with Pat O'Brien and Henry Fonda, and *Tiger Shark* (1932), which starred Edward G. Robinson as a hook-handed Portuguese fisherman. However, for this film, Raft did not exercise his contractual privilege to turn down remakes, though he did use his clout at the studio to veto his co-star. While Raft in his mellow later years would speak fondly of Humphrey Bogart, during their period together at Warners, there definitely existed some dissension, stemming back to *Invisible Stripes*.

One reason may have been offered by a former Warners executive who said, "Raft didn't want the competition." It was true that while Bogart was regarded in lower esteem than Raft at the studio, Warners was trying to build his career. To get him, as Jack Warner once said, "… to play something other than Duke Mantee."

Apparently, Raft used the same tactic to oust Bogart from *Manpower* that Bogart had employed to talk George out of doing *High Sierra*, telling Bogart's agent Sam Jaffe that his client was wrong for the part and that the film would hurt Bogart's career. Naturally, Bogart got wind of this and of Raft's adamant refusal to play opposite him. Finally, an ugly incident occurred when Bogart and Mack Gray got into a shouting match on the Warners lot. Bogart was particularly troubled that "nobody made any effort to stop it."

Bogart then attempted to speak directly to George to see what he was so upset about, but Raft wouldn't speak to him, prompting Bogart to write a telegram to Hal Wallis, which read in part: "Any remarks and accusations by Mack Gray which were attributed to me are completely and entirely untrue. I have never had anything but the very finest feelings of friendship for George. I understand he has refused to make the picture if I am in it ... I tried to get George to tell me this morning what he was angry about and what I was supposed to have said but he wouldn't tell me. I feel very hurt by this because it's the second time I have been kept out of a good picture and a good part by an actor's refusing to work with me ..."

What especially ruffled Bogart's ego was when the studio, perhaps trying to pacify him, sent him the script of a "B" Western, *Bad Men of Missouri* (1941). Rather than take on the unimportant assignment, and perhaps remembering his previous ludicrous Western casting in *The Oklahoma Kid* (1939) and *Virginia City* (1940), Bogart went on suspension, but not before returning the script to Steve Trilling with the scribbled message: "Are you kidding? This is certainly rubbing it in. Since Lupino and Raft are casting pictures, maybe I can."

In any event, by refusing Bogart, George Raft also relinquished top billing in *Manpower*. Although he later said the part of his friend-turned-romantic rival Hank McHenry should have been played by a bigger guy, someone like Victor McLaglen, Warners cast Edward G. Robinson, again thinking that they'd get more mileage out of pairing two of its Murderer's Row. Warners was counting on big box office since it was paying large salaries to its stars: Robinson got $100,000; Marlene Dietrich received $80,000; and George earned $60,000.

With Raoul Walsh set to direct, *Manpower* went into production. And almost immediately the troubles began. Raft, ever sensitive about his lack of schooling and uncertainty over his acting skills, felt that the educated and much-more accomplished Robinson was condescending to him. Robinson would give advice on how to play a scene or suggest bits of business for them to do which director Walsh would contradict, leaving Raft edgy and uncertain. Add to that Raft's infatuation with Marlene Dietrich (on whom, he felt, Robinson had similar designs), and a clash was inevitable.

A Warner Brothers affidavit detailed what happened: "[Raft] did violently rough-house and push the said Edward G. Robinson around the set ... directed toward him a volley of personal abuse and profanity ... threatened [him] with bodily harm, and in the course of his remarks directed and applied to Mr. Robinson in a loud and boisterous tone of voice, numerous filthy, obscene and profane expressions."

It was a disturbing scene to everyone on the set. Unfortunately for the principals, a photographer from *Life* magazine happened to be present and snapped a picture of the battle (which clearly shows Alan Hale restraining Robinson) that appeared on front pages across the country.

After the incident, Robinson walked off the set and neither he nor Raft wanted to go on with the picture. The conflict was finally resolved by Raoul

RAFT, MARLENE DIETRICH AND EDWARD G. ROBINSON IN *MANPOWER* (1941). THE OBJECT OF DIETRICH'S AFFECTION IS OBVIOUS

Walsh and representatives from the Screen Actors Guild, who held discussions with Robinson and George. While the two men managed to complete the movie, their confrontation created a rift in the friendship that might have been, and they would remain distant from each other for fourteen years.

In his posthumously published autobiography, *All My Yesterdays*, Robinson spoke of *Manpower* and succinctly recalled his working relationship with George: "Raft was touchy, difficult and thoroughly impossible to play with."

Marlene Dietrich retained a distinctly different memory of her co-star. "Raft was simply wonderful throughout the shooting ... His unique lovable kindness belied his appearance and his tough roles."

George had two other unfortunate experiences while making *Manpower*. In one scene, his character Johnny Marshall was supposed to slap Fay Duval (Dietrich) after bailing her out of jail following a police raid at the "clip joint" she had worked. George wasn't comfortable hitting a woman, but Miss Dietrich assured him it was all right. When George let loose with his slap, he connected so hard that she tumbled down the stairwell and broke her ankle. The shot remained in the movie.

Then it was George's turn to get banged around, although his could have had far more serious consequences. During one scene when Raft was climbing a utility pole, his safety belt broke and he fell almost forty feet to the ground, landing unconscious and winding up in the hospital with three broken ribs and contusions of the abdomen.

Despite all the production difficulties, *Manpower* emerged onscreen as an exciting, well-acted and directed drama. The posters for the film were as accurate a summation of the making of *Manpower* as the picture itself: "Robinson — He's mad about Dietrich. Dietrich — She's mad about Raft. Raft — He's mad about the whole thing." *The New York Times* wrote: "The Warner Brothers, like vulcan, know the pat way to forge a thunderbolt. They simply pick a profession in which the men are notoriously tough and the mortality rate is high, write a story about it in which both features are persistently stressed, choose a couple of aces from their pack of hard-boiled actors, and with these assorted ingredients, whip together a cinematic depth charge." A more ironic review from the *Brooklyn Citizen* read: "Robinson and Raft are ideally cast. They're hard as nails." (An interesting side note: In the nightclub scene where Raft's character has to slug his way out brandishing a broken chair leg, look closely at the girl he hands his "weapon" to as he exits. She was a bit actress named Virginia Hill, who would become more (in)famous as the girlfriend of "Bugsy" Siegel. The scene was later dramatized in the Warren Beatty film *Bugsy*, 1991.)

Raft's next passed on another Warners assignment — though this refusal would have a much more profound effect on Raft's subsequent film career.

The colorful and immensely talented John Huston was well-regarded by Warners for his brilliant screenplays, which included *Juarez* and, of course, *High Sierra* (along with his writing on *The Amazing Dr. Clitterhouse*, 1938, co-starring Edward G. Robinson and Bogart, and the Bette Davis-Henry Fonda classic *Jezebel*, 1938). But what the son of the respected thespian Walter Huston really desired was to prove his mettle as a director. Following the success of *High Sierra*, he finally received the opportunity. He chose as his directorial debut the third remake of the Dashiell Hammett masterpiece *The Maltese Falcon*.

Warners approved the project since it owned the story and, with a budget of $381,000, would be inexpensive to produce. However, for some inexplicable reason, Hal Wallis wanted to re-name the film *The Gent from Frisco*. Fortunately, Jack Warner intervened and ordered the film shot under its original title.

The most famous story regarding Raft's turning down *The Maltese Falcon* was that he didn't want to work with an inexperienced director, namely John

Huston. He even ignored the urging of William Wyler, who had proved right about *Dead End.*

"Huston is a brilliant guy and you can't miss with him," Wyler said.

"All right," Raft finally said. "I'll do the picture, if you direct my next picture."

To which Wyler replied, "Sure, George, if I have a role that suits you."

George took this as a rejection. At the very least, Wyler's response was evasive. At any rate, Raft couldn't muster any enthusiasm for the director, the story — or the character of private detective Sam(uel) Spade, whom he defined as "wishy-washy."

Raft was given a perfect opportunity to free himself from the assignment when a deal was arranged between Warner Brothers and Twentieth Century-Fox for an actor swap. Fox reportedly was interested in having George play the lead in *Hot Spot* (1941), to co-star Betty Grable. Warners wanted to borrow Henry Fonda for their comedy *The Male Animal* (1942). Jack Warner assured George that he could turn down *The Maltese Falcon* if he accepted the part at Fox. But George had only seven days to close his deal; otherwise, he would be expected to report to Warners to commence filming *The Maltese Falcon.*

Apparently, the Fox deal — if it ever existed in the first place — did not pan out (beefcake Victor Mature played the role of Frankie Christopher in the retitled *I Wake Up Screaming*) — but Raft failed to report to the studio as ordered. Instead, he wrote Jack Warner the following: "As you know, I strongly feel that *The Maltese Falcon*, which you want me to do, is not an important picture and, in this connection, I must remind you again, before I signed the new contract with you, you promised me that you would not require me to perform in anything but important pictures."

Finally, George's agent Myron Selznick called the studio to confirm that his client would not be doing *The Maltese Falcon.* Raft again enforced the "right to refuse remakes" clause in his contract.

Director John Huston was delighted. He'd wanted Bogart for the part right from the beginning. And had that not occurred, he certainly expected to have difficulties with Raft. He later said, "Just to show his authority, he [Raft] would be insubordinate on the set. He liked challenging directors." Huston went further by admitting that he was prepared to bring a blackjack to the set and use it, instantly, on Raft once he got out of line.

He also remarked, "He [Raft] fancied himself an actor, but he was not really a good actor."

In the 1997 book, *Bogart*, Jack Warner's secretary, William Schaeffer, commented on Raft, "He was never considered a big, big star. He played gangster roles and tough guy parts and he was good for those. He had a certain drawing power for a certain kind of picture. But other than that, why, he didn't have it. And he was always demanding things. Pushing people around …"

Unlike his refusals of *Dead End* and *High Sierra*, it was apparent that Raft did later regret turning down *The Maltese Falcon*. Not only did it solidify Humphrey Bogart as a bona fide star, the movie itself became a classic. The cast worked in a perfect synchronicity rare in motion pictures. And the "untried" John Huston's direction was flawless. He'd later say with uncharacteristic modesty, "All I did was film the book." Raft was mercilessly ridiculed for turning down this golden opportunity. Broadway columnist Ed Sullivan referred to "Raft's boner." *The Los Angeles Times* wrote that Raft was "doing a slow burn over Humphrey Bogart's hit performance."

Indeed, George very quickly realized his "boner." Spotted outside a New York theater where *The Maltese Falcon* was playing to an enthusiastic crowd, George was quoted as saying, "There but for the grace of me, go I."

Some years later, George offered another (self-revealing) reason why he turned down the role of Sam Spade. "I listened to my agent, Myron Selznick.... I didn't know much, so I listened to guys who were supposed to know something.... [He told me] 'Turn it down.'"

In a later interview with columnist James Bacon, George further explained, "I thought by that time I had played enough tough guys on the screen, and while John Huston was one hell of a screenwriter, Jack Warner only gave him his first directing job so he could hang on to him as a writer. Besides, the damn script had been done three other times before. I told J.L. to give it to Bogart."

If true, those words echo back to Jack LaRue's story that he'd suggested Raft for *Scarface*.

Regardless of how or why Raft turned down *The Maltese Falcon*, there can be no question that George's refusal provided Bogie with his best screen role to date. Bogart's success as Sam Spade finally freed him from roles where he played, what he termed, "George Raft's brother-in-law." His phrasing had almost the same bitter edge as Raft's when the latter said he did not want to "play parts that Humphrey Bogart should play."

Raft maintained that stance by turning down two other pictures that were inherited by Bogart: A semi-remake of *High Sierra* called *The Big Shot* (Bogie's last gangster role until *The Desperate Hours* thirteen years later) and the serio-comic gangsters vs. Nazis movie *All Through the Night* (both 1942). Reportedly, Raft refused this latter project because he was offended by the "heel"-like qualities of the character "Gloves" Donahue, who is a professional gambler yet who neglects to financially help his own mother. Of course, in the final film the character does not come off as quite like that — if he ever did in the script that Raft supposedly saw.

Fortunately for George, his personal life was faring better than his professional one. In 1941 he began dating Hollywood's soon-to-be World War II "Pin-Up Girl" Betty Grable, whom he had first met as a chorus girl on the set of *Palmy Days*. Apparently, George had already once dated Betty when he took her to the six-day bicycle races when she was just sixteen. Now Betty was a more mature twenty-four, beautiful, divorced from the child actor Jackie Coogan and a star in her own right at Twentieth Century-Fox.

Betty Grable would be the most serious of all of George's Hollywood romances. For one thing, she shared a genuine liking for all of his interests. In George's previous relationships with the refined Virginia Pine and cul-

NIGHTCLUBBING WITH "PIN-UP" GIRL BETTY GRABLE IN THE 1940s

tured Norma Shearer, they had accompanied him to his favorite outings more to please him. Betty, on the other hand, was fun and outgoing and enjoyed going to Sunday ballgames, Tuesday and Friday night fights, and especially the race track. She also loved going to nightclubs with George, where neither drank (except fruit juice drinks or ice cream sodas) but would dance for hours. Often, though, the two would just enjoy a simple evening at home, where after dinner they would play gin rummy or bridge. Betty admitted to falling in love with George almost immediately. "I would have married George Raft a week after I met him, I was so desperately, so deeply in love with him," she later told columnist Louella Parsons.

As for Raft, he said, "Betty is the first girl I ever went out with who could make me laugh, and I mean really laugh. When I'm with her, I'm completely happy and I don't give a hoot if the whole world topples on my shoulders — as long as she's with me and we're laughing."

One of the reasons Betty fell so hard for George was his constant thought-fulness and consideration. She recalled the time she had to go to the hospital for an infected wisdom tooth and received flowers from him every hour. Also, when George discovered that Thursday was the maid's night off he would never forget to invite Betty's mother to be with them. He even invited Betty's father to join them at Thanksgiving, even though Betty's parents were divorced.

As he was in all of his affairs, George was extremely giving, gifting Betty with furs, jewelry and even racehorses. Betty was later to say, "George was one of the kindest, most generous men I have ever known.

Naturally, movie magazines printed numerous stories and columns high-lighting George and Betty's romance. Most were rather silly offerings, catering to the public's insatiable appetite for details surrounding the domestic life of their favorite celebrities. One item, for instance, reported George and Betty's favorite nicknames for one another. George called Betty "Goodlookin'," while Betty would teasingly refer to Raft as her "straight man" or "Sinister."

Once again, Raft wanted to marry. He instructed his lawyers to give in further to Grayce's demands for granting him a divorce. Grayce said she might consider $300,000. The opportunity to raise half of that sum came in November 1941, when Universal offered George $150,000 to appear in a comedy with Rosalind Russell, with whom he had worked in *It Had to Happen*. George's only hurdle was, per his contract, he had to secure Jack Warner's approval for the loanout. When Warner did not return the tele-phone calls of either Raft or his agent, George took matters into his own hands and flew out to New York to talk with Warner personally at the mogul's Waldorf suite. According to George, the conversation went well and Warner gave a verbal okay for the deal. Raft was optimistic, even though a meet-ing later that day with one of Warner's associates planted seeds of doubt about Warner keeping his word. Doubts that were confirmed when George returned to Hollywood and found that Warner had indeed reneged on his agreement and that George was to report to Warners for a film titled *The Dealer's Name is George*. It was a project, George said, that was only a title — no script, intended to keep Raft contractually bound to the studio, thus precluding the loanout.

Raft felt betrayed and was livid. It was as if Jack Warner was exacting a kind of punishment on Raft for all the difficulties he had caused the studio. In any case, he never went to Universal and was unable to raise the cash needed to pay Grayce what she was asking.

Inevitably, the George Raft-Betty Grable romance began to erode. Despite her love for George, Betty realized there was no future with a man who could not marry. When the two would go out, Betty would become more atten-tive to other men, leaving George seething with jealousy. Finally, after two years together, Betty ended their relationship, but not before George had purchased a stone marten coat which he had intended to give Betty as a Christmas present. Although their affair was over, George instructed Mack Gray to deliver Betty the coat, and if she did not want it, not to bring it back but to leave it on her doorstep — which Mack was obliged to do after Betty refused to accept it.

Not long afterwards, Raft got into a fistfight at a Hollywood nightspot with bandleader Harry James, who was now involved with Betty. Fortunately, George's animosity did not last long and he subsequently forgot past grievances and became friends with the now-married Betty and James, and they occasionally socialized together. Harry James and Betty Grable would divorce in 1965, and Betty would die of lung cancer at age 56 in 1973, which affected George deeply.

George's breakup with Betty Grable was extremely difficult for him and he never again entered into a serious romantic relationship. As it was, George was always proud of the fact that in none of his relationships did he ever live with a woman. He was always a gentleman and would never disgrace a lady by subjecting her to such an arrangement.

Now surrendering to his inability to marry, he confined his romances to one-night stands with starlets and hookers, where there would be no painful emotional attachments.

But even when out with a prostitute, George always insisted that their evening be like a date. He was always a gentleman, would treat the girl well, as if she was his special girl — but if she did not reciprocate to his romantic gestures and wanted just to get it over with George would pay her and send her on her way. He also would not tolerate any girl he was out with to talk about other men she'd been with.

Despite his popularity with the opposite sex, George was surprisingly insecure when it came to women. He never thought that he was handsome (one of the reasons he refused to watch himself onscreen: "My face will scare babies," he'd once said) or sexy and believed that female attraction to him was based more on what he was than who he was. He always feared rejection and later said that he always waited until he knew that a woman was interested in him before he made an advance. That possibility of rejection was why he later preferred the company of prostitutes, because as long as one had the money, one would not be turned down.

George's reputation and generosity put him at the top of the list in every hooker's "black book," and so he was seldom in need of female companionship. His sexual proficiency was so astounding that once while doing a personal appearance he performed the near-Herculean task of bedding seven chorus girls in a single night!

Meanwhile, his troubles with Warner Brothers continued. He refused a loan-out to appear in RKO's *The Mayor of 44th Street* (1942) because the role was that of a reformed gangster (George Murphy replaced him) and he turned down the part that Ronald Reagan eventually played in *Juke Girl* (1942). (Interestingly, both of Raft's replacements would become active in California politics. Unlike Humphrey Bogart, however, inheriting these roles from George Raft would have nothing to do with their later successes.) He also failed to report for a picture to be directed by Raoul Walsh called *Deadline*, which was never produced.

BROADWAY (1942) IN WHICH RAFT ESSENTIALLY PLAYED HIMSELF, A HOOFER-TURNED-MOVIE STAR

Unsure of what to do with Raft, who was costing the studio a lot of money by agreeing to play a role to go on salary during pre-production, then would suddenly pull out of the film while still cashing his paychecks, Warners approved a loanout to Universal in exchange for the services of Robert Cummings, whom the studio wanted for their production of *Kings Row* (1942).

Although *Broadway* (1942) was a remake of a 1929 Universal film, which was based on a popular play by Philip Dunning and George Abbott, the film had surprising parallels to George's own New York experiences in the 1920s.

In the picture, George played "George Raft," now a successful movie star returning to New York who reminisces about his early years as a dancer in the city. Of course, his story is played out against the backdrop of Prohibition and the colorful characters with whom he associated: the gangster/bootlegger Steve Crandall (Broderick Crawford), speakeasy owner Nick (S.Z. "Cuddles" Sakall), the Texas Guinan-inspired "Lil" Rice (Marjorie Rambeau), dancing partner Billie Moore (Janet Blair) and cop Dan McCorn (Pat O'Brien). To further keep ties to George's past, Mack Gray was given the role of "Mack Gray."

The movie was a perfect showcase for George — because, in essence, he was playing himself. Reviewers took favorable note of this fact, particularly his fancy footwork. *The Brooklyn Daily Eagle* wrote, "Raft is comfortable in his role, dancing with a skill that hasn't tarnished in the years since he used it almost exclusively to earn a living." *The New York Times* said his acting was "more than ordinarily convincing."

It was on the set of *Broadway* that George was quoted, predicting his future at Warner Brothers, "I suppose I'll go back over there, turn down another story, and get suspended again. As far as I'm concerned, I don't care if I never make another picture on the Warner lot."

When Raft returned to Warner Brothers, he must have realized that his once-exalted status at the studio was in jeopardy. This was made evident when Warners was planning to film what was to become its most famous and endearing production, *Casablanca* (1942), based on the unproduced play *Everybody Comes to Rick's*. In casting the leading role of Richard Blaine, the proprietor of the Moroccan nightclub, associate producer Jerry Wald wrote to Hal Wallis: "This story should make a good vehicle for either Raft or Bogart." For the first time, Bogart's name was mentioned in the same breath as Raft's for a vehicle. He would no longer merely be "pinch-hitting" for his rival.

The casting of *Casablanca* has become Hollywood legend, ranging from a press release issued by the studio stating that the lead roles would be played by Ronald Reagan and Ann Sheridan, to later suggested casting for Ilsa of Hedy Lamarr and Michele Morgan, to that most intriguing question: Why did George Raft not appear in the movie?

Certainly, the dapper Raft was more suited to play a suave, white-tuxedoed nightclub owner than Bogart. Sartorially, at least, he would have been splendid. And while it has long been accepted that George turned down the role because he didn't feel it was right for him — or, according to another report, that he objected to the taint of ex-gangsterism in the character, the studio offers another story. A memo from Jack Warner to Hal Wallis read: "What do you think of using Raft in *Casablanca*? He knows we are going to make this, and is starting a campaign for it."

Perhaps George saw how his many rejections had raised the prominence of former B-player Humphrey Bogart both at the studio and with the ticket-buying public. While formerly Raft's status at Warners had been virtually untouchable, he must have become aware of how his refusals of roles and general troublesome behavior had begun to threaten his position at the studio. With this in mind, he may have seen *Casablanca* as the means to work his way back into the studio's good graces.

AN ELEGANTLY-ATTIRED RAFT GIVES A SUGGESTION OF HOW HE MIGHT HAVE APPEARED AS CASINO OWNER RICK IN *CASABLANCA*

But this time it was the studio that played hardball, particularly Hal Wallis. In response to Warner's query, Wallis wrote that he had discussed Raft's casting with director Michael Curtiz "and we both feel he should not be in the picture. Bogart is ideal for it and it is being written for him, and I think we should forget Raft for the property." Wallis further noted: "Incidentally, he [Raft] hasn't done a picture here since I was a little boy, and I don't think he should be able to put his finger on just what he wants to do, when he wants to do it."

The bitter truth was that although George's four films for Warners had all been successful, he had simply spent too much time on suspension to be considered a profitable asset to the studio. Warners definitely was an acrimonious studio, with walkouts and lawsuits the norm, but at least its contracted stars worked and made money for the Warners.[21] George, on the other hand, was proving to be a liability to the studio's accounting. And to Jack and Harry Warner, that was an unpardonable sin.

Bogart made screen history with *Casablanca*, earning a Best Actor Academy Award nomination (which he lost to Paul Lukas for *Watch on the Rhine*, 1943). Its enormous success transformed him from a "utility heavy" into a true cinematic icon, whose popularity continues to endure. His immortality was assured at a fee of $36,667, a bargain rate compared to the $60,000 that Raft would have pocketed for the role. Bogart's talent was unquestionable, but again, as with *The Maltese Falcon*, he benefited from a superior supporting cast, each of whom played his/her part, regardless of size, to perfection. One wonders how George Raft would have fared surrounded by such company as Ingrid Bergman, Paul Henreid, Claude Rains, Sydney Greenstreet, Peter Lorre and "Cuddles" Sakall.

Whatever the truth behind Raft's not doing *Casablanca*, in later years he would take credit for Humphrey Bogart's enormous success in the part. As he told his biographer Lewis Yablonsky, "I had many regrets after I gave Bogart the role of Rick ..."

Instead of taking part in the Oscar-winning movie, George took a leave-of-absence from Warners to do a gratis cameo in United Artists' all-star *Stage Door Canteen* (1943). Raft's few seconds oncamera had him cleaning plates alongside Mack Gray in the kitchen of the canteen, talking sports statistics with radio announcer Bill Stern, and opining that Henry Armstrong "pound for pound" was the best professional boxer. While his appearance was brief, he was no less noticeable than such other guest stars as George Jessel, Harpo Marx, Katharine Hepburn and even his *Scarface* co-player Paul Muni.

Not surprisingly, the enormous success of *Casablanca* prompted Warner Brothers to develop other projects that dealt with wartime espionage. One of those scripts found its way into Raft's hands: *Background to Danger* (1943), adapted from the novel *Uncommon Danger* by Eric Ambler. It was a choice role for Raft and he seized it. The character of Joe Barton was a heroic undercover FBI agent who, in the guise of an American machinery and tool salesman, exposes and foils a German plot to manipulate the Turkish government into forming an alliance with the Third Reich by falsely presenting a Russian plan to invade Turkey. Along the way, Joe encounters much intrigue, primarily in the persons of the sinister opportunist Colonel Robinson (Sydney Greenstreet) and double agent Nicolai Zaleshoff (Peter Lorre), the latter of whom is killed while attempting to escape with Barton. Raft's female co-star was Brenda Marshall (Mrs. William Holden, who was beginning to ease away from her professional career into a life of married domesticity), who, as Tamara Zaleshoff, was improbably cast as Peter Lorre's sister.

Although the plot was perhaps overly complex, the film included two action highlights: A thrilling car chase finale and the brutal beating Raft's character endures at the hands of Colonel Robinson's vicious henchmen. It was an effective bit of screen sadism, almost on a par with Raft's similar treatment at the hands of Jeff in *The Glass Key*.

While exciting in concept, *Background to Danger* could not help but to be compared to *Casablanca* and, as a result, failed to capture the same audience enthusiasm. For George, perhaps hoping to bounce back from his past errors, it may have been a case of too little too late.

Possibly George sensed this. Even though *Background to Danger* gave him the chance to play a bona fide hero, he still wanted his role to be beefed up and, during a script conference, requested a scene where the President of the United States personally thanks his character for the work he was doing. Needless to say, George didn't get his scene and John Huston, who had been working on the script with his *High Sierra* collaborator W. R. Burnett, merely got up from the meeting and announced that he was going off to war.

Far more interesting than the film, however, were the behind-the-scenes antics of Peter Lorre directed at George, and Raft's eventual (in character) retribution. Apparently, Lorre, besides being an inveterate scene stealer, was also a prankster who took George as an easy target. Certainly, Lorre did not consider Raft his equal, either in talent or intellect. He had a higher regard in both respects for his friend Humphrey Bogart.

Raft would later recall Lorre as a "mean little guy" who stole his hat from the wardrobe department and paraded around the set wearing it. But the topper came during the scene in the movie where Raft's character is tied to a chair and Lorre took advantage of Raft's helplessness by continually blowing cigarette smoke in his face. George repeatedly told Lorre to stop, but Lorre not only refused but also began flicking his cigarette close to George's eyes. Finally, after the scene was filmed and George was untied from the chair, he rushed into Lorre's dressing room and belted him, reportedly knocking Lorre unconscious for about five minutes.

While Raft may have been justified in slugging Lorre, he went further by calling him a German spy, which upset the half-Jewish Lorre and apparently was not much appreciated by others on the set, either.

Following the completion of *Background to Danger*, a dissatisfied Raft decided to terminate his contract with Warner Brothers. He met with little opposition from Jack Warner, who likewise no longer saw the need to keep the troublesome actor on his payroll. When the two met in December of 1942 to discuss the terms of dissolving their business relationship, Warner was prepared to offer Raft $10,000. George apparently misunderstood and

instead wrote Warner a check for that amount, which Warner accepted. ("I
practically ran to the bank with it before he could change his mind,"Warner
recorded in his autobiography.) George, however, would later say that he had
not misunderstood the offer — that he was aware that the studio still owed
him about $75,000, but had voluntarily paid the ten-grand just to get himself
off the lot. Perhaps this may be seen as a bad business deal on Raft's part, but
he still came out ahead of Jack Warner. During his three years at Warners, he
had earned a total of $288,396,82 — for appearing in only five pictures!

But apparently money had less importance for Raft than finally earning
his liberation after ten years of what he considered studio bondage.

RAFT POOLSIDE IN HIS FAVORITE SHOES WITH MACK GRAY'S SISTER MILLIE, IN THE EARLY '40S. PHOTO COURTESY OF THE MACK GRAY ESTATE

CHAPTER EIGHT

"IT DOESN'T ALWAYS TAKE THE IMPACT OF A BULLET TO CONVINCE A MAN THAT HE HAS MESSED UP HIS LIFE."

GEORGE RAFT

Now free from Warner Brothers, George Raft made the decision to never again commit to a long-term studio contract. Instead, he would freelance and chart his own career destiny, choosing only those projects that he felt personally comfortable about doing. Yet, as James Cagney and Humphrey Bogart would also discover upon severing studio ties, actors were not always the best judge at what they believed the public wanted to see them in. After watching the less-than-stellar box office returns from his three Cagney Productions releases, Jimmy would return to Warners to star in one of his most memorable and popular films, *White Heat* (1949), where, as the crazed gunman Cody Jarrett, he terrorized victims and movie audiences in a way Tom Powers or Rocky Sullivan never could have imagined. Humphrey Bogart's later Santana Productions produced a series of films that likewise made little impact on audiences, and he eventually returned — if briefly — to form at Warners in the crime drama *The Enforcer* (1951). Jack Warner had said of Cagney after the actor ventured independent (and it held equally as true for Bogart and Raft), "He'll find he needs us as much as we need him."

Raft would be among the first of the Hollywood Golden Age stars to find that his preferences concerning scripts and roles were not necessarily shared by movie audiences, and these miscalculations ultimately precipitated his decline. To make matters worse, this waning of public interest would coincide with a number of unpleasant personal episodes that would garner George plenty of bad press.

Before Raft went before the cameras again, he decided to do his part for the war effort and organized "George Raft's Cavalcade of Sports."[22] He spent $50,000 of his own money to bring his traveling boxing show to various army and navy bases on behalf of the U.S.O. The entertainment consisted of three-round matches featuring second-rate fighters, which Raft would usually referee unless a boxing "name" was present. He was helped in this venture by his friend and former ring protégé, Maxie Rosenbloom. In addition, George was among the first American stars to entertain the troops overseas. But even while performing this patriotic duty, George retained his

RAFT IN THE MID-1940S

underworld ties. While on a U.S.O. Camp Show Tour in Italy and North Africa, it was reported that he arranged for the employment of Vito Genovese by the Allied Military Government in Italy.

Raft also claimed to have done another favor for an underworld big shot during his overseas tours. He had collected a number of German and Italian pistols and rifles which he brought to Chicago to hand over as souvenirs to former Capone gang member Jake "Greasy Thumb" Guzik. Raft recalled that in accepting the guns, Guzik said to him, "Don't worry, Georgie. I'll never use them."

Raft's first post-Warners film found him in a role similar to the one he was performing for the U.S.O. In Universal's *Follow the Boys* (1944), Raft was Tony West, a hoofer-turned-movie star who becomes the chief organizer for the Hollywood Victory Committee. While the 122-minute movie is really a showcase for the talents of such stars as the Andrews Sisters, Marlene Dietrich, W.C. Fields, Sophie Tucker and Orson Welles, the wraparound plot

VETERAN ACTOR CHARLES GRAPEWIN (LEFT) PLAYED RAFT'S FATHER IN *FOLLOW THE BOYS* (1944). CO-STAR VERA ZORINA WOULD LATER CLAIM SHE DID NOT MUCH CARE FOR RAFT DURING THE MAKING OF THE MOVIE

finds Tony West so absorbed in his Committee work that he all but ignores wife Gloria Vance (Vera Zorina) and dies in a Japanese torpedoing of his ship before ever seeing his newborn son.

Besides the dizzying array of guest stars each performing a specialty act (W.C. Fields juggling, Orson Welles sawing Marlene Dietrich in two, etc.), the chief highlight of *Follow the Boys* is the opportunity to watch the 48-year-old Raft dance to his signature song of the 1920s, "Sweet Georgia Brown," which he performs not on the floor of a nightclub, but rather in the back of an open transport truck during a sudden downpour.

Apparently, George did not endear himself to his co-star Vera Zorina, who would later recall Raft without much fondness (to wit: "… he was so icky"), and admit that she was eager to complete the picture.

If Raft was aware of Miss Zorina's dislike of him, he certainly could not have been as bothered by that as what would become his next major career misstep. In 1944, director Billy Wilder approached George about returning to his former studio, Paramount, to play the lead role of opportunistic insurance agent Walter Neff in his upcoming *Double Indemnity* (1944), based on the famous James M. Cain novel.

Reportedly, George asked Wilder to tell him the plot rather than his reading the script and at one point inquired when the Neff character would flash open his badge and reveal that he was really a detective investigating the case. At that moment Wilder saw that Raft had no concept of the role, and George, in any case, turned down the plum part. ("That's when we knew we had a good picture," Wilder later admitted.)

Paramount's then-top star Alan Ladd had been the first choice for Neff, but he had graduated from sinister roles, such as hired gunman Raven in his breakthrough picture *This Gun for Hire* (1942), to pursue more heroic characters. Wilder then hit upon an unlikely, but ultimately inspired casting choice. Fred MacMurray, known previously for playing charming, easygoing types, somewhat reluctantly accepted the assignment and scored a career milestone, plotting murder alongside manipulative *femme fatale* Barbara Stanwyck.

Fred MacMurray reciprocated the favor to Raft the following year (but with far less satisfactory results) when he refused the role of Barbary Coast saloon proprietor Tony Angelo in Twentieth Century-Fox's Technicolor *Nob Hill* (1945). Despite being directed by action specialist Henry Hathaway, the musical drama was quite a dull offering focusing on Tony's romantic infatuation with a blue-blooded society woman, Harriet Carruthers (Joan Bennett), and eventual realization that his true love is singer Sally Templeton (Vivian Blaine), a girl closer to Tony's rough-hewn world. The earlier films *Barbary Coast* and *San Francisco* (1936) were much more successful renditions of colorful turn-of-the century San Francisco.

Nob Hill was the last of four pictures that Joan Bennett made with Raft, and she retained her impression of him as a gentleman, though apparently George had a run-in with director Henry Hathaway that resulted in Raft's walking off the set for a few days until producer Andre Daven could work out their differences. According to Miss Bennett, the Fox film was meant as a showcase for Vivian Blaine and moppet Peggy Ann Garner, who was riding high following her success in Elia Kazan's *A Tree Grows in Brooklyn* (1945). Moviegoers also got a glimpse of a handsome young (uncredited) Rory Calhoun in one of his earliest film roles.

During the filming of *Nob Hill*, director Hathaway asked George for his advice on how to make a bar fight sequence look more realistic. George remembered the often dirty street fighting techniques of his youth and suggested that his character smash his opponent's face against the mahogany bar rail. Hathaway approved, though later some critics complained that the scene was too brutal.

George entered the realm of *film noir* with his next picture, *Johnny Angel* (1945), produced by RKO. Raft fared well in this atmospheric mystery as the title character, a sea captain hunting for the men who murdered his father (J. Farrell MacDonald) and made off with the five-million-dollar gold bullion cargo. Johnny is aided in his search by Paulette Girard (Signe Hasso) and taxi driver Celestial O'Brien (Hoagy Carmichael). Among the many charac-

RAFT PLAYED THE TITLE CHARACTER IN *JOHNNY ANGEL* (1945), A SEA CAPTAIN SEARCHING FOR THE MURDERERS OF HIS FATHER. WITH A BESPECTACLED MACK GRAY

ters they encounter is the treacherous Lilah "Lily" Gustafson (Claire Trevor). Mack Gray also had another small part, as a bartender.

While *Johnny Angel* was a good film, it started the trend of Raft appearing only in pictures that featured him as the hero, a concept that soon would become redundant and tiresome for movie patrons. The movie also marked the first of six films Raft would make with director Edward L. Marin, which ultimately would prove an uninspired creative partnership.

Johnny Angel was a marginal success with audiences, but it was nowhere near as noteworthy as the film George Raft's rival Humphrey Bogart had appeared in the previous year, where he, too, had played a "man of the sea" — Harry Morgan, the skipper of a charter boat in *To Have and Have Not* (1944), based on Ernest Hemingway's (worst) novel. The picture was a critical and commercial smash, and was personally important to Bogart as it was during its making that he met his fourth (and final) wife Lauren Bacall.

Despite all his grumbling, Bogart had stayed on at Warners. While he admittedly played in a few post-*Casablanca* turkeys (*Conflict*, 1945, and *The Two Mrs. Carrolls*, 1947, both of which improbably cast him as a wife murderer), he also made a number of solid films that allowed him to display his versatility, while still capitalizing on his tough guy image. Unlike Raft, he went into combat in such films as *Action in the North Atlantic* and *Sahara* (both 1943), and became an accessible figure to wartime audiences. What is interesting, however, is that Bogart not only managed to retain, but expand upon his vast appeal while beginning to show the outward signs of his hard-living, chain-smoking and alcohol excesses. Makeup and careful studio lighting smoothed the rough edges somewhat, but Bogart, who was once considered a matinee idol, was not aging gracefully. Hormone injections following his marriage to Lauren Bacall had also caused him to start losing his already-thinning hair.

George Raft, on the other hand, was four years older than Bogart, and while his own hairline was receding, his appearance remained relatively youthful, his face still smooth and not a road map of endless morning-after hangovers. Perhaps that was part of the problem. Audiences saw in Bogart's tired, craggy features the tough guy they expected and admired. Raft's handsome, less-ravaged face suffered in comparison.

But if Raft's appeal as a cinematic tough guy was waning, a number of his off-camera exploits only strengthened the public's perception of him as a real-life gangster.

George's problems started in 1944, and this incident would not only garner him damning press, but resulted in the termination of his close friendship with Brooklyn Dodgers manager Leo Durocher. Raft and Durocher first met as young men in a 48th Street poolroom and had instantly hit it off. Through the years while each achieved success in his respective career, they had maintained their friendship, spending as much time together as possible and borrowing each other's clothes, cars and even girls. George was especially proud of the special Dodger uniform that Durocher had made for him.

George had just returned from an overseas U.S.O. tour and was in New York to promote *Follow the Boys*. George was always welcome to use Durocher's midtown apartment when Leo was away, as Raft reciprocated by inviting Leo to stay with him at his Hollywood home after the baseball season ended. Following the premiere of the movie, George invited some people up to a party at the apartment and someone suggested a dice game. George found a pair of Stork Club souvenir dice and began shooting. By the time the game folded toward morning, Raft was in possession of about $8,000 — mostly in checks. Raft, not normally a craps player, considered himself a lucky winner and thought no more about it. But seven months later while filming *Johnny Angel*, George discovered that the big loser in the crap game, a man named Martin Shurin, had issued a complaint with New

York District Attorney Frank Hogan, accusing Raft of using loaded dice and taking $18,500 in cash from him in thirteen straight passes. George naturally denied the accusation and Shurin's character would eventually come into question. But Raft had suddenly become the target of newspaper columnists, particularly the influential Westbrook Pegler, who apparently had a strong dislike for George Raft. The negative press became so vehement that Raft would later say, "You would have thought that I had personally dropped a bomb on Ebbets Field."

Leo Durocher, en route to Italy to play exhibition baseball for American soldiers, received a heated telephone call from Dodger owner Branch Rickey who made Leo promise to never again allow George to use his apartment. Durocher was further ordered to stop associating with other "undesirable" Raft companions, such as "Bugsy" Siegel and Joey Adonis.

Raft, meanwhile, received his own scolding from the New Jersey mobster Adonis, who told him: "You ought to know better than to get mixed up in a third-rate crap game with strangers. The papers will cut you and Leo to ribbons."

Unfortunately, Adonis's well-intended "advice" backfired when his telephone conversation with George was tapped and recorded by the police.

The incident continued to plague George as newspapers consulted professionals to analyze the game and comment on Raft's "luck." The nationally-known dice expert John Scarne, for instance, said that the odds against thirteen passes were 9851 to 1. A rival paper printed their findings that the true odds were 25 trillion to 1!

While George was publicly condemned for being a cheat, no one thought to ask him for his side of the story. According to Raft, he never made thirteen passes, he never collected all his winnings, and that his accuser Mr. Shurin was a draft dodger and swindler who passed bad checks.

Of course, Mack Gray came to George's defense. *The Washington Post* quoted Gray as saying that it sounded like a "frame-up," and that George made enough money in motion pictures that he did not need that kind of money. The article described Gray as Raft's "protector, chauffeur, fellow gambler and general handyman."

Raft maintained his innocence and was never convicted by D.A. Hogan due to a lack of any "hard" evidence. Later, a July 25, 1946 *Washington Times-Herald* newspaper article, captioned "George Raft's Dice Victim Craps Out as a Draft Dodger," would report that 33-year-old Martin Shurin had been arrested the previous day by the FBI as a draft dodger. But by then the damage had already been done. Raft's reputation with the public was tarnished, and his friendship with Durocher was over.

Leo had met secretly with baseball commissioner Happy Chandler on the fairway of the Claremont Country Club in Berkeley. Chandler offered Durocher the ultimatum: Either drop Raft or quit baseball. As tough as the choice was for him, Leo knew he could never leave his beloved sport and agreed to immediately vacate Raft's Coldwater Canyon home, where he had been staying at the time. It was a painful parting, and George would later say, "He [Durocher] had absolutely no choice, but my main regret is that he was forced into this decision by men who knew George Raft only from what they read in the papers."

Shortly after this episode, George had dinner in New York with Joey Adonis. During their meal Adonis said to him, "George, I like you and you like me. But it's no good for you to be seen with me. I'm in the rackets, and if the press ever connects you with me, you'll get hurt."

Unfortunately for George, his "connections" were already getting him into trouble. Particularly a dapper New York gangster named Benjamin "Bugsy" Siegel.

Ben Siegel was eleven years younger than George, but a product of the same Lower East Side environment and spent his early years getting into the same kind of trouble as Georgie Ranft. While their age difference made it unlikely that they hung out together as youths, they certainly would have known each other during the '20s when Raft was achieving success as a dancer and Siegel was making his own illegal reputation as half of the "Bugs-Meyer (Lansky) Combine."

Siegel was a vain, hot-tempered man who had earned his hated nickname "Bugsy" because of his crazy, irrational — indeed, violent behavior. He was cold and ruthless, but also fearless, and he became a valuable enforcer for Murder Incorporated. He was allegedly a participant in the assassinations of both Joseph Masseria and Salvatore Maranzano, when Charles "Lucky" Luciano decided to rid the underworld of the "Mustache Petes" and consolidate the various criminal organizations into one national Syndicate, run by committee, with Luciano as its CEO. Meyer Lansky, Frank Costello, Louis Lepke, Albert Anastasia and Joey Adonis served on the Board of Directors.

Paradoxically, Siegel could be utterly charming, and it was through his personal magnetism that he made his inroads into Beverly Hills society when he traveled west in 1935 to seek out lucrative new rackets for the mob.

Naturally, Ben's first move was to renew his friendship with George Raft. As with Mack Gray, Siegel could speak easily with George and shared many of the same interests. They were often seen together at the track or any one of Hollywood's hot night spots. Through George, Siegel very quickly became acquainted with many of the top names in Hollywood, including Gary Cooper, Clark Gable, Cary Grant, actresses Wendy Barrie and Barbara Hutton and even a reluctant Jack Warner. At the Hollywood Athletic Club, Siegel could be found playing handball with the likes of Pat O'Brien. Each was either charmed or intrigued by the mysterious transplanted New York "sportsman." These celebrities may have had hints or suspicions concerning Siegel's background and reputation, but as George would say, "In public he looked and acted about as tough as a cocker spaniel."

Siegel took up residence in opera singer Lawrence Tibbett's former home at 326 McCarthy Drive. Although he had no visible occupation, he lived lavishly and gambled prodigiously, attending the Santa Anita Race Track daily and almost always emerging as a cool winner. Behind the scenes, however, Siegel was busy with his various (mostly illegal) enterprises, such as establishing a drug smuggling operation between the U.S. and Mexico and operating a race wire service. He also owned pieces of the Tijuana racetrack and an illegal gaming room in Hollywood called the Clover Club. Siegel partnered with another hood named Tony Cornero to buy shares in the Rex, a gambling ship which was anchored offshore, past the twelve-mile limit, in Santa Monica Bay. Short of the necessary cash, he naturally approached his soft touch pal George Raft for a loan of $20,000.

Because George no longer had the financial security of a studio contract and was working at lesser fees as an independent, he had to drive 140 miles to Arrowhead Springs to borrow the money from his agent Myron Selznick as an advance against future pictures. When Raft later heard that the gambling ship was earning big profits, he approached Siegel about repayment of his loan and possibly a share of the dividends, as he was promised. Siegel was evasive, and finally George wrote him the following letter:

> Dear Ben:
> Between the Federal government, studios, and several other personal transactions, I've really been hard pressed for cash. I will surely greatly appreciate whatever you can possibly afford and spare for me, and I honestly trust that you will fully understand this request.
>
> Again, I'd like to remind you, Ben, that if my finances weren't as bad as they actually are, under no circumstances would I have ever asked you.
>
> Your friend and pal,
> George

Raft's poor grammar notwithstanding, his note got the desired result. A few days later when George was driving down Sunset Boulevard, Siegel's car came alongside and he motioned for George to pull over to the curb. Siegel handed George a check for $2,000 (on account) and explained that he was pulling out of the gambling ship deal and that he'd get him back all of his money (no mention was made of any "dividends"). Eventually, in small increments never exceeding $500, Siegel repaid Raft. But what puzzled George was that he was hearing that his pal was laying down big-time bets ranging from $2,000 to $5,000 a day on horse races, ballgames, and prizefights. Obviously, repaying a debt was not a top priority with the free-spending Ben Siegel.

Siegel was not the only man touched by George's generosity. Raft had lent about $1,800 to a "Bugsy" Siegel associate named Whitey Krakower — and had not been paid back. Siegel severely reprimanded George when he learned of the loan and promised that he'd talk with Krakower. Later, when George was on a personal appearance tour in New York, he received a telephone call at his Sherry Netherlands Hotel suite from an old friend, Ed Callahan, now a police lieutenant with the city's Homicide Squad. Callahan told Raft that there had been a killing on the Lower East Side and asked him if he wanted to ride along. George agreed, saying that it might give him an idea for a movie. When they arrived at the murder scene, Raft instantly recognized the body as that of Whitey Krakower; the victim either of mob violence (he was a suspected informer) — or perhaps "Bugsy" Siegel's rage over his taking advantage of Raft.

There was no question that "Bugsy" Siegel admired — even envied — his pal George Raft. He often visited George on the sets of his pictures and had Raft photograph him with his own camera equipment acting out scenes he had just watched George performing, claiming that he could act better than his friend. Because the Raft image was so strong and his sartorial preferences emulated by many men in America, Siegel likewise took to dressing like his pal, and he, too, cut a fashionable figure around Tinseltown. Siegel could also be extremely generous, both with picking up restaurant and nightclub tabs and handing out compliments. He made no secret of the fact that he considered George Raft the most authentic movie tough guy of them all.

But it was Benny Siegel, of course, who was the true tough guy. He was also psychopathic, with no compunction about committing cold-blooded murder. He'd killed an undetermined number of rivals during his time. But even among his closest pals he could suddenly turn violently unpredictable. George would recall a frightening incident when he almost became a victim of Siegel's homicidal tendencies. Raft had reluctantly found himself acting as a middleman in a few of Siegel's romantic escapades, and on one occasion Wendy Barrie came to see George to seek his opinion regarding her involvement with the charming gangster. George tried to warn her that being seen with Siegel would be bad for her career (advice that Raft himself failed to heed) and that she was, indeed, "playing with fire." Wendy reported this back to Siegel, who flew into a fury and sped out in his new Buick to Raft's Coldwater Canyon home, intending to kill him with the loaded .45 Colt automatic he'd brought along expressly for that purpose.

Siegel burst into the house, brushing past Mack Gray, and storming upstairs to Raft's bedroom, where the actor was still sleeping. Siegel crashed into the room, brandishing the .45, and threatened to shoot George for telling Wendy to stay away from him. To his way of thinking, Raft had double crossed him. While Raft always claimed he never knew the true extent of Siegel's criminal activities, he could not ignore the heated rage in "Bugsy" and truly believed that Siegel was capable of anything — including murder — at that moment.

George kept calm and tried to soothe his pal. Finally, he concluded, "Okay, Ben. You can shoot me if you want, but it'll be the finish for both of us. Look, put the rod away and let's forget it. What do you say, Baby Blue Eyes?"

Siegel's attitude instantly mellowed. Raft believed that Siegel was both amused and flattered by his calling him Baby Blue Eyes and it thereafter became George's pressure valve whenever he saw Siegel about to fly into a rage.

Another time his compliment came in handy was when Raft, as a joke, presented Siegel with a toupee as a surprise gift. The narcissistic Siegel was in the process of prematurely losing his hair and was frantically trying every known remedy and quack cure to impede his receding hairline. The last thing he expected or would appreciate was a reminder of approaching baldness from his friend. He blew up at Raft over his "gift," and once again George prevented a potentially violent situation by referring to "Bugsy" as Baby Blue Eyes.[23]

Apparently, George was the only person whom Siegel would permit to call him by that nickname. But not even Raft could get away with using "Bugsy" in his pal's presence. Or anywhere else for that matter. When Raft would be questioned by the police over some illegal activity of Siegel's, and the cops would ignorantly say "Bugsy," George would quickly correct them: "You mean Ben Siegel, don't you?" But it really made no difference. As far as the police and the press were concerned, Siegel was "Bugsy."

Siegel was obsessed with maintaining his handsome, youthful appearance. He used a variety of lotions and creams to keep his skin fresh and glowing, and he kept in shape by working out regularly at the Hollywood Athletic Club. He was compulsive about his personal hygiene and took long showers several times a day — an obsession that was shared, if not exceeded, by his pal and partner Mickey Cohen. Like Raft, Siegel wasn't a drinker and confined his smoking to only the occasional cigar. He also wasn't much of a nighthawk, preferring to retire to bed at 10:00 p.m. with a copy of *Reader's Digest*.

Although Siegel was married to his childhood sweetheart, Estelle, and the father of two daughters, he quickly gained the reputation of a Hollywood playboy. Among the women he was seen dating around town were actresses Wendy Barrie and Marie "the Body" McDonald, the Countess Dorothy di Frasso — and, most notoriously, mob tart Virginia Hill.

Virginia was born on August 26, 1916, in Lipscomb, Alabama. She moved to Chicago when she was seventeen and quickly became acquainted with the seamier side of the city. Later, in New York, she began seeing Joey Adonis, and it was through Adonis that Virginia first met Ben Siegel. After that, she traveled to Hollywood, where she enrolled in the Columbia Pictures drama school and attempted to break into pictures. Although she had little success as an actress (ironically, her nightclub "bit" with George Raft in *Manpower* was her most notable screen achievement), she maintained a lavish lifestyle thanks to her mob connections and became well known as a party "hostess." In Hollywood, of course, she hooked up with Ben Siegel, and soon the two became lovers. After Siegel finally divorced his wife, he and Virginia went to Mexico and were married in the fall of 1946.

In 1945, when Siegel got the mob's permission to start building a combination hotel/gambling casino on the outskirts of Las Vegas, he decided to name it the Flamingo, after his nickname for Virginia, so coined because of her long legs. Siegel's obsession to build his hotel to his expansive vision got him into serious trouble with the Eastern Mob who was backing the project. Construction costs skyrocketed far beyond the $1.5 million the Syndicate had approved, and soon Siegel, in his desperation to keep the project going, began selling shares that did not exist. On top of that, there were suspicions among the underworld hierarchy that Siegel was skimming cash off the construction budget.

Still, all could go well if the Flamingo turned a profit. Siegel was counting on a grand opening, planned for the day after Christmas, December 26, 1946. He asked George to see if he could line up some of his Hollywood movie friends to attend the opening, figuring that their presence would draw in the tourists. Unfortunately, George had to tell Siegel that the powerful William Randolph Hearst had informed all the studios that their stars were to stay away. Of course, Raft would be there, along with his old pals Jimmy Durante and George Jessel, and also Charles Coburn, Sonny Tufts and George Sanders. But these people were not the "names" Siegel had hoped for.

Still, the opening was successful — for the gamblers at least. By January 1947, the casino itself was in the red to the tune of about half a million dollars. Siegel was forced to close down the Flamingo until the hotel could be opened.

His New York mob pals — including boyhood friends "Lucky" Luciano and Meyer Lansky — had grown impatient with Siegel and his "dream." With the situation getting hot, Siegel asked George for a loan of $100,000 to help keep him and the Flamingo afloat. Again, Raft's own financial position was tenuous, but sympathetic to Siegel's desperation, he arranged for the loan by borrowing from an annuity fund. He met with Siegel on a street corner on Sunset Boulevard to hand over the cash. Raft neither asked for nor received a receipt for the $100,000 from Siegel.

The cash and other monies Siegel had managed to borrow made possible the reopening of the Flamingo in March 1947. With the hotel now operating, the venture had even begun to show a profit. But when the Syndicate received word that Siegel had somehow put together a personal bankroll of $600,000 and was planning to join Virginia Hill in Paris, they concluded that their former partner had become a liability.

"Bugsy" Siegel must have known that the end was near, though he probably hoped a vain hope that he could get away to join Virginia in Europe and start a new life.

On the morning of June 21, he stopped by Raft's house, and George later remembered that he "looked awful."

He admitted to his pal that he hadn't slept for days and was having trouble with his East Coast associates. No mention was made about the repayment of the $100,000 loan, though Siegel invited George to have dinner with him that evening at a restaurant called Jack's on the Beach. George had to decline because he already had an engagement with producer Sam Bischoff to discuss a three-picture deal. Siegel understood, but asked Raft to drop by Virginia Hill's house on Linden Drive later where they could talk further.

George's business meeting finished early, but because he didn't think Siegel would be back from dinner until maybe around eleven, he decided to go over to a Beverly Hills bridge club he frequented to play a couple of hands. It was while he was there that he got the news. Benny Siegel had been shot to death by an unknown assassin while sitting on the living room couch reading a newspaper. Ironically, one of the 30-30 carbine slugs blew out one of Ben Siegel's Baby Blue Eyes. Equally ironic was the advertising label pasted to the cover of the *Los Angeles Times* newspaper found resting on the dead gangster's lap: "Good Night. Sleep well with the compliments of Jack's Restaurant."

"Bugsy" Siegel's murder was deliberately plotted to take place outside of Las Vegas. The men who ordered the killing wanted no violence to tarnish the image of the new gambling mecca.

Raft was in a daze and later admitted to hopping into his car to drive out to the Linden Drive house, only to turn back once he saw the convergence of police and photographers around the place. But later that night he was visited and questioned by representatives of the District Attorney's Office, who knew of his friendship with "the Bug."

There was nothing George could tell them, except to say, "When they shot Benny, they shot me."

George later explained what he meant by his mysterious statement. "They say you can't take it with you, but Benny did. My $100,000, I mean."

George was also philosophical about missing his meeting with Siegel that fateful night. "As for me, I might have been sitting there in that living room that night, right next to Benny. I guess it was fate, or just not my time to go."

BENJAMIN "BUGSY" SIEGEL WAS MOVIE STAR HANDSOME BUT DEADLY AS A COBRA. THE INFAMOUS "KISS OF DEATH" PHOTO TAKEN FOLLOWING SIEGEL AND AL SMILEY'S LENIENT SENTENCING ON A 1944 BOOKMAKING CHARGE

However, there was no denying that George was genuinely upset over his friend's murder. Besides lending money whenever Siegel asked, Raft had even risked his shaky professional reputation by testifying on Siegel's behalf when the gangster was arrested on a 1944 bookmaking charge. George had been present at the Hollywood Towers when members of the Los Angeles County's Sheriff's Vice Squad, led by Captain William Deal, burst in on him, Siegel and Siegel's friend Allen Smiley (who would be seated next to Siegel on the night of the gangster's murder). Since George was only a bettor and not "making book," he was not charged. But he was furious at what he saw as a "bum rap."

Ignoring the warnings of studio executives that going to bat for Siegel could jeopardize his movie career, Raft went to court and became so outraged in his defense of Siegel and Allen Smiley that he was warned more than once by Judge Cecil Holland not to risk putting himself in contempt. George asked heated questions to Captain Deal while himself being interrogated by the District Attorney, and when told by the judge that he was not permitted to question people from the witness stand, he retorted, "Why not? I'm entitled to free speech, aren't I? Besides, I think this whole thing is ridiculous." He maintained that at the time of the raid he and Allen Smiley were playing gin rummy with friends and making telephone bets on horse races in Nevada, where off-track betting was legal. Whether Raft's testimony was a factor, the prosecutor offered to drop the felony charges if Siegel and Smiley would plead guilty to one bookmaking charge. They accepted and were each fined $250, received 180-day suspended sentences, and were placed on probation.

Taking his friendship and loyalty to Siegel one step further, George agreed to pose for photographers outside the courtroom, grinning and with his arm around his pal's shoulder. The photo was printed in newspapers all across the country. Raft later said that certain people referred to that picture as "the kiss of death."

Raft's film career was already entering a decline, and so it is debatable whether his "noble gesture" had any detrimental effect on him professionally. What it definitely did do was further cement George Raft's reputation as a genuine gangster in the eyes of the public.

More trouble arose for George when he received a handwritten envelope addressed to his Coldwater Canyon home, postmarked July 19, 1947. The enclosed unsigned letter was a poorly-composed demand for blackmail — and is printed as written.

Dear George

Well George did you receive my letter? & do you remember or still can't remember? You know anyway this was in Hollywood during night can't tell you where or when, this is up to you to remember, anyway its some sort of photo even you could hardly remember how or when, & also you didn't know how it got into my hands, its a certain negative which FBI would like to have. You was under investigation couple times but didn't get any clue on you, but the clue they are looking for is in my hands — not only negative, but some sort of other things too. Maybe you was drunk or etc didn't know anything, if I mention where & when & with whom, you would be more excited but won't mention it cause this evidence is too strong, & you will be glad to have in your hands to read all. Well my friends told me he didn't receivd your answer yet. You know he don't know anything about this, if he tell or phone to me again in Las Vegas I am going to mail this envelope to the FBI. & so thinkit oer either you buy this or jail to you & I know what you are thinking now, (what evidence & what kind,) well don't think & you will soon know your memory if you see it. I will mail it to you if my friend received your $6 grand or more, not less. Then you can have it & destroy yourself Well Ill be seen you think it oe'r? Your friend in Las Vegas Maybe I might ask for more soon I hope, cause this cost more than your life to you when you have it.

It is not known whether George ever responded to this blackmail — or what exactly these incriminating items were.

Perhaps this was another reason why he tried even harder to distance himself with movie hoodlum roles. While his characters might have some shady leanings, they usually emerged heroic — or at least as redemptive good guys. Sadly, most of the pictures themselves were poorly written and produced with low budgets. In the first of two mediocre pictures for United Artists, *Whistle Stop* (1946), George played small-town gambling layabout Kenny Veech, who is loved by Mary (Ava Gardner). Mary eventually leaves Kenny because of his shiftless nature for club owner Lew Lentz (Tom Conway), who later tries to frame a murder rap on Kenny and his pal Gillo (Victor McLaglen). At the climax loyal Gillo and Lew kill each other in a shootout and Kenny and Mary are reunited.

Director Philip Yordan apparently had problems coaxing performances out of Raft and Gardner. He suggested that neither could act, and claimed both had difficulty speaking their lines and for that reason much their dialogue consisted of monosyllables.

Despite this, the *Motion Picture Herald* gave the film a surprisingly good review. "With the dynamics of Gardner and Raft in it, *Whistle Stop* is certainly not a dull place."

But, overall, critics were not generous either to the movie or Raft's performance. *The New York Times* called *Whistle Stop* a "plainly remote and artificial concoction," while saying that Raft "plays the bum in a bored gangster style."

Leonard Maltin's annual *Movie Guide* refers to *Whistle Stop* as an "Unusually stupid Raft vehicle ..."

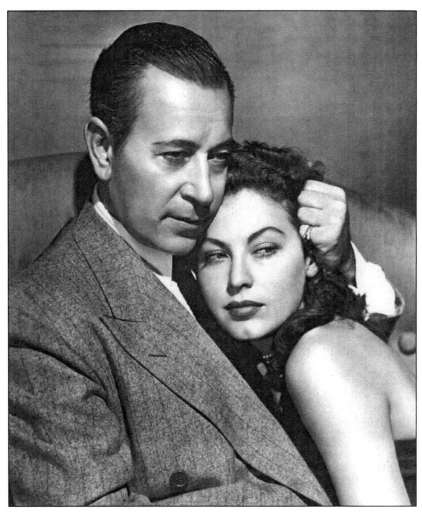

RAFT APPARENTLY FELL FOR THE GORGEOUS AVA GARDNER OFF THE SET OF HER BREAKTHROUGH PICTURE *WHISTLE STOP* (1946)

While reviewers may not have thought much of Raft in the picture, his co-star Ava Gardner was of an entirely different opinion. In her autobiography, *Ava: My Story*, Miss Gardner wrote: "I enjoyed [*Whistle Stop*] so much because George Raft, great actor or not, was such fun. George was one of the sweetest, nicest men I've ever met, and he made *Whistle Stop* worthwhile."

Miss Gardner was not the first actress considered for the role of Mary, but was chosen when MGM agreed to loan her to United Artists at a bargain rate. Previously, her most noteworthy credit was alongside Bela Lugosi and the East Side Kids in *Ghosts on the Loose* (1943). George may have also been instrumental in promoting Gardner for the picture. She later related that she and George went out dancing on a few occasions — and that she got the distinct impression that Raft would have liked their relationship to go further. She finally had to admit to him that she looked at him as more of a "father figure" (having watched him on the screen since she was a young girl). While his ego may have been somewhat bruised, George — ever the gentleman — did not insist, and the two remained friends.

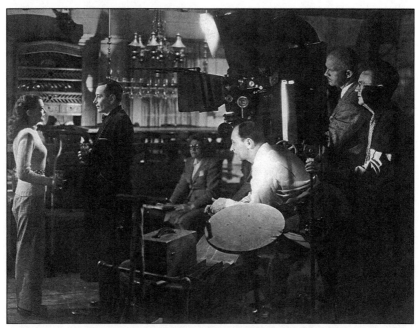

MR. ACE (1946) WITH SYLVIA SIDNEY, WHO THOUGHT HIGHLY OF RAFT IN THE THREE FILMS THEY MADE TOGETHER. DIRECTOR EDWIN L. MARIN IS SEATED AT RIGHT

Raft's second movie for United Artists fared little better with the critics or the public. *Mr. Ace* (1946), a dreary film dealing with political ambitions, offered George little more than the opportunity to again co-star opposite Sylvia Sidney. In the film, Sidney is Margaret Wyndham Chase, a wealthy but ruthless congresswoman who seeks the support of Eddie Ace (Raft), an underworld character with political influence, in her run for governor. Tough guy Eddie, however, firmly believes that "beautiful women and politics do not mix," and, in fact, conspires against Margaret. Of course, Eddie eventually falls in love with her and rights all wrongs, with Margaret picked to run on an independent good-government ticket.[24]

In his second film with director Edwin L. Marin, George received mostly negative reviews for his performance. *Silver Screen* offered the most blunt and succinct observation: "George Raft still can't act."

Once again, Sylvia Sidney retained warm feelings toward her co-star. She remembered that during the shooting of *Mr. Ace*, which was just after the war, it was still very difficult to get silk stockings, and that George would furnish her with them. Also cigarettes — and never just a pack, but a carton.

"And he never made a pass at me," Miss Sidney added. "He was a perfect gentleman."

Raft's career received a brief reprieve from its downward trend with *Nocturne* (1946), another *noir* drama which he made at RKO. Again directed by Edwin L. Marin, *Nocturne* at least put George back in more comfortable territory: as Detective Lieutenant Joe Warne, out to solve the murder of a composer with the title musical number as the link to the killer. As with the previous *Johnny Angel*, *Nocturne* had plenty of *noir* atmosphere, but was hampered by slow pacing and a pedestrian storyline. Reviews for Raft's performance were mixed, with *Variety* writing that Raft "gives his usual, slow-paced, tough touch to the assignment to make it thoroughly effective." The *New York Herald-Tribune*, on the other hand, reported: "George Raft has even less animation than in his former pictures, entering a rough-and-tumble fight or a love scene with almost the same mask-like expression."

As if George wasn't having enough trouble professionally, once more he found his personal life in serious question. Raft, along with a number of prominent studio executives and celebrities, was named as a purchaser of obscene motion pictures produced by an underground pornography ring. It was alleged that the elaborately staged and technically perfect films sold for more than $500 per reel with the primary customers being the Hollywood elite.

Even more potentially damaging was Raft's suspected violation of the White Slavery Traffic Act arising out of his affair with a nineteen-year-old starlet (prostitute) who was in contact with George while he was staying at the Sherry Netherlands Hotel in New York. However, he was never prosecuted due to a lack of sufficient evidence. A January 31, 1946 FBI memorandum noted: "I think it is useless to try and obtain anything against Raft re: White Slavery for his victims are often even lower than he is if that is possible ..." In questioning Raft, it was reported: "Agents observed that Raft is small in stature, has a very limp handshake and gives the personal impression quite contrary to that which he portrays in motion pictures and television shows."

He was further briefly investigated that year by the FBI in connection with general criminal activities in the Los Angeles area.

Then, the December 14, 1946 *Los Angeles Daily News* headline read: GEORGE RAFT ACCUSED OF GANGSTER BRAWL IN $300,000 DAMAGE SUIT

Since his break-up with Betty Grable, George had been dating many movie starlets, among them the 19-year-old Betty Doss. Apparently, Miss Doss was one of George's more serious flirtations as he had presented her

SETTING UP A SHOT FROM *NOCTURNE* (1946). DIRECTOR EDWIN L. MARIN IS STANDING BEHIND THE CAMERA. BARNEY RUDITSKY IS TO RAFT'S RIGHT, WEARING SUNGLASSES. RUDITSKY WAS A LEGENDARY N.Y. CITY DETECTIVE DURING PROHIBITION WHO LATER BECAME A PRIVATE EYE IN HOLLYWOOD. HE WORKED AS TECHNICAL ADVISOR ON THE FILM AND WAS A FRIEND OF "BUGSY" SIEGEL, MICKEY COHEN, JOE DIMAGGIO AND FRANK SINATRA

with a number of expensive gifts valued at over $6,000, including a Persian lamb coat, a charm bracelet, a diamond and ruby mesh ring, a wristwatch and a platinum diamond cross. However, when the affair ended shortly before Christmas, 1945, Raft, according to Miss Doss, "by [unspecified] trick and device" managed to reclaim possession of the gifts he had given her.

Several days later, Miss Doss retained Los Angeles attorney Edward Raiden to recover the alleged "love gifts." Raiden claimed that he first made

WITH ACTRESSES LUCILLE CASEY (CENTER) AND LYNN BARI ON THE SET OF *NOCTURNE* PHOTO COURTESY OF LUELLEN SMILEY

a telephone call to Raft, whereupon the actor allegedly threatened Miss Doss, her mother and Raiden himself. The following day Raiden said he was paid a visit by Mack Gray and a Raft crony named Ben Platt, who told the attorney that Miss Doss had settled her claim against Raft, and who then, according to Raiden, threatened him to "convince" Raiden to drop the suit. Raiden later heard from Miss Doss that Raft wanted her to leave the state and would only return the gifts one piece at a time, providing that he felt "she was acting white towards him." She pressed forward with her claim and further wanted to bring suit against both Raft and Mack Gray for slander and to restrain them from harming her screen career and forcing her to leave the state.

On the night of December 21, Raiden was summoned by Miss Doss to her apartment at 1782 Orchid Avenue after she received a call from Raft telling her that he was on his way over. Raiden arrived at about 8:30, and when George came a short time later, Miss Doss disappeared into the bathroom. Things quickly turned ugly.

According to Raiden, he was standing with his back to the door when it was suddenly opened by Mack Gray's brother, Joe, who pinned Raiden's arms in back of him while Raft proceeded to beat him with his fists and then kick him in the groin and stomach with his knee. Raft then threatened Raiden with further physical violence when he left the apartment.

The following day, Miss Doss and her mother went to the office of Raft's lawyer and signed a letter discharging Raiden as her attorney. Later, Raft and Mack Gray accompanied her to a train that was leaving the state. Miss Doss stated simply that she was going to visit an aunt.

In an attempt to explain his client's actions, Raiden said, "She's probably afraid of him [Raft]. Raft told me he would never let her get a job in the studio and that he'd make her leave the state if she didn't drop the suit."

But Raiden was not so easily intimidated. He immediately filed suit, demanding $50,000 compensatory damages and $250,000 exemplary and punitive damages.

Surprisingly, Betty Doss came to Raft's defense, stating, "George is one of the finest men I ever met. I have no complaint against him and no feud." As to the alleged assault against Raiden and the reclaiming of gifts by Raft, Miss Doss said, "I never witnessed any fight. And furthermore I never received any presents from him [Raft] except this charm bracelet that I am still wearing."

Mack Gray was quoted as saying, "The whole thing is ridiculous. The matter has been settled a long time ago."

In an article printed in the December 16 issue of the *Los Angeles Examiner*, Raft's friend Ben Platt likewise called the whole affair "ridiculous," claiming that he had never been present at any time Raft or Mack Gray had encountered Edward Raiden. He also offered several observations of George based on their 20-year friendship. "I'm just gonna say George is the swellest guy in the world and he never belted nobody ever. He's got a heart as big as an apple — as big as the whole world. He'd give you a handout if you needed it, but George don't go around beltin' guys. At least I never seen him do it. He even thanks movie fans who ask him for his autograph." Concerning the Betty Doss matter, Platt said, "As for Betty Doss, this guy Raiden don't know none of the answers. That dame is just a simple, sweet kid trying to get along, and Georgie still wants to see her make the grade. Why his agent

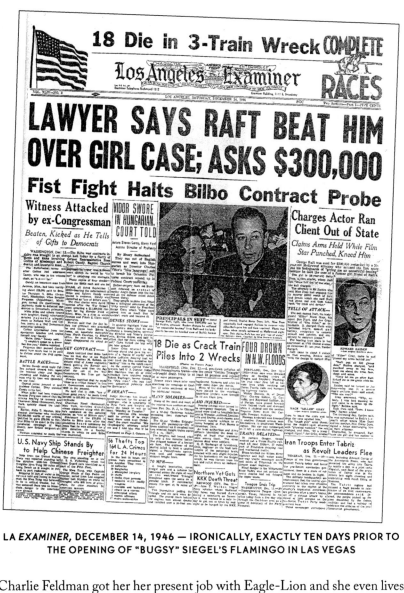

LA *EXAMINER*, DECEMBER 14, 1946 — IRONICALLY, EXACTLY TEN DAYS PRIOR TO THE OPENING OF "BUGSY" SIEGEL'S FLAMINGO IN LAS VEGAS

Charlie Feldman got her her present job with Eagle-Lion and she even lives with her own mother. We — I mean — Georgie wouldn't drive no skirt out of any town."

George later claimed that he had never even met Raiden, though the lawyer produced a $400 check given to him in payment by Raft's attorney, Loyd Wright, for services rendered Miss Doss.

The suit was eventually settled out of court with George paying Raiden a substantial amount, though apparently far less than the $300,000 the lawyer demanded.

With all this bad publicity surrounding him, Raft must have been somewhat gratified by the article printed in the May 16, 1947 issue of the *Washington Times-Herald* headlined: MISUNDERSTOOD GEORGE IS SWEET AND GENTLE AT HEART.

The story painted George Raft as a kind-hearted man who had risen from the slums of Hell's Kitchen and remained loyal to his old pals. It further stated that Raft's tough guy reputation was merely the result of the types of characters he portrayed on movie screens, and that the real George Raft was extremely fond of children and baseball. Of course, the author of the article had spoken with George's closest friend Mack Gray, who likewise presented a favorable image of his friend. He mentioned how his nickname "Killer" had originated with Carole Lombard and further remarked: "I'm no killer. I've never even had a traffic ticket. They say I'm Raft's bodyguard. Look at George. Does he look like a guy who needs a bodyguard?" Gray spoke about the regrettable Leo Durocher incident and said of Raft accuser Martin Shurin, "A war worker in 1943 who was sore because he lost money gambling with Raft," adding, "He is behind bars now as a draft dodger, too. The only sport Raft lays lettuce on is horse racing and he belongs to a bridge, not a poker club." As to George's other positive traits, Gray commented, "In a town where more corn goes into liquor than fritters, Raft is a teetotaler. The only thing stewed at his night club table are the tomatoes, his favorite dish." Finally, Gray defended those damning accusations regarding Raft's shady associations: "George danced in New York for years and met a lot of guys who ended up on the other side of the fence. But just because they did doesn't mean they're not his friends now."

Not all of Raft's friends were on the wrong side of the law. Shortly after their arrival in Hollywood to appear in movies for producer Hal Wallis, nightclub comics Dean Martin and Jerry Lewis were invited to George's Coldwater Canyon home, where they became fast friends with the actor. Martin in particular was a huge Raft fan and considered him a "superstar." His wife Jeanne would later say, "Dean adored George."

Around this time another actor new to Hollywood made a surprising discovery about George Raft. As Kirk Douglas recounted in his 1988 autobiography, *The Ragman's Son*, he was at a party and wandered into the kitchen to find the movie tough guy at the sink … washing dishes. When a curious Douglas inquired about this, he was simply told that George enjoyed washing dishes.

On the professional front, George's career continued to slide. In United Artists' *Christmas Eve* (1947), he played Mario Torio, another initially unscrupulous character on the lam from the authorities who becomes a prosperous café owner and tangles with a Nazi war criminal before returning home to assist his brothers (played by Randolph Scott and George Brent) in thwarting the schemes of Phillip Hastings (Reginald Denny)

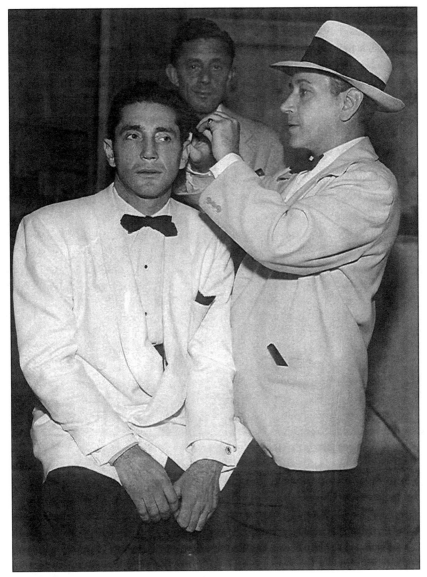

RAFT PREPPING UP HIS FRIEND AND LONG-TIME STAND-IN JOE GRAY TO DOUBLE FOR HIM IN A STUNT FIGHT FOR *CHRISTMAS EVE* (1947), WITH JOE'S BROTHER MACK IN THE BACKGROUND PHOTO COURTESY OF THE MACK GRAY ESTATE

against their adopted mother Matilda Reid (Ann Harding). In the process, Mario is vindicated when Phillip is revealed as the true crook for whom Mario took the rap.

Though certainly well-cast, the convoluted but dreary, multi-story film was ignored by the critics and movie audiences. About its only note of interest was that its reissue title, *Sinner's Holiday*, also happened to be the name of James Cagney's debut film.

For his next feature, George decided to go into production for himself, though his project hardly varied from form — including his choice of releasing company: United Artists, and director: Edwin L. Marin. Initially, his female co-star in *Intrigue* (1947) was to be Jane Greer, but George vetoed

RACE STREET (1948) WITH WILLIAM BENDIX AND EDNA RYAN

her in favor of June Havoc. The film itself was a quite ordinary crime story set in post-war China with Raft's Brad Dunham, an ex-Army pilot dismissed from service on a smuggling frame, infiltrating a gang of black marketeers who murder his reporter friend Mark Andrews (Tom Tully), but through him discovering that it was the Russian Tamara Baranoff (Havoc) who was responsible for his frame. Tamara is killed at the climax and an exonerated Brad is free to romance young Linda Arnold (Helena Carter).

To help hype the film, George's surname was highlighted as a synonym for action in the ad copy for *Intrigue*: "A Raft of lightning action. A Raft of racy romance. A Raft of heart-stopping thrills!"

Needless to say, this absurd wordplay did little to attract a substantial audience. George Raft's post-war film career had slipped another notch.

He went more or less back to form in *Race Street*, his only 1948 release, co-starring with William Bendix, Marilyn Maxwell and Harry Morgan. While still a budget-conscious effort, this RKO crime drama was more effective than most of Raft's films of the period. In it, he played Dan Gannin, a successful San Francisco bookie who takes matters into his own hands when his pal Hal Towers (Morgan) is brutally murdered by an extortion syndicate planning to muscle in on Gannin's racket. Dan's search to locate the killers takes him through a *noirish* labyrinth of treachery and deception, including his betrayal by fiancée Robbie Lawrence (Maxwell), who is actually wed

RAFT, MACK GRAY AND WILLIAM BENDIX TAKE CENTER STAGE IN *RACE STREET*, ONE OF RAFT'S BETTER LATE 40s FILMS

to syndicate chief Phil Dickson (Frank Faylen). The film ends with Dan taking a fatal bullet intended for boyhood friend-turned-cop Barney Runson (Bendix). A heroic demise that must have overcome Raft's desire not to die on camera.

Unfortunately, critics did not think much of *Race Street*. The *New York Post* wrote: "It's stodgy and trite, and hero-worshipful without a hero," while *Time* magazine noted: "There is nothing in this show that cannot be found in most tough-mug movies — and nothing that isn't passably watched through half-closed eyes."

Despite these negative reviews, Raft's co-star Harry Morgan, some years away from memorable supporting roles in television's *Dragnet* and *M*A*S*H*, held only positive memories of working with George. "I did two pictures with George and in both of them he was a complete gentleman — no ego and very kind, at times giving me lines that really belonged to him. I wound up liking him enormously and would have done ten more pictures with him had that been possible. He was a complete pro."

While George was struggling to keep his career afloat with formulaic crime pictures at such lower-echelon studios as RKO and United Artists, Humphrey Bogart was enjoying the creative and financial prestige of the fifteen-year, $3-million deal he had signed with Warners in 1946. In 1948 he had appeared in two classic movies that far outshone Raft's meager and undistinguished efforts. Both were helmed by John Huston, the director with whom Raft had refused to work. *The Treasure of the Sierra Madre* was a towering success that garnered three Academy Awards, including two for Huston. And in *Key Largo*, Bogart got the satisfaction of top-billing over Edward G. Robinson and had the added pleasure of gunning down his co-star in a kind of retribution for all those years Bogie was on the receiving end of a Robinson bullet.

Although 1948 had proved a professionally slow year for George, he was kept busy in 1949 by appearing in five films, though again the standards of each were barely mediocre. He made *Johnny Allegro* for Harry Cohn's Columbia Pictures, a studio that had risen above its Poverty Row origins thanks mainly to the films of Frank Capra. But, as with most of the Hollywood studios at the time, Columbia's output consisted of too few "A" pictures and too much "B" and "C" product.

Despite Raft's presence and a storyline that borrowed heavily from *The Most Dangerous Game*, *Johnny Allegro* emerged as one of the studio's lesser offerings. The rather far-fetched plot had George as the title character, an ex-gangster now running a florist shop who is hired by the Treasury Department to halt the efforts of villain Morgan Vallin (George Macready), who is planning to overthrow the United States government by flooding the American economy with counterfeit money. Posing as a wanted criminal, Johnny works his way into Vallin's confidence on a Caribbean island. However, once Johnny is exposed, he truly becomes a man on the run as Vallin chases him through the jungle with an arsenal of deadly silver-tipped arrows. The climax features a two-fisted battle between hero and villain, with Vallin plummeting to his death. Johnny ends up in the arms of Glenda Chapman (Nina Foch).

In its review of the film, *Variety* merely said that Raft performed with "his usual deadpan style that appeals to his fans."

George then reappeared at RKO for *A Dangerous Profession* (1949), co-starring for the second time with his friend Pat O'Brien, with Ella Raines providing the romantic interest. The movie was another familiar budget-conscious crime drama where Raft and O'Brien play bail-bondsmen involved in embezzlement and murder. Also on hand is a pre-*Gilligan's Island* Jim Backus as a police detective, Nick Ferrone. The director of the film was former Paramount cameraman Ted Tetzlaff, with whom Raft had refused to work on *The*

Princess Comes Across because of his suspected favored photographic treatment of Carole Lombard.

While critics were unanimous in praising Humphrey Bogart's latest work, the *New York Times* simply said that Raft was "laconic and familiarly tough" in his latest role.

During the filming of *A Dangerous Profession*, George recalled sitting on the set with O'Brien and Miss Raines and listening with envy and a little bitterness as both bragged about the scholastic accomplishments of their children, some of whom were celebrating a birthday that same day. Suddenly, George snapped, "Oh, yeah, I'm celebrating, too. My kid gets out of San Quentin today."

To ease the tension, O'Brien quipped, "Great, George! Now he can enroll at Joliet without any entrance exams."

Raft returned to *noir* for *Red Light* (1949), where he co-starred opposite Virginia Mayo, Harry Morgan and a menacing heavy still relatively new to the film scene, Raymond Burr. In a movie that can almost be taken as a follow-up to *They Drive by Night*, Raft played John Torno, the head of a prosperous trucking company who sets out to avenge the murder of his priest brother, Jess (Arthur Franz), at the hands of a vindictive former employee, Nick Cherney (Burr). While single-minded in his purpose, Torno is spared committing the ultimate revenge by a posthumous message from Jess, which is found written in the margin of a bible: "Johnny — Thou Shalt Not Kill." However, the brutal Nick still pays for his crimes — perhaps by divine intervention — when he is electrocuted while trying to escape.

The film demanded more of Raft than had been displayed in most of his previous pictures, including a myriad of emotions ranging from extreme sorrow over the death of his brother to explosive anger as he tracks the killer. And, as directed by an old Raft hand, Roy Del Ruth, George performed his duties mostly admirably. Of course, it helped that he was surrounded by a cast of capable co-players, including film bad guy Barton MacLane in a rare sympathetic role as a cop and Arthur Shields as an understanding priest. George had particular praise for the Canadian-born Raymond Burr, whom he felt "had a lot of talent."

It was during the filming of *Red Light* that George remembered "Bugsy" Siegel's hair-combing compulsion and suggested to director Del Ruth that it might make a good mannerism for his character, much as his coin-spinning in *Scarface*. Del Ruth declined, explaining, "It looks exaggerated. You couldn't convince an audience that a guy would really do this."

A film intended for George was Don Siegel's *The Big Steal* (1949). However, when the cameras rolled, it was younger and rougher RKO star Robert Mitchum who stepped into the role of Lieutenant Duke Halliday. The picture's exploitive tagline indicated that the studio was as eager to promote Mitchum as the movie itself: "Mitchum is HOT! — HOT ... off location

in the heart of Mexico ... HOT ... after a girl with a million-dollar figure!...
HOT ... at the nation's boxoffices ... HOT ... in his newest picture!"

Perhaps the nadir of Raft's 1949 cinematic output was his appearance in
United Artists *Outpost in Morocco*, in which he was improbably cast as French
Foreign Legion officer Captain Paul Gerard, opposite Marie Windsor as the
doomed Cara. Even with the talented Akim Tamiroff on hand as Paul's sub-
ordinate officer Lieutenant Glysco, the film failed in its absurd title casting
and lukewarm action scenes, and was quickly and mercifully forgotten. Bosley
Crowther of the *New York Times*, one of George Raft's most consistent critics,
was particularly cutting in his review of Raft's performance, citing that he
" ... plays his wild adventures as though he had all day and speaks his lines
with the effort of a five-year-old reading a book."

Perhaps George was hoping to expand his range (*a la* Humphrey Bogart
in *The Treasure of the Sierra Madre*) by taking on such an unconventional
assignment, but his decision (and the film itself) proved laughable, uninspired and ill-conceived.

George's final film of the year was a cameo as himself in *Nous Irons a
Paris* (a.k.a. *We Will All Go to Paris*), which he made while on vacation in
France. Little seen in the United States, the slight plot deals with three
young people who operate a radio station called Radio X, whose purpose
is to poke fun at advertising. Raft's bit finds him as one of the people the
small group meets in their travels to elude the police. Although the movie
proved quite popular in the European market, it did nothing to enhance
Raft's waning career.

This was made evident by the fact that George did not make a single film
in 1950. However, it appeared that Raft was keeping himself busy with other
ventures. In 1949, it was reported in the *Los Angeles Herald and Express* that
George Raft, together with financier Todd Horn and others, had purchased
the Desert Retreat Hotel in Palm Springs, California, with the intention of
upgrading the establishment. Todd Horn was listed as the General Manager
with George acting as a silent partner. That same year, federal authorities in
Los Angeles noted that Raft was reported to have a large amount of control
over the gambling activities in the Los Angeles area. It was later reported that
his official function in that regard was as a "steerer" of motion picture celebrities to gambling games.

The report also said that Raft frequently visited known underworld figures in such centers as New York, Miami, Chicago and Kansas City. His
name came up in a Chicago Crime Commission report that said he had
participated in large gambling card games which were held at the Sheridan
Hotel. Among the other players was mobster Frank Costello, who at some
point asked Raft for advice prior to appearing before the televised Kefauver
Rackets Committee hearings. Raft's only advice was for Costello not to get
into word duels with the experts.

George's ties with underworld figures made newspaper headlines when the *Herald and Express* reported that a telephone tap on mobster Mickey Cohen by the Los Angeles Police Department revealed that Cohen and a couple of other "fellows" had spent a night "out at George Raft's ..." where they had a "grand dinner" and enjoyed themselves very much. Cohen's wife later said that "... they always have a wonderful time when they go out to visit George and think nothing of staying out all night."

The 1950s would be George Raft's last years of screen prominence. As the decade would draw to a close, it would mark the virtual end of Raft's featured movie career ... which unfortunately would once more coincide with a public image further marred through scandal and association.

RAFT, SPORTING AN UNCHARACTERISTIC MUSTACHE, EN ROUTE TO NEW YORK AFTER FILMING *OUTPOST IN MOROCCO* (1949), ABOARD THE HOLLAND-AMERICAN LINER NIEUW AMSTERDAM

**RAFT AND FORMER NEW YORK CITY DETECTIVE-TURNED-HOLLYWOOD-
PRIVATE EYE BARNEY RUDITSKY**

**RAFT WITH LEGENDARY GAMBLER SWIFTY MORGAN, WHO WAS THE MODEL FOR
DAMON RUNYON'S "LEMON DROP KID"**

"THIS IS NOT A GOOD PLACE TO BE OLD. YOU GO OUT AND PEOPLE NUDGE EACH OTHER AND SAY: 'THAT'S GEORGE RAFT. HE IS FINISHED.'"

GEORGE RAFT

With film offers rapidly drying up, yet faced with ongoing expenses to maintain the high lifestyle associated with his image, George looked to the new medium of television as a way to earn much-needed cash. He began appearing as a guest on some of the most popular video programs of the day, such as *The Colgate Comedy Hour* with Abbott and Costello, likewise at a low cinematic ebb as the 1950s began.

On one of the live episodes, George appeared to display some of his pugnaciousness when Lou Costello began roughhousing with him and it looked as if Raft was beginning to take the matter seriously, turning on the fat little comedian and manhandling him with a bit more intention than what Costello was probably expecting.

George also continued his association with radio, starring in the CBS series *The Adventures of Rocky Jordan*, where he performed in 58 episodes, running from June 27, 1951 to June 26, 1953. Raft was not the first actor to play the role; he was preceded by Jack Moyles, as the hard-boiled owner of the Café Tambourine, who in each episode found himself embroiled in a mystery. Though forgotten today, it was quite highly regarded in its time. Raft's premiere episode was titled "The Man from Damascas."

George's career also, rather unflatteringly, made the press on March 14, 1951, when Paul V. Coates, a columnist for the *Los Angeles Mirror*, wrote that the early films in which Raft appeared as an actor caused the public to become a "nation of hoodlum coddlers. It is customary now to think of these bums as romantic personalities. Hollywood's slightly dim-witted café society is probably the worst offender in this respect. Some years ago Benny Siegel came out here and was immediately accepted as a social leader."

Another unpleasant experience occurred that year at Hollywood agent Swifty Lazar's New Year's Eve party, held at Romanoff's restaurant. Both George and Humphrey Bogart were present when a fistfight broke out between Oscar Levant and producer Walter Wanger, the husband of Raft's old co-star Joan Bennett. Raft attempted to break up the scuffle and was

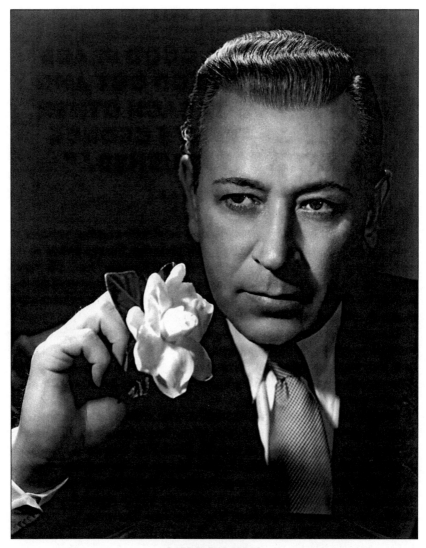

RAFT IN THE 1950S

punched by Levant for his trouble. George retreated to a corner where it was said he had tears in his eyes, either from the painful sock or by the humiliation of being on the receiving end of a blow. In any case, with this incident the tough guy image had started to fade.

The following year George would receive an even more crushing professional blow when he saw his old rival Bogart climb up to the podium of the Pantages Theater to accept the Best Actor Oscar for his outstanding portrayal of gin-guzzling riverboat pilot Charlie Allnut in the John Huston-directed *The African Queen.*

Raft's next film took him to Italy: *Lucky Nick Cain* (1951), which he made for Twentieth Century-Fox. In the picture, which co-starred the lovely Coleen Gray, Raft played the title character, an American gambler vacationing in Italy, who is slipped a Mickey Finn and framed for the murder of a U.S. treasury agent. In his efforts to clear himself, Nick teams up with an American tourist, Kay Wonderly (Gray), and young Toni (Enzo Stafolo, who had appeared in the classic *The Bicycle Thief*, 1946).

While the film was praised more for its beautiful location shooting along the Italian Riviera than its pedestrian storyline, critics were generally kind toward Raft's performance. *The New York Times* said George Raft is "… working in a tailor-made role. He is laconic, a smooth tango dancer, tough on dastards and easy on the eyes of several ladies."

Coleen Gray remembered working with Raft: "He was very shy. I think it was because he knew I had gone to college and he hadn't had much education. I don't think he even finished high school. But he took me out to dinner in Italy and we got along fine. He even taught me how to dance the tango, and that was special. Later he gave me the trench coat that he wore in the picture. I still have it."

Prior to leaving for Italy to shoot *Lucky Nick Cain*, George was visited in his New York hotel room by an associate of "Lucky" Luciano and asked to personally deliver a small suitcase to the crime boss, now living in exile in Naples. Raft agreed, though the secret contents of the suitcase concerned him. His work schedule, however, precluded his leaving the San Remo location and he asked two elderly schoolteachers whom he had met through mutual friends, and who were on their way to Naples, to deliver the suitcase for him. A couple of weeks later, George met up with the two women, who were beaming and who had obviously been charmed by Luciano, of whose true identity they remained ignorant. They spoke of the faithful "servants" (bodyguards) who followed him around everywhere. When George asked what had been in the suitcase, thinking it cash or perhaps contraband, one of the women replied, "Little coffee candles."

George recalled that when he told Luciano about the naiveté of the two old ladies a couple of years later, the gangster enjoyed his first good laugh in eight years of exile.

After completing *Lucky Nick Cain*, George returned to the States, where Republic Pictures offered him a role in *Hoodlum Empire* (1952). Even though George was offered $150,000 to play the part of gang boss Nick Mansani, he turned it down, feeling that real-life mobster Frank Costello, on whom the character was based, would not like the film. He was replaced by Luther Adler in a movie that few critics admired.

Again seeking an alternative to his slowing film work, George decided to move into series television. Fortunately, he found a role suited to his "good guy" preferences. On *I Am the Law*, he played the part of Lieutenant George

Kirby of the New York Police Department. Although early '50s television offered plenty of police dramas, such as Jack Webb's *Dragnet*, *I Am the Law* was the first program to be based on the NYPD. The series was financed by George's old chum Lou Costello, but unfortunately never caught on with viewers. Critics, though, were more kind. *Variety* said: "Raft's a natural in his role of the cop, a role he's done often enough. He commands attention throughout, without overplaying."

Apparently, the FBI was less pleased with the series. The Los Angeles Office noted in a memorandum that the shows "did not always picture law enforcement in a favorable light." It further went on to report: "Raft continued to play his 'tough type' roles and used many slang expressions which have long since become obsolete in law enforcement. The general impression of the programs gathered from viewing them was not favorable to law enforcement."

Only twenty-six episodes were filmed before the program was cancelled. George was reportedly offered $90,000 for doing the series, but claimed he received very little after expenses were deducted from his salary. When the show was later syndicated in the U.S. and in England under the title *Briefcase*, it again failed to catch on. George himself didn't think much of the series, which was probably why he rejected an offer of $125,000 from his agents Jules Levy and Charles Feldman to buy three of the episodes and tie them into a feature. Raft would never again venture into series television, though throughout the 1950s he would turn up as a guest star on such popular programs as *What's My Line?*, *I've Got a Secret* (as the "mystery guest"), *The Buick-Milton Berle Show*, *Texaco Star Theatre* with Jimmy Durante, *The Jack Benny Program*, *The Tonight Show* with Jack Parr, *The Gisele MacKenzie Show*, *The Ed Sullivan Show* and *The Arthur Murray Dance Party*.

By 1952, Raft's financial position was in such shaky shape that he reluctantly parted with his longtime friend and assistant Mack Gray. While Gray offered to stay on for room and board, both knew that it was impractical and that it was time to move on. Gray would go on to assume similar duties with Raft admirer Dean Martin, before his death in January 1981.

What George could not cut back on, though, were his romantic affairs. Although he had not entered into anything approaching a serious relationship since the Betty Doss scandal, he dated many beautiful women, among them starlet Barbara Payton, whom he'd met at Slapsie Maxie's nightclub in 1949. As he was with all his girlfriends, he was generous with his gifts and in his affections, and while their affair was to be short-lived, Raft left a favorable impression on Miss Payton.

To keep active, George accepted a six-week European personal appearance tour, booked by then-agent Lew Grade, which he concluded at the Prince of Wales Theatre in London. Here he met Bernard Luber, an executive with Lippert Pictures. With no Hollywood offers awaiting him, Raft signed with the company to appear in three pictures, the first of which was the American-lensed *Loan Shark* (1952), directed by Seymour Friedman. With George Raft attached to the project, the movie was afforded a higher budget than most of Lippert's output: $250,000, with George receiving a salary of $25,000. While a modest sum given Raft's past earnings, he was also offered 25% of the profits.

Gail Russell, whose own career was on the decline due to personal problems, was originally announced as Raft's co-star. However, she was replaced on short notice by Dorothy Hart. George was also joined in the cast by two solid veteran "B" performers: Paul Stewart (memorable as the villain in *The Window*, 1949) and John Hoyt. The small role of Thompson, the loan shark "lure," was played by Russell Johnson, later the Professor of *Gilligan's Island*.

Raft plays Joe Gargen, an ex-con looking for work, who is hired by a tire manufacturing company to investigate the loan-sharking activities that are taking a toll (including threats, beatings — and murder) on the plant's employees. To achieve his purpose, Joe pretends to join up with the racketeers, alienating his sister Martha (Helen Westcott) and girlfriend Ann Nelson (Hart), but at the end exposes the gang and guns down its leader Walter Karr (Larry Dobkin).

While the film itself received moderate reviews, Raft again was not spared criticism. *The New York Herald Tribune* wrote, "Someday a movie racket buster may be found who can modulate his voice differently during a love scene and while facing the muzzle of the big boss's gat. This, apparently, is not one of Mr. Raft's talents."

As for George's percentage of the film's box office earnings — the picture never showed a profit, which may well have been the result of Hollywood accounting.

Raft traveled to England for his next Lippert venture.[25] Nineteen-fifty-three's *I'll Get You* (a.k.a. *Escape Route*), was again directed by Seymour Friedman, and co-starred Sally Gray and Clifford Evans. For this picture, George received $31,655.59. While ads for the film promised: "It's loaded with searing, screaming suspense!," *I'll Get You* proved a rather dull offering with a walk-through performance from Raft as FBI agent Steve Rossi.

Even worse was George's final film under his Lippert contract. Also released in 1953, *The Man from Cairo*, directed by Ray H. Enright and filmed in Italy and North Africa, found Raft as Mike Canelli, an American who gets involved in a search for a hundred-million-dollar gold shipment hidden in the North African desert during World War II. In its review of the film, *Variety* wrote, "*The Man from Cairo* takes all the prizes for inconsequential 'B' productions." Of its star, *Variety* offered a more generous assessment: "Raft does his best to make something of the confusion."

Yet Raft's indifference is evident in another tired, uninspired performance. His opening scene of his "pretending" to read a newspaper set the tone for his unconvincing work throughout the film.[26]

However, it is certain that upon his return to California George read the September 30, 1953 edition of the *Los Angeles Times* with much more intent. Its headline announced:

RAFT FREES CAPONE

According to the article, Raft was in John Capone's Beverly Hills hotel room on September 29 when police burst in to arrest the younger brother of "Scarface" Al and an associate named Joe Laino on suspicion of robbery. The pair claimed they were preparing to leave for Las Vegas on their way to Chicago, with Capone explaining that he was in Los Angeles to collect money that was owed him. Capone had in his possession $5,362 in cash. Raft simply told the police that he was an old friend of Capone's and had gone to the hotel, where they had a couple of drinks. Following the arrest, Raft went to Police Chief C.H. Anderson to request the release of the pair and guaranteeing they would "take the first plane out of here."

The story George offered differed significantly. He claimed that he had gone to the Beverly Hills Hotel as a favor to his old pal Jimmy Durante to pick up a friend of his named Lou Cohn. When he went upstairs, he found Cohn with John Capone, who, though a gambler, had no criminal background that he knew of and was, in fact, so embarrassed by his notorious surname that he had taken to calling himself John Martin. However, as soon as Raft entered the room, he said two Beverly Hills cops broke inside and hustled Capone to the police station. Raft said he then put in a call to his lawyer to have Capone released.

The true facts notwithstanding, George resented the sensational head-lines that implied that it was Al Capone, not brother John, whom Raft had helped to free. Such publicity may have made the public momentarily forget that Al Capone had died in 1947.

The negative press may have contributed to George's rejecting his next film offer. He had been offered the role of gangster Marty Brill in Colum-bia Pictures' *The Miami Story* (1954), but before the cameras were set to role, Raft vacated the part and was once again replaced by Luther Adler. Another reason for his refusal may have been that he'd heard that some of his under-world pals were not enthusiastic about him taking on the project. George knew better than to disappoint his "friends."

Yet it was those same friends who had caused some earlier problems for George prior to his leaving to Europe for his two Lippert pictures. A couple of girls had been sent to George by someone in the mob to see if they could borrow his Coldwater Canyon estate while he was away. They promised to maintain the upkeep, water the lawn, etc., and kind-hearted George agreed. When George returned, however, he found that all twelve rooms of his home had been burglarized. The only thing ever recovered — from a pawnshop —

was a gold watch with an engraved message on back, which was given to him by Norma Shearer.

The underworld connection continued when George visited San Juan, Puerto Rico that year, where he gave a statement to a San Juan newspaper that he and some "associates" were planning to rent or construct in Puerto Rico a gambling casino similar in design to the large casinos in Europe.

ANNE FRANCIS, RAFT AND ROBERT TAYLOR IN *ROGUE COP* (1954)

Reportedly, their attempt to obtain a license was unsuccessful.

A professional high point for Raft during these bleak days came on the evening of March 24, 1954 when George was the "honoree" at a Silver Anniversary Testimonial Dinner presented by the Friar's Club. The lineup of stars and bigwigs on hand to "roast" George was impressive: Jack L. Warner, Darryl Zanuck, Jesse L. Lasky, Joseph Schenck, Dore Schary, Maxie Rosenbloom, George Burns, Ronald Reagan, Dean Martin and Jerry Lewis, and famed celebrity attorney Jerry Geisler. According to an article in the *Los Angeles Herald Express*, Raft "wept openly" during the dinner. But there was also much levity. George Burns quipped, "Raft and Gary Cooper once played a scene in front of a cigar store, and it looked like the wooden Indian was overacting."

When it came time for "Slapsie" Maxie Rosenbloom to speak, he looked at the heavy-hitters seated around the dais and said in his inimitable style,

RAFT AS CRIME KINGPIN DAN BEAUMONTE IN *ROGUE COP* (1954), ARGUABLY HIS BEST FILM ROLE OF THE 1950s

"Gents, when I met dis bum Raft, I din't have two bits to my name. Now I owe twenty-five thousand dollars. Tanks, Georgie."

George appreciated and enjoyed the good-natured ribbing. But when he stepped up to the lectern, he became emotional and spoke about how badly his career was doing. George never looked for or expected pity; he was just speaking what he felt.

In any event, the next day MGM head Dore Schary called George over to the studio and offered him the strong supporting role of gangster Dan Beaumonte in *Rogue Cop* (1954). Based on the hard-hitting novel by crime specialist William P. McGivern (who also penned *The Big Heat*), and directed by Roy

Rowland, the movie top-lined Robert Taylor as crooked cop Christopher Kelvaney, accepting "graft" from the city's underworld ruled by Beaumonte and Ackerman (Robert F. Simon), but who has a change of heart after his honest patrolman brother Eddie (Steve Forrest) is slain by the gangsters. In the *noirish* shootout that concludes the film, both Beaumonte and Ackerman are killed, and Kelvaney is prepared to make amends for his past mistakes.

RAFT AS DAN BEAUMONTE TAKES AIM IN THE VIOLENT CONCLUSION OF
***ROGUE COP* (1954)**

Rogue Cop was arguably Raft's best film of the fifties. Critics unanimously praised his performance. In short, George Raft was back in his element. His Dan Beaumonte performs as a totally ruthless specimen without any of the redeeming traits Raft once insisted his villains must possess. It was a role that George most likely would have turned down as a "dirty heavy" during his "starring" days. Now, though, it was a part imbued with comeback potential.

Of course, it should not be overlooked that Raft was once again supported by a strong cast and an able director. He always fared well when working with superior talent, which had been lacking in most of his previous movies.

The late Janet Leigh played the role of Karen Stephanson, Eddie Kelvanney's girlfriend, in the movie and had fond recollections of working with

Raft. "I had a wonderful time making *Rogue Cop*. I especially enjoyed working with Robert Taylor and George Raft. He [Raft] was a legend when I worked with him. I remember that he was so unlike the awful character he was playing. He was very personable and always very professional."

George's next film, *Black Widow* (1954), was made for Darryl Zanuck's Twentieth Century-Fox and likewise appeared to have good potential. Apparently, Zanuck, like Dore Schary, offered his friend George a part in the movie as a goodwill gesture following the Friar's Club dinner. In the film, Raft was allowed a complete role reversal from *Rogue Cop*. His Lieutenant Detective Bruce is investigating the apparent suicide of young Nancy "Nanny" Ordway among a glittering array of suspects, including Broadway producer Peter Denver (Van Heflin), playwright Brian Mullen (Reginald Gardiner), his actress wife Carlotta "Lottie" Marin (Ginger Rogers) and Nanny's law student boyfriend John Amberly (Skip Homeier). The role of Peter Denver's wife, Iris, was played by the beautiful Gene Tierney. While a glossy, expensive (filmed in color and CinemaScope) and well-cast production, *Black Widow* proved a tedious mystery, not helped by George's rather bored playing, his eventual exposing of the murderer generating no tension or excitement.

While George's career hit a temporary high with *Rogue Cop* (Steven H. Scheuer, in his book *Movies on TV and Videocassette*, raved: "Raft is a standout as a syndicate czar who is more than a bit sadistic"), it once again appeared on a downward spiral with the release of *Black Widow* (of which Leonard Maltin's annual *Movie Guide* judged, "… with remarkably poor performances by Rogers as a bitchy star and Raft as a dogged detective").

His sole 1955 release, *A Bullet for Joey* (a.k.a. *Canada's Great Manhunt* and *The Kill*), offered the promising re-teaming of Raft and his old Warner Brothers rival, Edward G. Robinson, but the final product seemed to just miss the mark. George was back as a gangster, an exiled racketeer named Joe Victor who is illegally sent to Montreal, Canada from Spain to aid a Communist plot to kidnap atomic physicist Carl Macklin (George Dolenz, father of future *Monkees* drummer, Mickey). Robinson was Inspector Raoul Leduc, who attempts to foil the nefarious plan.

The two aging leads played their parts effectively, but were ultimately defeated by the film's slow pacing and a so-so storyline. The finish finds Joe Victor teaming with Leduc to thwart the Communists, shooting down ringleader Eric Hartman (Peter Van Eyck) before somewhat improbably walking into a bullet that brings about his own demise. Leduc speaks his epitaph: "He died a hero and never knew it."

The film received the expected lukewarm reviews. *The New York Times* wrote: "We need only scan the details of Mr. Raft's laying out the job and Mr. Robinson's patient checking of him every step of the way. These are the things Mr. Raft and Mr. Robinson can act with their eyes shut — and some-times do."

Perhaps the only satisfaction George received from doing the film was that it mended the fourteen-year rift between him and Robinson, and the two became good friends. In fact, Robinson wrote in his autobiography that during a later hospital stay one of the first bouquet of flowers that he had received

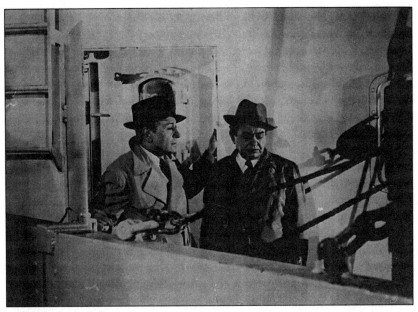

WHILE ONCE MORE PLAYING RIVALS ONSCREEN, RAFT AND EDWARD G. ROBINSON ENDED THEIR FOURTEEN-YEAR FEUD WHILE MAKING *A BULLET FOR JOEY* (1955)

had a card attached that read: "Get well soon. Your pal, George Raft."

Audrey Totter played Joyce Geary, Joe Victor's former girlfriend, in the picture, and echoed the sentiments of many of Raft's co-stars: "Mr. Raft was a charming man — a delight to work with."

At some point during the 1950s, George had a brainstorm. He drove out to visit the semi-reclusive Paul Muni to discuss with him the idea of remaking *Scarface*, with both he and Muni recreating their famous roles. But apparently Muni wasn't interested.

George's response to Muni's refusal was, "I guess he was having too much fun making plastic ashtrays."

The January 24, 1955 issue of *Sports Illustrated* printed an article entitled "The Boxing Monopolies Put on the Squeeze." The story told how one Donald Rettman was frozen out of the management of a promising middleweight fighter named George Johnson. Raft figured into the article, and again in connection with his underworld influences.

"One day in November 1953, Rettman ran into his old friend, the Wilmington syndicate man, who listened to his troubles and then produced an idea which Rettman, in the state of mind he had reached, was glad to hear. George Raft, the movie star, will be in Wilmington soon, the gambler said. Raft was interested in boxing and liked to have pieces of fighters and was on close terms with the hoodlums whose prototypes he played on the screen. For instance, Frankie Carbo. Carbo liked Raft so much, in fact, that instead of insisting on the usual 15% minimum as his share of the management contract, he asked Raft for only 10% on fighters Raft owned; sometimes even less. If Rettman could make a deal with Raft, the gambler pointed out, he and Johnson would have Raft's influence working for them on the West Coast and Carbo's protection in the East, a wonderful combination. However, as it turned out before a deal could be consummated with Raft, promoter Herman Taylor in some way managed to inveigle Johnson into signing a contract with Taylor."

Despite the negative light cast on George in the article, it was true that he retained a lifelong interest in the sport of boxing. He was even asked by heavyweight champ Rocky Marciano if the plastic surgeon who had fixed George's ear could repair Marciano's nose after the first Ezzard Charles fight. Raft told him that it would heal by itself, which it did.

Because of the reduction of his film work and movie earnings that were far less substantial than those he had pulled in during his studio years, George accepted a part-time job as an entertainment consultant for the Flamingo Hotel. The hotel had prospered in the years following the murder of "Bugsy" Siegel, but had lately fallen on hard economic times through competition, profit skimming and general mismanagement. It looked as though the Flamingo was headed toward bankruptcy when a man named Al Parvin, who was a successful Beverly Hills businessman, together with other investors, took control of the hotel. It was Parvin who approached George about taking the job. In his capacity, George was able to book into the Flamingo such top-flight talent as Frank Sinatra, Dean Martin and Pearl Bailey, who had had a major musical success on Broadway and was signed to a three-year $15,000-per-week contract for performing eight weeks a year. So delighted were Parvin and his partners with Raft's work that they offered him the opportunity to buy stock in the hotel.

But a golden opportunity suddenly turned sour. To raise the needed capital, $65,000 for two points, George first had to sell his Coldwater Canyon house, furnishings and all, for which he took a loss. On top of that, half of the profits went to his estranged wife Grayce. He also had to borrow $20,000 on his insurance annuities and $10,000 from his agent, Charles K. Feldman. But his problems really began when he filed an application with the Nevada State Gaming Control Board.

Once again his past was made public.

George was driving home after a bad day at Santa Anita and happened to switch on the radio. He heard the news broadcaster say: "George Raft, the movie star who made his reputation playing gangster roles, had his past catch up with him today. The Nevada State Tax Commission denied Raft a gambling-casino stockholder's permit because he was friendly with such underworld figures as Owney 'The Killer' Madden, Joe Adonis, 'Lucky' Luciano and 'Bugsy' Siegel."

George was stunned by the news, but he still went out to a dinner appointment he had at the Beverly Hills home of his close friend, producer Jack Dietz.[27] Dietz tried to reassure George that the problem could be worked out, and then suggested that he sit down and watch some television, adding, "You might see one of your old pictures and that might give you a laugh."

Dietz's ten-year-old son Jackie was very fond of George and always called him "pal," and Raft likewise felt great affection for the boy. Jackie climbed up onto George's lap, and George switched on the TV. What appeared on the screen proved far more embarrassing and humiliating to Raft than watching any of his old movies.

Newscaster George Putnam repeated in detail the story about Raft's being denied a stockholder's permit, again mentioning George's gangland associations as the reason for the refusal. Raft swiftly turned off the set, but the damage had been done. Young Jackie Dietz began crying and said in disgust, "You're nothing but a gangster and I'm not your 'pal' anymore," and ran out of the room. Raft was so upset that he had no appetite for dinner, and so grabbed his hat, said goodbye to Jack, and went home.

Many of Raft's respected and influential friends went to bat for him. George himself appeared before the board in Carson City and answered questions for about an hour. He admitted to knowing "Bugsy" Siegel, adding, "Like everyone else in Hollywood." He also was upfront about the other underworld characters he had known. But as he rather reasonably stated, "I couldn't very well have gone around asking who was the real owner of every speakeasy I worked in. I was a guy trying to make a living; I had to work ... "

Six months later the Committee unanimously reversed their decision and George was awarded a stockholder's permit. Prior to the board voting, Committee chairman Robbins Cahill said that he was satisfied that none of Raft's early connections still existed. But in the interim Raft was subjected to ongoing negative press concerning his gangster pals and underworld affiliations. The scandal magazine *Hush Hush*, for example, carried an article entitled "Why George Raft Was Blackballed in Las Vegas." All his past sins were once again dragged out, including the Betty Doss and Ed Raiden incident. Certainly not the kind of press George needed or was looking for at the time.

Two points in the Flamingo may not have seemed like much, but the hotel/casino prospered under Parvin and his partners' management. By the

SHOT OF RAFT SANS HAIRPIECE IN THE MID-50s

time Parvin and company sold the Flamingo in 1960, Raft's two-percent interest would have been worth about half a million dollars, and George could have once more been financially solvent. Unfortunately, this was not to be the case. Shortly after receiving the Committee's approval, George had to sell his two points because he had a desperate need of cash.

By 1956, George was living in a bachelor apartment on Charlesville Boulevard in Beverly Hills. His landlady was Joan Crawford. That same year he consented to be interviewed by journalist Dean Jennings that resulted in a five-part series of articles that were published the following year in *The Saturday Evening Post* under the title "Out of My Past." George spoke candidly about his life and career, but was reportedly very upset with the printed results, claiming that he had never been given the opportunity to see the galleys, and that he was seriously misquoted. He was further disappointed that the articles focused more on his hoodlum associations than on his show business career and that the text was accompanied by graphic photo images of murdered gangsters, such as Willie Moretti, Dutch Schultz and "Bugsy" Siegel. The series frequently quoted him as living an almost friendless existence, visited infrequently, receiving very few telephone calls, and no longer getting complaints from the postman about the sacks of fan mail he was delivering.

In one of the installments, George freely admitted his compulsion for thievery — even after he became a Hollywood success. He'd estimated that he'd earned about $10,000,000 from his movie work, yet could not quite curb the temptation to "lift" merchandise that he really neither needed nor wanted. He would walk into a store and spend a thousand dollars in cash on clothing and suits and still steal a five-dollar tie. He recounted one incident when he was traveling West on the 20th Century Limited and stole the silverware from his table in the dining car. The next morning, after a light breakfast of orange juice, toast and coffee, he was presented with a bill for forty dollars. When Raft protested, the waiter smiled and explained that the breakfast cost a dollar and a half, the rest was for the silverware he had taken. George claimed it was the first and only time he had ever been caught stealing.

Raft further stated that prior to agreeing to "tell his story," he had received threatening telephone calls from anonymous sources, perhaps afraid that he would reveal too much.

Still, the multi-part publication of Raft's "biography," such as it was, led to interest by major film studios to turn his story into a motion picture. Paramount and Twentieth Century-Fox made offers, and such stars as Tony Curtis, Dean Martin and even Robert Evans were considered for the lead. Raft said his choice was Tony Curtis. However, it was a lesser studio, Allied Artists, headed by a man named Steven Brody, that eventually acquired the rights. George was dissatisfied with the various shooting scripts he saw and soon dissociated himself from the project, though he allowed some production shots to be taken of him and his film alter-ego, Ray Danton.

When the movie was finally released in 1961, *The George Raft Story* proved to be an inaccurate account of his life. In fact, there were more real-life parallels in the earlier fictional *Broadway*. Impressionist and future "Riddler" Frank Gorshin played Moxie, a part loosely modeled on Mack Gray, and Neville Brand recreated his Al Capone role from *The Scarface Mob* (1959) in what is perhaps the one (reasonably) honest scene in the film: Raft's Chicago meeting with Capone following the release of *Scarface*. Brad Dexter played "Benny" ("Bugsy" Siegel), Barbara Nichols was "Texas," and the fictional women in George's life were portrayed by Julie London and Jayne Mansfield. No mention was made in the photoplay of any character resembling wife Grayce or even Owney Madden, perhaps the most important influence in George's professional life.

As upset as he would be over the finished product, Raft was equally disappointed by the poor box office returns of the film. It likewise did little business in England, where it was released under the title *Spin of a Coin*.

Raft's film work continued to diminish. Hollywood proved to be a humiliating experience for the once big-name actor. In 1956, his only credit was a cameo as a Barbary Coast saloon bouncer in Mike Todd's all-star widescreen extravaganza *Around the World in Eighty Days*. Although George knew the role would do nothing for him professionally, he at least had the satisfaction of sharing his segment with friends Red Skelton, Marlene Dietrich and Frank Sinatra.

While filming the final moments of his scene, Raft was instructed by director Todd to pitch a knife into the table where Phineas Fogg (David Niven) is sitting, as a warning to Fogg to back off from saloon singer Dietrich. The trick had to be done just right and Todd offered to get a professional knife thrower to teach George how to perfect the toss. George suddenly recalled the infamous knife fight he'd had as a youth with Sammy Schwartz where his ear was gashed open. He admitted that old hostile feelings were aroused and that he felt it hard to restrain a quick, violent impulse when he saw Todd walking toward him on the set holding the ten-inch blade. But George recovered, took the knife and when the director called "Action," he flung it expertly into the surface of the table. The scene required a second take and once more Raft hit the target with precision aim. Impressed, Todd said to George, "You've obviously handled a knife before."

To which George replied, "Yes. Kid stuff. Used to go hunting."

Around the World in Eight Days proved to be a huge commercial hit and earned the Academy Award for Best Picture of the year. But as George had expected, he was lost in the shuffle. George's cameo in the movie would be his last film work for three years. As Raft would say, "And then … the phone just seemed to stop ringing."

Apparently, he was offered a role in another movie to be filmed in England titled *Women of the Night*, but was refused a work permit by the Ministry of Labor. George returned to the States and tried to keep busy by appearing as a guest on more television shows.

He even announced his interest to move into directing, stating, "I believe I know more about directing than ninety percent of the men in the industry today," and asked his close friend Darryl F. Zanuck if he could help in any way. Zanuck wrote George a letter from London explaining that with movie studios cutting back on experienced personnel, it was unlikely they would hire someone as-yet unproven as a director. Zanuck did suggest, however, that Raft should consider buying story properties and developing them on his own, which apparently George never did.

However, a short time later, Zanuck did propose to George the starring role in a feature film. George remembered the incident that he would later call "a swift kick in the ass." While he was in San Francisco, George received a telephone call from a man named Robert Goldstein, who was Darryl Zanuck's production chief in London. He was asked if he would fly to London to appear in a movie to co-star Bella Darvi. Raft agreed. He received a $5,000 advance and flew to London, where almost immediately he was entangled in a web of confusion and, ultimately, deceit. He was upset to find out that the picture was not a Twentieth Century-Fox production, but a movie Zanuck was producing independently — as a project for Miss Darvi. The script he was given was an amateurish jumble, with him as an American detective returning home who is called back to where he had just solved a case. Raft's attempts to meet with Zanuck to make some sense out of this mess initially proved unsuccessful, and by the time he finally caught up with Zanuck at his hotel, he was furious. He had determined that there was to be no movie, and he demanded to know exactly why he'd been brought over to London. Zanuck was evasive, and promised George that they'd talk later to sort things out. But when George next tried to contact him, he discovered that Zanuck had flown back to the States. George later discovered that the whole movie project was bogus from the beginning, and had been designed by the jealous Zanuck to keep his mistress Bella Darvi occupied while he was away. Raft's participation was merely a façade to add authenticity to Zanuck's scheme. Raft's humbled position in the film industry had evidently made him the perfect patsy. When George later ran into Zanuck at a club in New York, he was prepared to beat the daylights out of him, but after some discussion and apologies, Raft and Zanuck shook hands and the matter was dropped, though George was still hurt at being deceived by someone he considered a close friend.

On January 14, 1957, Hollywood received the news that Humphrey Bogart had succumbed to throat cancer at the age of 57. It was no secret that he had been ill, but his passing affected many because it signaled the beginning of the end of an era. Within a few years, Bogart would be followed into death by Tyrone Power, Errol Flynn, Clark Gable and Gary Cooper — each a relatively young man.

One wonders what George Raft felt. He'd never been friendly with Bogart; in fact, he probably inwardly resented him, and certainly had never visited the dying actor at his Holmby Hills home as had Spencer Tracy, Frank Sinatra and others. Still, at the time of Bogie's death, it would have been fitting for the press to ask him to provide a few words, given the enormous impact Raft had had on Bogart's career. As it was, George would not really speak publicly of his rival until many years later when the "Bogart cult" was firmly established. And, as George was wont to do, he would speak respectfully of Bogart's talents, without envy or bitterness.

Humphrey Bogart died just a few years after his career had reached a new plateau, one that elevated him from supporting roles and particularly the gangster parts by which he had become almost fatally typecast. (Of these roles, Bogart once grumbled to Jack Warner, "You can make a card index of the lines they speak. 'Get over against the wall.' 'Get your hands up.' 'Don't make a move or I'll shoot.'") It would have seemed appropriate that the passing of one of the original movie tough guys should have opened new doors for George Raft. But that was not to happen. In an ironic reversal of roles, Humphrey Bogart had become a star; George Raft was relegated to the ranks of a (rarely employed) supporting player.

George was again obligated to seek work outside of the motion picture field. An opportunity presented itself when in the spring of 1958 he received a telephone call from an old Broadway acquaintance named Jerry Brooks, who offered Raft the position as "Director of Entertainment" for his Havana-based hotel/casino The Hotel Del Capri. Raft accepted the assignment and soon was responsible for booking into the Capri such talents as singer Tony Martin, world-renowned flamenco dancer Jose Greco — and even Marlene Dietrich.

George's efforts paid off as tourists and locals alike flocked to the hotel — as much to see Raft as the various entertainers who played there. George was a gracious "hands-on" host and hand-shaker and mingled with the crowds as well as occasionally dealing blackjack hands. He made a special effort to be accommodating to the guests. Once when an American tourist remarked to the head clerk at the hotel that his wife was a huge fan of Raft's, the clerk promised that the next morning Raft would personally serve her breakfast in bed. Sure enough, the following morning George, dressed in a bellman's uniform, showed up at their room with a breakfast tray.

The Capri was a pleasant and rewarding environment, and George basked in the respect and recognition that now seemed to elude him in Hollywood.

When the tourist season slowed in summer, George requested a leave of absence to return to Hollywood. As it turned out, his timing could not have been better. Billy Wilder was preparing to shoot his new movie, *Some Like It Hot* (1959), and, perhaps forgetting his earlier experience with Raft on *Double Indemnity*, offered George the fourth-billed role of gangster "Spats" Columbo, whose St. Valentine's Day Massacre-like slaying of rival mobsters sets the comedic story in motion. Raft's co-stars were Marilyn Monroe, Tony Curtis, Jack Lemmon, old pal Pat O'Brien and wide-mouthed comedian Joe E. Brown.

Unemployed musicians Joe (Curtis) and Jerry (Lemmon) witness the Chicago mob killing and to escape "Spats" and his gang, disguise themselves as "Josephine" and "Daphne" and join up with an all-girl orchestra heading for Miami. Onboard is Sugar Kane Kowalcyzk (Monroe), whom Joe romances in Florida by shedding his "Josephine" masquerade and posing as a wealthy playboy, calling himself "Junior." "Daphne," meanwhile, has her hands full as she/he is pursued by a determined Philadelphia millionaire, Osgood Fielding III (Brown). The complications really arise once the Chicago underworld appears in Florida for a mob convention. Despite their best efforts to avoid the gangsters, Joe and Jerry are soon recognized by "Spats," but are saved almost at the last minute when Columbo and his gang are assassinated at a banquet presided over by the big boss "Little Bonaparte" (Nehemiah Persoff). The hilarious denouement finds an exasperated "Daphne" revealing his true self to the amorous Osgood, who merely replies, "Well, nobody's perfect."

Some Like It Hot was a bona fide hit. Critics raved and the box office grossed over $8.3 million. What made its success so astounding was that it was a modestly-budgeted black-and-white film competing in an era of Technicolor and widescreen blockbusters. *Variety* said that Raft "hams it up as a caricature of himself." Indeed, in a film filled with memorable moments, one of the best belongs to George, when "Spats" snatches a coin being flipped by his soon-to-be-assassin "Paradise" (Edward G. Robinson, Jr.) and snarls: "Where did ya pick up that cheap trick?"

Edward G. Robinson (Sr.) was originally offered the role of "Spats" Columbo, but declined when Billy Wilder (with whom Robinson had worked in *Double Indemnity*) would not pay Robinson's standard screen salary. Not even the incentive of having his son play a small role in the film could persuade Robinson to lower his price. Instead, the actor took on the co-starring part as Frank Sinatra's brother in Frank Capra's *A Hole in the Head* (1959).

Even with the film destined to become Raft's biggest hit of the decade, George spoke resignedly about playing another gangster. "Typecasting again. But what can you do? I just never seemed to make the break away to other roles the way Cagney and Bogart did."

Still, George enjoyed making the film and was even patient during the lengthy on-set delays caused by Marilyn Monroe, which stretched Raft's short contracted work period into sixteen weeks. During these periods he would reminisce with Pat O'Brien and Joe E. Brown, or else give lessons in the tango to Jack Lemmon and Brown for their comical dance scene together. In fact, Marilyn Monroe had suggested to director Wilder at one point that the film should end with her character and "Spats" tangoing off into the sunset. Fortunately, Wilder declined. Not only did the murderous "Spats" have to pay for his crimes, but Wilder was not about to change his classic finale.

The versatile Nehemiah Persoff played the volatile "Little Bonaparte" in the film. He spoke about working with George: "I met George Raft briefly when we worked on *Some Like It Hot*, but I really know nothing about him, except that he did his job in a business-like way; he was relaxed and friendly."

The late Mike Mazurki, best known for his "dumb" (which in real life he most definitely was not) tough guy roles, played one of "Spats" Columbo's henchmen, and remembered George shortly before his death in 1990. "George was a quiet guy, but we had the chance to speak between scenes. He was always very interested in sports and that's what we mainly talked about since he knew I had been a professional wrestler."

Even though *Some Like It Hot* was intended as a zany comedy, Raft played his role absolutely straight, and his "Spats" Columbo was just as ruthless and menacing as the crime lord he'd essayed in *Rogue Cop*. Unfortunately, he couldn't capitalize on this success. There just weren't that many gangster films being made, and fewer yet that afforded parts to an aging actor.

With his work completed on the picture and no other movie work forthcoming, George responded to Jerry Brooks' urging that he return to the Capri for at least the two weeks of Christmas and New Year's. George's reluctant decision to do so provided him with an adventure far greater than any he had ever played onscreen.

The political climate in Cuba was becoming uneasy as rebel guerilla forces under the command of Fidel Castro made steady inroads to overthrow the government of General Fulgencio Batista, a government which had allowed American interests, such as gambling, to flourish in the country.

George arrived in Havana on Christmas Eve, 1958, and resumed his duties. Once again, everything seemed to be going smoothly. Actress and former Miss California 1939 Margia Dean, who had played a role in *Loan Shark*, was also in Cuba at the time and recalls her experience.

"I was invited to a New Year's Eve party hosted by Batista at the Isle of Pines, Cuba. The night before, we were in Havana and I went to the casino that George Raft was running. He was a friend of mine socially and I also appeared in the movie *Loan Shark* with him. I told him that we were hearing rumors of political unrest there, and he said that it was just Florida trying to keep the tourists away from Havana! He said not to worry, that if there was any problem he would be the first to know! (I still have a $10 chip from the casino.) The morning after the party, we awakened to bearded soldiers with machine guns circling us. Batista fled during the night on Trujillo's [Dominican Republic dictator] yacht along with Porfirio Rubirosa. There was a 'Who's Who' group at the party and we all had to rough it. The help had run off so the men were fishing for food and the women were cooking. We were bitten alive by mosquitoes; no one knew how to run the DDT machines. The revolutionaries freed the jailed prisoners on the island and killed the commandant. His daughter ran to us hysterically. We were afraid that they would attack us, but I guess they just wanted to get home. The airport was sandbagged so we couldn't leave. I believe it was George Skagel [one of the Kennedys] who had the private plane and he, Eileen Mehle [*Suzy the Jet Set*], my date and I dared to take off from the beach with all the armed soldiers standing around watching us. They could have shot us down but probably believed we had permission! There was so much confusion. We were the first to get out of Cuba and hit the headlines. Everyone else was stuck there for many weeks."

On New Year's Eve, Raft was present in the club, meeting and greeting the revelers, not imbibing but making the rounds holding a soft drink. He retired to his suite and his Cuban girlfriend at around six a.m. the following morning. Just as he climbed into bed he heard machine gun fire shattering the dawn. A quick call to the desk informed George that Castro's armies had broken into Havana and that Batista had fled the country. Pandemonium raged outside as people were shot and killed by the advancing rebels. About a hundred revolutionaries had even broken into the Capri and began to smash up the casino.

Because of Raft's tough screen reputation, the terrified hotel occupants immediately looked to him to take charge of the situation. George managed to convince the rebels that he was an American and neutral, and that they could help themselves to food and other items inside the hotel provided they cooperated. Surprisingly, they agreed, and after stocking up with provisions, most of the rebels left. While some measure of calm was established inside the Capri, it was still much too dangerous for Raft and the other guests to venture outside into the ongoing carnage.

Later explaining his calm control of the precarious situation, George said modestly, "I never told anyone I was an actor. But I guess I fooled a lot of people."

George attempted to call J. Edgar Hoover, but was unable to get through to Washington. He then tried the American ambassador, only to be told that he couldn't speak to Raft, but was working on the problem.

Two days later Castro's regular army entered Havana and about 175 of the rebels came to the hotel for rooms, though they preferred sleeping on the floor to using beds. Raft later said of these soldiers, "Nicest, quietest guys I ever saw."

George was asked to appear on Cuban television, where he made an appeal for peace, reminding the rebel forces that the Americans were neutral and should be treated fairly. But George and the others remained trapped inside the Capri for two weeks, subjected to occasional bursts of machine gun fire from revolutionaries housed across the street at the National Hotel, which had become Castro's headquarters in Havana.[28] Fortunately, there was still enough food inside the hotel to see them through.

Finally, after sixteen days, with the food supply running low, now consisting of warm beer, sardines and dry English biscuits, George received word from an official that he and the others were free to leave and that a plane was waiting at the airport. George may have felt a momentary relief that his ordeal was at last over — but, in fact, his troubles were just beginning.

He and the hotel manager were driven by two Cuban soldiers to the airport, which had been completely taken over by armed troops who had thoroughly vandalized the terminal. George had just gone through immigration when he was suddenly approached by four men with machine guns and marched into an office. Inside, the soldiers removed the twenty-eight hundred dollars in cash Raft had on his person, then slammed him up against a wall and aimed their weapons at his head.

Raft felt as if he were awaiting execution before a firing squad and admitted that he was about to ask for a priest. Drenched in sweat, George didn't know why they were threatening him, only that the soldiers demanded to know where the money was. George still did not understand.

Finally, a big, fat captain named Nunez entered the room and ordered Raft and the others to follow him out to the gangplank where George was told to pick out his luggage. He obliged. George was always meticulous about his clothes and stood in silent fury as the soldiers began ripping apart his two suitcases. Although the soldiers had suspected Raft of smuggling large sums of Capri cash out of Cuba, their search turned up nothing more than clothing, cologne and some publicity glossies. The soldiers then carelessly tossed George's belongings back into the suitcases, and Raft was allowed to board the plane leaving for Miami — but not before suffering one final insult when Captain Nunez asked George to autograph one of his photos for him. George suppressed the anger he felt at his unjust treatment, and complied. He said without embarrassment that when the plane finally landed safely in Florida, he got down on his knees and kissed the ground.

George had garnered a significant amount of publicity from his Cuban ordeal. But it did little to rekindle interest from film producers. The old studio system was virtually finished, and Raft was just one of the Golden Age stars who was cast adrift — though, of course, his release from studio bondage was his own decision and preceded the final collapse of the long-term contract player by many years. While John Wayne, James Stewart and Spencer Tracy still continued to be major draws at the box office, and names such as Henry Fonda, Cary Grant and Katharine Hepburn maintained a respectable audience following, others like Bette Davis, Errol Flynn and Mickey Rooney found their once-potent popularity waning. They were often forced to appear in low-budget pictures of far less quality than those produced by Warner Brothers or MGM.

Of the screen toughs, Bogart and John Garfield were dead, and Cagney was just a couple of years from retiring (for twenty years) from the screen. Only Edward G. Robinson was working steadily after nearly having his career destroyed during the HUAC hearings.

Rather than humble himself with interviews and auditions in the changing Hollywood, George attempted to establish himself in a couple of business ventures. He made a proposal to purchase New York's The Roundtable restaurant, but the owner, Morris Levy, was not interested in selling. George's attempt to promote a heavyweight bout between Archie Moore and Sugar Ray Robinson, to be held in Miami (reportedly under the sponsorship of the Miami mob), likewise did not pan out.

Instead, George recorded dialogue from *They Drive by Night* on a Roulette album called "Co-Star." The idea was to allow the listener to "act" scenes opposite Raft from a script provided along with the record.

George then received a contract from Inter Continent Films to appear (third-billed) with Guy Madison and his *Red Light* co-star, Virginia Mayo, in *Jet Over the Atlantic* (1959), directed by Byron Haskin. In this low-budget precursor to *Airport* (1970) and other airborne disaster movies, Raft was FBI agent Stafford who is accompanying alleged murderer Brett Matoon (Madison) on a trans-Atlantic flight from Madrid to New York City. Also onboard is Lord Robert Leverett (George Macready), who has planted a bomb aboard the jetliner. Brett, a former air force pilot, is forced to take control of the plane after the crew is killed, and is also compelled to kill Lord Leverett. He lands the plane safely, but then attempts to escape, his action earning him a bullet from Stafford. The predictable windup finds the wounded Brett cleared of his murder charge when the real culprit is arrested and confesses to framing him. Stafford assures Brett and his dancer girlfriend Jean Gruney (Mayo) that Brett will soon be a free man.

Unfortunately, while the picture should have been a taut, suspenseful airplane drama along the lines of *The High and the Mighty* (1954), the action never really takes off. The pacing drags, the cardboard characters fail to arouse audience sympathy and the film's low budget is apparent throughout.

Raft's harshest critic, Bosley Crowther, reported in *The New York Times*: "A melodrama in which George Raft, Guy Madison and Virginia Mayo get caught aloft in a crippled plane. By some miscarriage of justice, they all get down alive."

Jet Over the Atlantic would prove to be George Raft's last major film role. He would continue to make occasional movies and show up on various television programs for the next twenty years, but the parts offered were usually "bits" or even cameos whose only purpose, apparently, was to exploit his fading though still-recognizable image.

His 27-year reign as one of the great stars of Hollywood was over.

CHAPTER TEN

"I'VE NEVER BEEN LOCKED UP. I'VE NEVER TAKEN A DRINK. I NEVER HURT ANYBODY, AND I GAVE ALL MY MONEY AWAY. SO HOW COME I GOT THIS BUM REPUTATION?"

GEORGE RAFT

In 1960, George Raft's address was 1275 Beverly Estates Drive in Beverly Hills. He lived in a $70,000 mortgage-free home with a swimming pool that, while certainly not the showplace his Coldwater Canyon residence had been, was still a reflection of his former Hollywood status.

Even living a more modest lifestyle, Raft needed to keep working. Although he was nearing sixty-five, he could not afford a comfortable retirement due to the fact that he hadn't saved any money. His pal Frank Sinatra invited George to come aboard for the small role of Las Vegas hotel owner Jack Strager in the first of the so-called Rat Pack movies, *Ocean's Eleven* (1960). Strager appears late in the film, after the successful New Year's Eve multi-casino heist, where he enlists the conniving Duke Santos (Cesar Romero) to recover the stolen money. Although little more than a cameo, Raft performed convincingly in his single scene. The major parts of the ex-army buddies who execute the crime were played by Sinatra, Dean Martin, Sammy Davis, Jr., Peter Lawford, Joey Bishop, Richard Conte and Henry Silva.

He also made an appearance on the January 26 telecast of *The Red Skelton Show* spoofing his gangster image as "Mister Lasagna," with Mary Beth Hughes as his moll. But lucrative entertainment offers were not forthcoming.

George Raft may have been forgotten by the motion picture community, but he still had an important name that an enterprising man named Bud Kiley sought to use in promoting his new chain of discount stores: Consumer Marts of America. George was paid a very modest $150 per week salary as C.M.A.'s Public Relations Director — a position that involved making personal appearances at store openings (for which he received additional fees) and meeting with the stores' employees. He was also promised that he would share in the company's stock when C.M.A. went public.

George did so well in his job that after only a year Bud Kiley and his partners made him a vice president in the company. Even though his "promotion"

203

offered no increase in pay, Raft accepted the responsibility and signed the necessary papers. Only a few years later this decision would cost him dearly.

Meanwhile, he appeared in another cameo, this time for director-star Jerry Lewis in *The Ladies Man* (1961). Raft's bit had him appearing near the beginning of the film, as the date of one of the girls living at the boarding house where Herbert H. Heebert (Lewis) works as a houseboy. There was

A.J. "TOT" O'DOWD, RAFT, NEWARK BUSINESSMAN CHARLIE DEROSA AND RICHIE "THE BOOT" BOIARDO IN THE 1960S PHOTO COURTESY OF JOHN O'DOWD

little need for George's participation in the movie (which also featured Harry James, at the time still married to Betty Grable); it was evident that Lewis, an admitted Raft admirer, just wanted to do his friend a favor.

A much more substantial part came George's way when he was asked to come to England to appear with Maxie Rosenbloom in a comedy called *Two Guys Abroad* (1962). George was optimistic about the Don Sharp-directed movie in which he and Rosenbloom played a pair of Piccadilly club owners, with Rosenbloom, naturally, getting into all sorts of trouble and Raft on hand to bail him out. George even thought that the picture might spin out into a television series. Unfortunately, audiences never got the chance to see *Two Guys Abroad* as producer Ian Warren decided not to release the picture after viewing the final edit.

Outside of some television spots, such as the game show *Your First Impression* and *The Ed Sullivan Show*, George remained professionally inactive until 1964. And once more his return to movies consisted only of a couple of insignificant cameos. Again for Jerry Lewis, he appeared for a few non-speaking seconds in *The Patsy*.

While Hollywood bellboy Stanley Belt (Lewis) is being "groomed" to replace a deceased singer, he remarks that he wants to look like George Raft. Stanley's hair is styled in a similar fashion and while being fitted for wardrobe by Sy Devore (Richard Deacon), he sees the reflection of George Raft in the mirror — which indeed turns out to be the aging though still dapper actor.

To Jerry Lewis's credit, he did his part to keep the George Raft image alive. But the bits he offered did nothing to further Raft's career.

Neither did his cameo in *For Those Who Think Young* (1964), a teen-oriented film intended to capitalize on the success of the Frankie Avalon-Annette Funicello "beach party" movies being made by American-International Pictures. The title itself derived from a then-popular Pepsi slogan. A fedora-wearing, trench coat-clad George Raft and Roger Smith appear as a couple of detectives late in the movie, but perhaps the main attraction for nostalgia watchers are the somewhat larger roles of veteran actors Robert Armstrong, Allen Jenkins and Raft's old pal Jack LaRue as ex-gangster Edgar J. Cronin's (Robert Middleton) henchmen.

Around this time George openly socialized with a well-known New Jersey mobster named Richie Boiardo. Author John O'Dowd shares the story:

"One night in the 1960s, my late parents, Bette and A.J. O'Dowd (better known to his family and friends as 'Tot'), dined with George Raft at an Italian restaurant in Newark, NJ., and I've been told they were very impressed with him. They met him through a mutual friend, Mr. Richie 'The Boot' Boiardo, who lived on a sprawling estate in nearby Livingston, New Jersey. In the early 1960s my father had somehow become acquainted with Mr. Boiardo, a flashily-dressed, elderly man with an admittedly somewhat mysterious demeanor, and 'Mr. B' began inviting him and my mother up to his house every week for dinner.

"As I was very young during the time, my family was dinner guests of Mr. B's, and all I really remember about him is how generous and almost grandfatherly he was to us. Mr. B gave my sisters and me silver dollars every year for our birthdays and in the summer months we swam in his built-in swimming pool, which was so huge it even had a rowboat in it!

"Despite Mr. B.'s always kind and generous demeanor, I have recently learned that there was a lot more to him and to his life than what met the eye.

"According to noted author and confirmed 'mob-a-phile,' Alan K. Rode, Mr. B. led a whole other existence of which I was not aware until recently … a rip-roaring and dangerous life that I'm not convinced even my parents knew about! Says Alan, 'Boiardo was nominally a captain in the Vito Genovese family but he also operated as an independent power, particularly in Newark, N.J.'s First Ward, where his presence was felt for decades.'

"This description of Mr. B. was enough to spur me on to research his life further and what I have learned about him has been quite a revelation to me. According to material I have gathered from various sources on the Internet,

Mr. Boiardo came to Chicago at the turn of the century when he was nine. As a young man during Prohibition, he allegedly built a reputation as a no-nonsense bootlegger in Newark, N.J. By 1930 he was an associate (and some say, a bitter adversary) of notorious gangster Abner 'Longy' Zwillman, who was often referred to as 'the Al Capone of New Jersey.' As the aforementioned 'Mak' writes, 'Through the 1930s and later, Boiardo was connected by state and federal investigators with bootlegging, numbers and lottery rackets.' In the 1950s, Mr. B. was reportedly involved in mob gambling and loan-shark-ing activities, and in 1963 a man named Joe Valachi exposed him as a power in the 'Costra Nostra' or Mafia crime syndicate. There were supposedly mob killings with which he was involved and other nefarious activities and they allegedly continued right up until his death in 1984. Needless to say, this is more than a bit shocking to someone who saw none of that in the years my family knew Mr. B.!

"As I stated earlier, my parents first became friendly with Mr. B. in the early 1960s and their meeting of George Raft took place, I believe, in the middle part of the decade. In addition to the Thursday night dinners at his home, Mr. B. often hosted several Saturday night gatherings for his adult friends at various Italian restaurants in and around Newark. It was at one of these eat-eries that my parents met George Raft. I recall my dad later telling my sisters and me that his first impression of Mr. Raft was that of a suave, impeccably-dressed and down-to-earth gentleman. He said that although he was a bit on the quiet side at first, Raft was extremely cordial to everyone in Mr. B.'s party and that he didn't act at all like 'the movie star.' Dad said that Mr. Raft asked him about his business and seemed very interested when Dad told him how he had his pilot's license and how he had met Howard Hughes one time when he landed a small airplane at the family hangar in Pine Brook. My mother, who was part Italian and part Slovak, was a very glamorous woman in the 1960s and apparently Raft was impressed with her appearance as he told her that she reminded him of 'a blonde Sophia Loren.' My parents evidently got a real kick out of that as they later told all their friends in suburbia about it!

"As far as we know, our folks only had that one meeting with Raft, but we know they enjoyed it greatly. It also appeared to them that Mr. B. and Raft knew each other quite well as they were seen engaging in several intimate con-versations that night—you know, just the two of them. They were apparently serious discussions, too, as Dad said that both men had very intense looks on their faces. Oh, to be a fly on the wall of that restaurant all those years ago!"

In September 1965, shortly before his seventieth birthday, George's name again made the headlines:

GEORGE RAFT ACCUSED OF TAX EVASION

The Washington Daily Post article read: "Actor George Raft was accused yesterday in a Federal grand jury indictment of evading payment of income taxes by understating his income in the amount of approximately $85,000 for the years 1958-1963. The indictment carried six counts — five of evading taxes and one of making a false statement.

"Mr. Raft, 69, is expected to surrender on the indictment and would be arraigned. September 7."

The unfortunate matter developed through George's association with Consumer Marts of America. He discovered in a 1964 meeting with Jarvis Weiss, the corporate accountant, that the firm had gone into bankruptcy. Because of his "position" with the company, George found out that he was financially responsible for C.M.A., and in the bankruptcy proceedings, he lost (temporarily) his Beverly Estates house along with his other tangible assets.

Investigating further, the Internal Revenue Service discovered that Raft had not paid taxes on his earnings from C.M.A. George, who admitted that he had never been a good businessman, had assumed that the company had been taking care of his deductions.

At any rate, George did not have the money to pay what he owed — and he was too proud to ask for assistance from any of his friends.

Raft was indicted and the case went before a grand jury. It was charged that he had falsified his gross earnings in 1958 by $12,000, $7,668 in 1959, $17,500 in 1960, $30,000 in 1961, and an undisclosed amount in 1963. Further, he was accused of claiming a capital loss of $25,000 on Capri stock in 1962.

The seriousness of the situation was not lost on Raft. As he later told his 1974 biographer Lewis Yablonsky, "… Now, finally, I'd really go to the can — not for knowing or associating with hoods, but with businessmen."

With the case now made public, many of Raft's friends came forward, offering financial help and writing to U.S. District Judge Pierson M. Hall pleading for leniency. Those included Lucille Ball, Jimmy Durante, Bob Hope, Frank Sinatra, and Senator George Murphy.

George was deeply appreciative of the support, particularly Frank Sinatra's generous offer of any amount Raft needed — up to one million dollars — to help his case. But, again, George's pride and fierce independence would not allow him to accept Sinatra's financial assistance.

On the day of sentencing after Raft pleaded guilty to one count of tax evasion, the former movie tough guy stood in the courtroom clutching his grandmother's rosary with tears running freely down his cheeks. Although George could have been handed a minimum sentence of three years in prison and a $5,000 fine — or both, he received only a $2,500 fine and a suspended sentence. After the sentencing, Judge Hall told Raft that he would not have been surprised to see a not-guilty verdict if the case had gone to trial.

Outside the courtroom, a weeping Raft apologized to the public, saying, "I never had any intention to defraud the government." He also told reporters, "I am very happy with the court decision. It was most fair. The judge was wonderful … I feel great that people really like you for what you are — not for the company you sometimes keep."

While George was both pleased and relieved with his lenient sentencing, he was also saddened to learn that during the trial his boyhood friend and later mentor Owney Madden had passed away from emphysema at the age of seventy-three. Though he and Madden had not seen much of each other over the years, Raft felt the loss deeply. A vital link with his past was gone.

In January of 1966, George was called to appear before a New York Grand Jury investigating possible underworld influence with Scopitone, "a film juke box," purchased by a company called Tel-A-Sign. George was subpoenaed because he had apparently been given 1,000 shares of stock in the Tel-A-Sign Corporation. He gave a brief testimony, but had nothing to offer, and was naturally upset by the resulting publicity, which he felt exploited him and again connected him with the underworld.

But at least something good came out of his trip to New York when he met with French film star Jean Gabin, who hired George to appear in his upcoming film, *Du Rififi a Paname* (*Rififi in Panama*, 1966) — to be filmed in Europe. Even though the role was that of an aging gangster, it was a substantial part and after Raft's recent ordeals, he could appreciate a trip abroad.

In the movie, released in the United States in 1967 under the title *The Upper Hand*, Raft's Charles Binnaggio is an American Mafia leader trying to muscle control of the international gold-smuggling organization run by Paulo Berger (Gabin). When several of his key men are killed, Paulo agrees to meet with Binnaggio, but brings along a time bomb which effectively eliminates his enemy.

Unfortunately, the film was an almost total misfire (*The New York Times* called it a "pushy but dull gangster melodrama"), suffering most prominently from poor dubbing in its U.S. release and the wooden playing of the two veteran screen gangsters. Gabin, of course, had made his reputation in France, where he had appeared in films since 1928, most notably as the title character in the pre-*Algiers* (1938) *Pepe Le Moko* (1937). Also in the supporting cast of *Du Rififi a Paname* was Gert Frobe, who had previously made his mark as James Bond's nemesis *Goldfinger* (1964).

Although *Du Rififi a Paname* did nothing to revitalize a film comeback, once more George Raft's name and reputation led to an offer in another branch of entertainment. He had traveled to London to appear live on the *Eamon Andrews Show*, then the most popular television program in Britain. His success on the show led to a booking for an October 30, 1965 television broadcast from the London Palladium, where the 70-year-old Raft performed a 1920s gangster shtick, then danced the Charleston. After this, he was the subject of a British TV version of *This is Your Life*. Concurrently, he was in meetings with a couple of men named Andy Neatrour and Dino Cellini, who were proposing that George take on the role of host at their

Colony Club, a classy and successful gambling establishment in the Mayfair section of London. George presented certain conditions for accepting the job, which were met. He would receive a two-bedroom apartment, complete with a full-time maid, at the posh Belton Towers in Marble Arch nearby the club, a chauffeur-driven limousine, free meals at the Colony, a $200-a week salary, and five points in the club. Raft would begin sharing in the profits once the investors were paid. In addition, the nightspot would be called "George Raft's Colony Club." However, at first George was not too sure about this billing. Almost repeating what he'd said thirty-three years earlier when Paramount wanted to "star" him in *Night After Night*, Raft remarked, "Suppose they put my name out there and no one comes?"

But they did come. The Colony soon became the most popular nightclub in London, and George was once again enjoying the success, respect and admiration that had been denied him in Hollywood.

"It was a piece of luck I needed," Raft said of the opportunity.

The club reflected the Raft image: from its tasteful décor, highlighted in George's favorite colors, red carpeting and gold chandeliers, to the attire of the staff. Of course, George had played the role before: in motion pictures and in Havana at the Capri. But there were no movie cameras rolling or no threat of revolution hanging over London, and George was completely happy and comfortable in his new surroundings. He was a gracious host, ensuring that guests (which included celebrities, politicians and other assorted American and British VIPS) received first-class treatment and were pleased with the food and entertainment provided by the Colony.

The late Marc Lawrence remembered the Colony: "I visited the club when I was in London in the sixties. I had a very good time there. George was a good host. He was nice and friendlier than I remembered him in the movie we made [*Invisible Stripes*]."

A GAMBLING TOKEN FROM GEORGE RAFT'S COLONY CLUB

There was even the offer of film work. Producer Charles Feldman (who had worked with Raft in Universal's *Follow the Boys*) asked George to perform a bit as a casino host, like his real-life role at the Colony, for his extravagant all-star spoof of James Bond films, *Casino Royale* (1967). George appears onscreen at the madcap finale, involving a casino invasion by the French Foreign Legion, United Nations paratroopers, American Indians, the U.S. Cavalry — even the Keystone Kops! As himself, the dapper Raft flips his famous coin before pulling out a revolver. "I've been framed," he says. "This gun shoots backwards. I've just killed myself." Then he drops to the floor.

Surprisingly, these few seconds of celluloid afforded George his best reviews in years. *Newsweek* enthused, "Raft's bit, a cameo miracle of timing in a morass of footage, is the best in-joke in the film because Raft is simply himself."

However, critics were less complementary about the rest of this $12 million cinematic hodgepodge.

There was also talk about George starring in a film called *The Midnight Man*, but the picture was never made. Not that it mattered since George found himself in demand to headline many charity sporting events sponsored by various British organizations, such as "The George Raft Colony Sporting Club Trophy Meeting."

George decided to return home to Los Angeles as the Christmas season approached. He fully intended to return to his duties at the Colony after the holidays, but a telephone call from a *New York Times* reporter permanently halted his plans. According to the reporter, who contacted Raft at his Beverly Hills home, the *Manchester Guardian* had printed a front-page story headlined: GEORGE RAFT BARRED FROM LONDON. George immediately placed a long-distance call to London, where Joel Tarlo, the attorney for the Colony Club, assured him that there was no truth to the story. George felt relieved … until a short time later when Tarlo contacted him to tell him that the story was indeed true.

The British Home Office had denied George Raft re-entry into England. They said in their official announcement, "Raft's continued presence in the United Kingdom would not be conducive to the public good. He should be advised that under the circumstances he should not seek readmission here."

While never declared publicly, the probable reason for the British Home Office's decision was Raft's high-profile association with the underworld. The Office had been investigating ownership of the Colony and discovered such mob names as Meyer Lansky, Charley (The Blade) Tourino, Carmine Mastrototaro and Raymond Patriarca connected with the club.

George placed a telephone call to Senator George Murphy (Republican — California), requesting that Murphy write a letter on his behalf to the British Government. When Murphy declined, Raft asked if Murphy could arrange it so that he could review any files the FBI might have on him. Again,

Murphy refused, though he offered to line up an appointment so that Raft could make whatever statements he wanted to the FBI. The Bureau agreed to meet with Raft, but made it clear that they would not divulge any of the information they had of Raft on record.

George attempted to defend himself in an interview printed in the March 30, 1967 issue of the *Los Angeles Herald-Examiner*, in which he said, in part, "... I'm not a member of any mob, never was. Sure, I know some guys that are, but I know a lot of people. What am I supposed to do when these guys say hello to me — tell them to get lost? What have I got to do to clear myself? I lead a quiet life. I don't ask for any trouble. I have never taken a drink. I don't get in any fights. If broads are an offense, then I plead guilty."

Raft was further quoted as saying, "The only thing I can figure is that it was the FBI. And so I'm going to try to see J. Edgar Hoover and find out what they have got against me ... I suppose the British had some information on me and it must have come from the FBI. I'm going to New York this week to see about a job and I plan to drop down to Washington and wait in Hoover's office until he sees me ... "

Regarding his treatment by the British government, George said with bitter irony, "Funny, they remember that I used to know Benny Siegel, and that he knew Lansky and that I maybe once said hello to a couple of mob guys. Do they remember that I used to get a big hello from the guy who was their king? Or that it was me who helped get a house for him and the duchess when they came out to California in the 30s? No ... they don't remember that."

George's wish to speak personally with J. Edgar Hoover never came about as he was advised that the FBI Director could not meet with him.

But George maintained his determination and wrote the following letter to J. Edgar Hoover on March 28, 1967, requesting the Director's help in determining why he had been declared persona non grata in England:

> Dear Mr. Hoover:
> I am writing you this letter as a last resort.
>
> No doubt you have heard the story about my being barred from coming into England. All the letters that I have received from my solicitor in England all indicate that the crux of my problem stems from the Federal Bureau of Investigation of the United States having informed the English government, or their agency, of my affiliation with gangsters. I have never been known to be affiliated with any gangsters, and there are no records to show any tie-up with me and any gangster elements.

It is true that, being in the entertainment world for forty years, you are bound to be associated by friendships with all kinds of characters from all walks of life. But this happens to all entertainers, especially entertainers such as myself who have played in pictures and worked in cafes during the Prohibition days.

I have all my personal belongings stored in England.

I would be most grateful if I could come to Washington and discuss with your Federal Bureau of Investigation anything that they may feel makes me an undesirable through association. I have always known for many years what an honorable and fair person you have been. I am sure you would like to help me and see that I could get justice and have a fair hearing in England. I would appreciate your advising me as to what would be the proper procedure for me to take to get my name cleared to enable me to get back into England.

I realize you are awfully busy and have many important duties without worrying about me. But a lot of our mutual friends told me to write to you direct, that you are never too busy to help a person if it is honorable. I sincerely in my heart feel that I am as honorable a citizen as any person can be in the United States.

In fact, the Friars Club of Los Angeles is paying honor to me with a testimonial dinner on Tuesday evening, June 13. I hope if you are on the West Coast you will do me the honor of attending. The biggest names in show business are going to pay me homage ...

Hoover's succinct reply was dated April 4, 1967, and did not offer George much encouragement.

Dear Mr. Raft:
This will acknowledge your letter of March 28, 1967, concerning the actions of the British government in excluding you from the United Kingdom. I am certain you realize that the FBI has no jurisdiction in England and has no control over governmental action taken by a foreign country.

In the event you desire to supplement your letter with additional data, you may be certain that such will be made a matter of permanent record upon receipt at this Bureau.

George even received the support of influential columnist Walter Winchell.[29] In a letter, dated April 4, 1967, Winchell wrote the following to J. Edgar Hoover in Washington (excerpted):

Dear John:

I have known George Raft, the movie star, since the 1920s when he appeared in the best Broadway nightclubs and stopped the show cold with his "Charleston" to the rhythm of "Sweet Georgia Brown." I have never known him to do anything that would be in violation of the law.

I ran into George today and he told me he was unhappy over Britain's ban and the stigma that followed him because the general public assumes that he is guilty of some illicit and illegal deeds. It has cost him several movie and television jobs. He asked me to tell you all this and also that "one of those" hard-to-pin-down tips is that the "FBI informed Scotland Yard that he was a dangerous character, etc." I assured him I never knew John Edgar Hoover or Clyde Tolson (or any of the FBI chiefs) to punish or slander anyone who never had a criminal record …

Hoover's reply to Winchell, dated April 6, 1967, again stated that the Bureau had no influence over the actions of the British government.

George wrote a second letter to J. Edgar Hoover on April 21, 1967, in which he stated that his solicitor in London had learned that the United States Ambassador in London had supplied an FBI dossier on Raft to the British Home Secretary. In his letter, George wanted Hoover to verify whether the FBI did furnish the U.S. Ambassador with such a dossier.

However, this was denied by the U.S. Ambassador, who said he did not even know Raft was in England until the papers reported that he had been "kicked out." It was suggested that Raft's solicitor had been furnishing the actor with false information to "earn his fee and to convince Raft his difficulties are attributable to the FBI, when actually they are with the British Government."

George applied for a renewal of his permit and requested a hearing with the Home Office, but was refused. The British Home Office would not reverse its decision, and Raft was forbidden to return to London. What made this additionally frustrating for Raft was that, prior to this ruling, he had been signed for a small role as, ironically, a London casino host, in Joseph E. Levine's *Robbery* (1967), loosely based on *The Great Train Robbery*, starring Stanley Baker. But as the film was to be shot entirely in England, he had to be replaced in the part.

Back in the U.S. George bitterly told reporters, "All my life I've tried to be a nice guy. But what's the use of being a nice guy when they hit you like this? I have no idea what this is all about. I haven't done anything. I'm not a criminal. I never drink. I pay taxes in Britain as well as America."

Although George's barring from England received the most publicity, seven other Americans had also been expelled from the country. These included: Angelo Bruno, a Philadelphia racketeer, Anthony ("Tony Ducks") Carollo, Dino Cellini. Flamingo Hotel owner Morris Lansburgh and his son Leonard, Meyer Lansky, and Charles ("Charlie the Blade") Tourine.

One theory as to why George was banned was that rival casino owners were envious over the Colony's success, and that they had conspired to keep Raft out of the country. It was suggested that Raft's high-profile public expulsion was conceived as a deliberate example to discourage other Americans who might decide to invest in London's profitable gambling business.

George would never really recover from his barring from England. At the age of seventy-one he had endured another painful and humiliating experience — one that again was the result of his mob friendships. He himself firmly believed that the only reason he was "kicked out" was because of guilt by association. He said, "I'll never forget what happened to me in England. I look back at my life and wonder what the hell I had done to deserve that kind of a kick in the balls."

Prior to the British Home Office decision, the *New York Post* columnist Pete Hamill wrote a sympathetic tribute to Raft that was titled "The Last Caper" (March 4, 1967).

"... He was the last one left, the only survivor of that gaudy mob that had marched so boldly through the land of Warner Brothers. They were the best film actors America had produced, and with their pearl gray hats and the sub-machine guns, the tight coats and polished shoes, the glittering blondes and black limousines, they showed a whole generation of big city kids a style that would allow them to last. But with Bogart, Lorre, Greenstreet dead, and the best of them all — Mr. Cagney — in retirement, all we had left was George Raft ...

"... We always knew that the heroes of gangster pictures were part of our secret mind, the cowboys working the big town; the British thought they were documentaries.

"... At 71, Raft is not about to make any more movies. A few years ago he was bankrupt. They probably won't put him to work in Las Vegas, because he has had a cup of coffee from time to time with the wrong guys. So he will sit around the ruins of Hollywood, serving the last years of the longest bit there is, and I for one only wish that someone would give him a long coat and a machine gun, a pair of spats and a blonde, and let him flip a silver dollar in the air, before shooting it out with the cops. George Raft, of all people, should be allowed to go out in style."

George was later quoted by his biographer, Lewis Yablonsky, "I don't live in a palatial home. I don't go out much, I'm home most of the time. I go out to dinner, wait for the paper, come home and take a sleeping pill. I live the life of a hermit. If, as some of them say, the FBI is really watching me all the time, those guys must be leading an awfully dull life."

One night that certainly could not have been dull for Raft was June 13, 1967, when he was honored at the Friar's Roast (which, despite Raft's invitation, J. Edgar Hoover did not attend). It was a star-studded affair, with many show business friends (and even former enemies, such as Jack L. Warner and Edward G. Robinson) and colleagues on hand to pay tribute to Raft.[30] The special evening coincided with a low point for George, but he did his best to enjoy the festivities, which was hosted by Frank Sinatra. Perhaps the highlight of the evening was a specially arranged song performed to the tune of My Favorite Things:

> Silk ties from Sulka, and hankies to weep in;
> Lounging pajamas a fag wouldn't sleep in;
> Ten-dollar hookers who bounce off the springs –
> These are a few of his favorite things ...
> When his luck fails, like in London,
> When they said, You're through,
> He simply remembered his favorite things
> And said to the Queen, "---- you!"

In September, George's name again made the news in connection with the Friar's Club when he was called upon to testify before the Federal Grand Jury convening in Los Angeles to investigate illegal surveillance equipment being used to monitor card games at the club. Raft himself was never accused of any wrongdoing in the affair, and there was little information he could offer.

George Raft was one of many stars who performed a cameo on TV's popular *Batman* series. On the March 15, 1967 episode, "The Black Widow Strikes Again" (which featured Tallulah Bankhead as the week's villain), Raft was seen as a suspicious, coin-flipping bank customer who exchanges a few words with the Caped Crusaders before exiting with the farewell: "Ciao," leaving Batman and Robin to look momentarily puzzled.

George was also offered a couple of movie roles. He was set to do another cameo in the Tony Curtis comedy *Don't Make Waves* (1967), until his legal affairs conflicted with the shooting schedule, and he had to drop out. A strange independent film titled *Silent Treatment* was next on the agenda, but the comedy, which was shot without dialogue, was never released, and if Raft did appear in it, his footage most probably ended up on the cutting room floor.

The following year he did appear as one of the *Five Golden Dragons* (1968), a secret criminal group which also included veteran actors Brian Donlevy, Dan Duryea and Christopher Lee, each of whom performs his function in Oriental masks and attire (only Lee manages to look comfortable, probably due to his previous playing of Fu Manchu). A Warner-Pathé/Anglo Amalgamated co-production, the movie starred Raft's *Souls at Sea* co-player Robert Cummings as an American playboy tourist in Hong Kong who becomes entangled with the title organization. The film did little business at the box office and was even less profitable professionally for Raft and his aging co-stars. In his entertaining autobiography, *Tall, Dark and Gruesome*, Christopher Lee recalled that during a lull on the set Raft fired a gun under the table to liven up the action. Perhaps a necessary maneuver given the lethargic playing by the cast.

Lee also told authors Tom Johnson and Mark Miller that on location in Hong Kong, he "spent several hours alone with George Raft, and I must say it was an unforgettable experience. There wasn't much he hadn't done in or out of pictures." He clarified in his autobiography, that after listening to Raft talk about his career for six straight hours, "A film of *that* would have been of better value."

Another film that also did little to boost the reputation of George or co-stars Groucho Marx (as a crime boss named "God"), Jackie Gleason, Burgess Meredith, Cesar Romero and Mickey Rooney was Otto Preminger's disastrous misfire *Skidoo* (1968). *Variety* called it "a dreary unfunny attempt at contemporary comedy. Overproduced, underdirected and lifelessly acted …" Fortunately, Raft's role as Garbaldo, the captain of "God's" yacht, was so small as to be virtually overlooked.

George then signed for the role of Mike Madigan in Sidney Pink's production of *Madigan's Millions* (1968), to be filmed in Italy and co-starring Elsa Martinelli and an unknown 30-year-old actor named Dustin Hoffman. However, when Raft discovered that his character was a deported gangster who dies while in exile, he felt the role hit too close to home and decided not to make the movie. He was replaced by Cesar Romero. Even with movie roles at a premium, George held firm to his principles.

In 1968, George, deeply in debt, was forced to sell his Beverly Estates home and move into an apartment. One way he managed to keep solvent was by appearing in television commercials. In a commercial spot for Pontiac, he was a chauffeur to George Brent and Ursula Andress. He also appeared in an ad for Maxwell House coffee. Perhaps his most popular commercial was as one of three tough convicts (the others being Mike Mazurki and Robert Strauss) in the prison mess hall demanding Alka Seltzer to ease their indigestion from eating bad jailhouse food. For his one day's work on the ad, Raft was reportedly paid $3,000, plus airing residuals. Because of the commercial's success, George also went on a nation-wide tour to promote Alka Seltzer.

George did another bit, as "himself," in a comedy made in Mexico called *The Great Sex War* (1969), starring James Franciscus, Joan Marshall and Cantinflas (once proclaimed by Charlie Chaplin as "the world's greatest comedian"). The picture holds the distinction of being one of the most obscure of all of Raft's movies.

Performing in such minor film roles was hardly enough to keep Raft ahead of his creditors. It was reported that he owed the IRS about $75,000 in back taxes. His only other source of income was a pension he received from the Screen Actors Guild, which he used to cover his living expenses.

Hoping to turn things around, in 1970 he reapplied for permission to return to England — but was again denied.

Instead, he endured more bad publicity when he received a subpoena to appear before a Manhattan Grand Jury Rackets investigation. The reason he was called was that his name was mentioned in a nine-year-old taped telephone conversation between organized crime figure Charlie ("The Blade") Tourine and a movie executive in which Tourine demanded payment of a gambling debt, whose check would be delivered to and endorsed by George Raft — a favor Raft had apparently performed for Tourine before.

Raft was dismissed after providing whatever testimony he could. But instead of returning directly to California, he made a brief stopover in Connecticut to visit the grave of his long-estranged wife Grayce, who had died the previous year. Although Grayce had exhibited much bitterness, if not outright greed, toward George by her stubborn refusal to divorce him, any resentment that Raft felt was kept private, and when he spoke of her it was always with courtesy and respect. While finally after forty-seven years Raft was truly a bachelor, it was unlikely at the age of seventy-five that he ever would remarry.

Shortly after returning to Los Angeles, George popped up a couple of times on Rowan and Martin's *Laugh-In*, came out of the "closet" on *The Dean Martin Show*, and was a guest on the April 4, 1971 telecast of *The Tonight Show* with Johnny Carson. It was on this program that Carson showed a clip of *Bolero* and was surprised to see George turn away. When Carson later asked why he wouldn't look at the clip, Raft replied, "I'm afraid to look, because I'm probably awful."

Certainly producer-actor Tony Bill didn't think Raft was "awful" when he invited him to appear with Ida Lupino for a small part in his trucker comedy *Deadhead Miles* (1971). One of Bill's favorite movies was *They Drive by Night*, and he planned the Raft-Lupino pairing as an inside joke. The film's star Alan Arkin said of their cameos, "Their scene isn't just a gag. It's homage."

Paramount, however, decided not to release the movie and it was not seen by audiences until 1982.

George then had the misfortune of playing a bit in the eleventh screen pairing of Elizabeth Taylor and Richard Burton in the Peter Ustinov-directed *Hammermith is Out* (1972). Raft appeared as Guido Scartucci, the owner of a topless go-go club called The Tit, which escaped mental patient Hammersmith (Burton) and his male nurse Billy Breedlove (Beau Bridges) plan to take over. Scartucci meets with Hammersmith in a high-rise office building, where he is tossed out the men's room window and lands as a corpse in the back seat of his own automobile. George could consider himself fortunate that the film and his humiliating cameo were not widely seen by audiences.[31]

George returned to television, though his appearance on the short-lived (thirteen episodes) 1971 Dean Jones Prohibition comedy *The Chicago Teddy Bears,* in an episode titled "The Rivalry", which also featured Ann Sothern, again consisted only of a cameo, with Raft briefly glimpsed as a passenger in a car driven by the series star.

George was far more visible in a couple of commercials he did with Aldo Ray for Merchant's National Bank, both of which capitalized on his gangster image. Yet he could not have been further away from that role when he provided the narration for the "Peter and the Wolf" children's LP. That same year he lent his familiar voice to United Artists' *The Golden Age of the Hollywood Musical,* which was a tribute to the classic Busby Berkeley musical numbers of the 1930s. Raft's narration provided the right nostalgic touch.

It was rumored that George's name briefly came up when casting discussions opened for pivotal roles in Paramount's upcoming production of Mario Puzo's bestselling *The Godfather* (1972). Edward G. Robinson was another momentary consideration for the part of Don Vito Corleone. While Raft would have been visually perfect for the role of an elderly Mafioso, with his slight resemblance to Carlo Gambino, he, like Robinson, was too old for the title role, and if he'd ever been considered in the first place, the powers-that-be quickly passed on using him.

As Raft aged he began to develop problems with his health. Although he had given up his heavy cigarette smoking, he still suffered from crippling bouts of emphysema, which was further aggravated by the Los Angeles smog. In 1972 he entered a Los Angeles hospital for surgery on a double hernia. Remarkably, despite all his personal and professional difficulties, and now with health concerns, George did not look like a seventy-seven-year-old man. As Jack LaRue quipped, "George wore his age probably better than any other man in Hollywood — except for me."

While George remained absent from motion picture and television screens, he appeared at several Hollywood functions, such as the 100th birthday celebration for former Paramount president Adolph Zukor, and at gala tributes to Mae West and director Henry Hathaway.

He also received some much-needed positive publicity when Jack Parr announced on his late night ABC talk show that George Raft had taken charge when Mrs. Parr suffered a heart attack at a Beverly Hills restaurant. George's cool yet swift action likely saved the woman's life. As Parr related on national television, "There was this seventy-seven-year-old man taking over while I could do nothing."

Raft now resided in a small apartment in Century City. He spent most of his time watching television, though avoiding showings of his old movies. Most of his outings consisted of going out to dinner at the Brown Derby, his preferred restaurant, or visiting the racetrack at Santa Anita every weekend, where he was a great fan of Willie Shoemaker. Raft would later run into actor Dick Van Patten at the track and confess to him that his favorite television program was *Eight is Enough*.

Although it appeared that George Raft was forgotten by all but his closest friends, two books appeared on the market that suddenly generated new interest in the former star. *The George Raft File* was an unauthorized biography published in 1973 by Drake (co-authored by James Robert Parish and Steven Whitney), and the following year Lewis Yablonsky secured George's co-operation in the writing of the simply-titled *George Raft*, published by McGraw-Hill and later released in paperback by the New American Library. Although George claimed to have never read either book, he did his part to help promote the latter effort. He showed up as a guest on *The Tonight Show* with Johnny Carson, and then made a memorable appearance on *The Merv Griffin Show*. When asked by the host why he wasn't working so much anymore, Raft candidly replied that he suffered from breathing difficulties and often had long periods where this made it hard for him to speak. The highpoint came when he was followed out on stage by his old friend Pat O'Brien. The gregarious O'Brien talked about the days when George would enjoy a night out with the Boy's Club — or "Irish Mafia" (O'Brien, Cagney, Spencer Tracy, Ralph Bellamy, Frank McHugh, Frank Morgan and Lynne Overman), and then in a touching moment presented George with a walking stick he had brought back from a recent trip to Ireland. George was visibly moved by the gift.

George hoped that with the passage of time he might be allowed back into England to publicize the book, but was again denied entry.

George was later asked by a reporter that should a movie be made of his autobiography, who would he like to see play him. Raft responded, "Al Pacino."

George turned up at the 1974 American Film Institute Salute to James Cagney, where he was introduced by host Frank Sinatra and rose to applause for a quick table bow. Others in attendance among the old Warners group were Mae Clarke, Allen Jenkins, Frank McHugh and Ronald Reagan.

He was also briefly seen on the motion picture screen in archival movie footage of him and other vintage stars in the British documentary on the Great Depression titled *Brother, Can You Spare a Dime* (1975), which was nominated the following year for a Golden Globe.

Early the following year George was admitted to the hospital where he underwent serious aneurismal surgery. Though weakened both by the operation and his emphysema, Raft apparently made a satisfactory recovery. When Raft had surgery for hernias on his chest and abdominal walls, he said, "It's the coughing that does it. Every time I have a coughing attack I run the risk of a hernia."

Raft's respiratory problems necessitated the use of a special machine which he used twice a day, for fifteen minutes at a time.

Raft also told how the emphysema had limited his activities. "… But I really don't do much anymore. If anyone told me I'd be getting to bed each night by 9:30, I'd have told them they were crazy."

George did work part-time in the Beverly Hills office of Las Vegas' Riviera Hotel. As he explained, "I'm their official ambassador of goodwill. It's at least something." Perhaps what George enjoyed most about his job was that it gave him the opportunity to meet with old friends and talk about old times.

Contrary to his former image as a "rough customer," George was a well-liked man in his later years. Author Jon Tuska, who interviewed Raft for a chapter in his book, *The Detective in Hollywood*, wrote: "George Raft is the sweetest, gentlest, most charming man in all of Hollywood."

In fact, it was surmised that the reason George lived so comfortably for a man in his poor financial state was that he was provided for by many of his friends.

George also had another hit television commercial for a chain of auto tune-up shops where he played a gangster on the lam. A few years earlier he had played a convict behind bars in an ad for Stick-Up Air Freshener, where he quoted the famous slogan: "You know, this is a good place for a stick-up."

In an interview with *Los Angeles Herald-Examiner* columnist James Bacon toward the end of his life, George spoke reflectively: "I wish I had taken up some hobby like golf or stamp collecting. You know me, I had only one hobby — broads. Now, here I am eighty-five and how in hell can you have a hobby like that at my age? Worse, with this damn emphysema, I can't even smoke anymore. But I still love to look at all those beautiful dames who walk down Wilshire Boulevard."

George was interviewed by the *Los Angeles Times* around the same time, where he spoke about his life and regrets. "Funny, I don't feel like an old man. But I'm in my 80s. And I don't feel poor. But I'm sure not rich. Maybe I should of done something different. Maybe I shouldn't smoke — should have stopped before the lung got so bad. And maybe I should of kept some of the dough. But I didn't. And I don't feel too sorry. Funny, I still got the feeling I could get it all back. Like I was still a young guy and could do it. Yeah."

In the same interview, George admitted what may have been his greatest mistake. "I should of done at least one thing: that silver half-dollar I used in *Scarface*. I should have kept that, at least."

Perhaps George's most amusing comment concerned the loss of the fortune he had earned in show business. "I must have gone through $10 million during my career. Part of the loot went for gambling, part for horses and part for women. The rest I spent foolishly."

The late actress Liz Renay, who knew Raft through their mutual association with Mickey Cohen, recalled seeing Raft in Las Vegas in the late '70s. Although never a man given to self-pity, George said to her, "You know, I envy you. I'm a forgotten man. No one knows me anymore."

But he wasn't totally forgotten. Certainly not by old friends. In 1978 he was asked by Mae West to appear in her upcoming movie *Sextette*, based on her notorious stage play *Sex*, to be directed by Ken Russell.[32] Although he again played "himself" in yet another cameo, there was definite nostalgia value in his elevator scene with West. Raft appears quite well and younger than his eighty-two years as he chats for a few moments with Miss West before departing. But the film itself, Mae West's last, was a critical disaster on a par with her earlier *Myra Breckinridge* (1970). Some reviewers even commented that the plot detailing younger men's attraction to the much-married octogenarian "sex symbol" Marlo Manners (West) was almost a nod to necrophilia.

At the age of eighty-four, George appeared in his final film. He played the role of club owner Petey Cane in the movie *The Man With Bogart's Face* (1980), based on the novel of the same name by Andrew J. Fenady. Raft had aged considerably since his last screen outing and in his dialogue was clearly plagued by his emphysema. In the film, Bogart impersonator Robert Sacchi plays a former cop who undergoes plastic surgery so that he can resemble the pre-eminent purveyor of private eyes, Humphrey Bogart, appropriately changes his name to Sam Marlow, opens a detective agency and then becomes embroiled in a case to recover two priceless blue sapphires, the "Eyes of Alexander." The film attempted to be an affectionate modern-day spoof of classic detective movies, and to that end the supporting cast was peppered with such genre veterans as Yvonne DeCarlo, Mike Mazurki, Victor Sen Young and Martin Kosleck. The movie succeeded quite well in its aspirations and was nominated for an Edgar Allan Poe award for Best Motion Picture. Unfortunately, the terrible title tune was likewise nominated and won … a Razzie Award for Worst Original Song.

Raft had only one scene in the picture, where he is confronted behind his desk by Marlow. His memorable piece of dialogue is: "I came across guys like this before." One wonders what Raft must have been thinking as he spoke that line at the climax of his career.

Michelle Phillips, formerly of the '60s pop group The Mamas and the Papas, played the role of Gena. She remembered working with Raft in his final scene in his last movie. "I know I did his last scene in the movie and I can tell you he was a beautiful creature — very dignified — quiet — professional. We did that scene in one take. He had — and I know this is an overused term — an aura about him. And in that white suit it was magnified. He only worked one day on the film, so we didn't get to know each other — but he was sweet, and boy, you sure knew that George Raft was on the set. We were in awe of him."

The Man with Bogart's Face was not released until after Raft's death, and his image was featured on the poster. Strangely, his final two movies reflected the irony of his former stardom. Both a major highpoint (his first starring feature, with Mae West) … and what would ultimately turn out to be the low (the enormous success he'd handed over to Humphrey Bogart).

Another low point came on January 29, 1980, when George's longtime friend Jimmy Durante passed away at the age of eighty-six. Raft thought highly of Durante and always appreciated the kindness he'd shown during George's early days of struggle.

In April of that year, Raft's ongoing bout with respiratory problems developed into pneumonia, which kept him hospitalized for seven weeks. His physician Dr. Rex Kennamer was later to explain that Raft had been "a respiratory cripple" for years.

It was also discovered that George had leukemia, though the diagnosis was kept from him. Shortly after Raft was admitted to New Hospital in Los Angeles, for what would be his final stay, the news reached the world that Mae West had passed away on November 22, 1980. George, gravely ill and drifting in and out of a coma, was told of her passing, but it was doubtful he either heard or understood.

Two days later, on November 24, George Raft, at age eighty-five, the second last surviving member of Murderer's Row, succumbed to his illnesses.[33] Raft biographer Lewis Yablonsky, who visited George toward the end, believed Raft finished life an essentially contented man. "He didn't dwell on the past or the errors that he made," Yablonsky said.

But apparently one aspect of his past never left him. A source revealed that in his final days George received visits from what he perceived as his underworld pals, who sat at his bedside.

Just as appropriate to the George Raft legend — though in a macabre vein — was that following his death, Raft's body and that of Mae West were similarly placed in the same mortuary.

George Raft's funeral on November 28 was attended by more than 100 mourners, including an ailing Mack Gray (who would succumb to cancer less than two months later), Danny Thomas, Jack LaRue and Raft's *Nob Hill* co-star Vivian Blaine. Afterwards, his casket was interred at Forest Lawn, Hollywood Hills in the Court of Remembrance, Sanctuary of Light, #2356. His crypt is located next to that of the tragic comedian Freddie Prinze.

After his passing, George received many tributes from people who had known him. Perhaps these sentiments were best expressed by Raft's longtime friend and attorney Sidney Korshak. "He was a kindly man and gentleman, and a legend in his time."

Besides the televised showings of his movies, George Raft also made a unique sort of posthumous comeback, *a la* Bela Lugosi in Tim Burton's wonderful *Ed Wood* (1994). The films *The Cotton Club* (1984), directed by Francis Ford Coppola, and Barry Levinson's *Bugsy* (1991) each either directly or indirectly featured the character of George Raft. In the former, Dixie Dwyer (Richard Gere) is a trumpet player in the employ of Owney Madden (superbly played by Bob Hoskins), who is sent to Hollywood by the gangster to preclude his involvement in a mob war, and subsequently becomes a sensation in gangster movies. Despite the difference in their club specialties (trumpet player as opposed to Charleston dancer), the parallels between Raft and Dwyer are significant. It was a role offered to and rejected by Al Pacino, who certainly would have been better suited to playing "George Raft" than Richard Gere, *sans* silly pencil-thin mustache.

In *Bugsy*, the character of "George" (strangely, no mention is ever made of the famous last name, not even in the closing credits) is already a top Hollywood star, appearing in the nightclub scene from *Manpower*. It is George who welcomes Siegel (Warren Beatty) to Hollywood and provides the inroads to Tinseltown society for the charismatic gangster. The role of George was played by the talented Joe Mantegna.

Perhaps more than any other star of his era, George strongly identified with his film roles. It was important to him that he be liked as much on camera as off. To that end, when he reached the point of stardom where he could start being selective about the material he chose, he often exercised a judgment that was … eccentric, to say the least. Particularly in his choice of criminal or gangster parts. One wonders how Raft could have embraced a minor B-film film such as *The House Across the Bay* while firmly rejecting *High Sierra*, a quality A-picture on his home lot. Today, it is almost inconceivable to fathom Raft's inability to recognize the merits of *The Maltese Falcon*, the character he rejected destined to become the screen's quintessential private detective. Of course, Raft's career would never recover from these mistakes. But in an odd way, one cannot help but respect Raft for these decisions. Because, for better or worse, like many of the characters he created on film, he played the game his own way.

George Raft may have been forgotten by audiences during his final decades, and his reputation is perhaps even less remembered today, but it cannot be denied that among the galaxy of great movie stars who graced the majestic silver screen during the '30s and '40s, George Raft was in a class by himself and, as such, is truly a legend.

AFTERWORD

When I came back to Hollywood from New York in the early 1960s, I bought a wonderfully large home on Mulholland Terrace at the very top of the Santa Monica Mountains near Laurel Canyon Boulevard. While I was living in that elegant house I met George Raft at one of the many parties I was accustomed to throwing. We got along famously, as they say, and soon George and I started dating. His home was just down the hill from mine in Hollywood and two or three times a week he would invite me to have dinner with him at his impressive estate or go out with him "on the town." George was an exceptionally fine dancer; not as athletic as my former boyfriend Ed Wood, but graceful and smooth. We were an item for a couple of years. George was very interested in my career and even seriously promoted me with Darryl Zanuck and other important people in the industry. Unfortunately, nothing came from his efforts.

George rarely spoke about his own career. Surprisingly, a lot of our talks revolved around interior decorating, probably because I admired the tasteful décor of his home and had a long-standing interest myself in decorating. I remember that George had a hardwood floor in one of his many rooms that was used for dancing. He had a long bar along one side of the room and a fine high-fidelity system for playing his large record collection. With such an elaborate set-up, you might think that his private parties would include a lot of people. But that wasn't the case. Customarily, he would invite another couple or perhaps two more couples to dine with us. The most I remember at any dinner party was eight people, including us. That followed the old saying that the best discussions are always with a number of people between one more than the trinity (four) and one less than the number of the muses (eight).

Unfortunately, I don't remember much about any of the discussions, only that they were interesting. George and I enjoyed dancing together, and that was probably the strongest bond between us.

Eventually, our relationship came to an end, primarily because George could not get a divorce from his wife for religious reasons. He was at least twenty years older than I was and definitely from another era: "Classic Hollywood." I always had a feeling that George might have been "connected" with the underworld without ever having a single specific reason to think so. Perhaps it was because of his movie roles, where art is stronger than reality.

For example, I never cared for his gangster part in Billy Wilder's *Some Like It Hot*. Maybe it was because I always liked George so much that the nasty, evil character he played in the film irritates me. I always wanted to see him in a picture that would take advantage of the smooth, sophisticated, generous, considerate gentleman that he was. The perfect movie script would portray George as a graceful dancer whose character is outgoing, popular and friendly, yet underneath it all, mysterious, sad and thoughtful.

George Raft might have come from a crime-ridden New York neighborhood, but he was a polished gentleman with fine manners whom I respected without ever quite falling in love.

The last time that I saw George was, I believe, at the Las Vegas Hilton. That was about 1968 or '69 when I had moved to Vegas because my partner, Hank Levine, and I were putting together shows for the hotels and I was spending so much time in Las Vegas that it made sense to buy a home here and not keep running back and forth to Hollywood. I'm not sure that George had a scheduled appearance in Las Vegas or if he was just visiting, but I remember clearly that he looked a lot older and not at all well. It made me quite sad to see him so much less dashing than I had remembered. I recall feeling the same about Elvis Presley shortly before he died when he had trouble remembering lyrics to songs and struggling to keep up appearances. But George, of course, was much older than Elvis and lived a few more years, even making a few more films after the last time I saw him.

I have only wonderful memories of George Raft and am privileged to have known him both as a fine gentleman and a cherished friend.

Dolores Fuller
Las Vegas, Nevada

1929	*Queen of the Night Clubs*	Gigolo
1929	*Gold Diggers of Broadway*	Dancer
1929	*Side Street*	Georgie Ames
1931	*Quick Millions*	Jimmy Kirk
1931	*Goldie*	Pickpocket in carnival crowd
1931	*Hush Money*	Maxie
1931	*Palmy Days*	Joe the Frog
1932	*Taxi!*	Willie Kenny
1932	*Scarface*	Guino Rinaldo
1932	*Night World*	Ed Powell
1932	*Love is a Racket*	Sneaky — Scenes deleted
1932	*Winner Take All*	Bandleader (scene from *Queen of the Night Clubs*)
1932	*Dancers in the Dark*	Louis Brooks
1932	*Madame Racketeer*	Jack Houston
1932	*Night After Night*	Joe Anton
1932	*If I Had a Million*	Eddie Jackson
1932	*Under-Cover Man*	Nick Darrow/Ollie Snell
1933	*Pick-Up*	Harry Glynn
1933	*The Midnight Club*	Nick Mason
1933	*The Bowery*	Steve Brodie
1934	*All of Me*	Honey Rogers
1934	*Bolero*	Raoul DeBaere
1934	*The Trumpet Blows*	Manuel Montes
1934	*Limehouse Blues*	Harry Young
1935	*Rumba*	Joe Martin
1935	*Stolen Harmony*	Ray Angelo/Ray Ferraro
1935	*The Glass Key*	Ed Beaumonte
1935	*Every Night at Eight*	Tops Cardona
1935	*She Couldn't Take It*	Spot Ricardi/Joe Ricard
1936	*It Had to Happen*	Enrico Scaffa
1936	*Yours for the Asking*	Johnny Lamb
1937	*Souls at Sea*	Powdah
1938	*Spawn of the North*	Tyler Dawson
1938	*You and Me*	Joe Dennis
1939	*The Lady's from Kentucky*	Marty Black
1939	*I Stole a Million*	Joe Laurik (Harris)

1939	*Each Dawn I Die*	Judson "Hood" Stacey
1939	*Invisible Stripes*	Cliff Taylor
1940	*The House Across the Bay*	Steve Larwitt
1940	*They Drive by Night*	Joe Fabrini
1941	*Manpower*	Johnny Marshall
1942	*Broadway*	George Raft
1943	*Stage Door Canteen*	Himself
1943	*Background to Danger*	Joe Barton
1944	*Follow the Boys*	Tony West
1945	*Nob Hill*	Tony Angelo
1945	*Johnny Angel*	Johnny Angel
1946	*Whistle Stop*	Kenny Veech
1946	*Mr. Ace*	Eddie Ace
1946	*Nocturne*	Lieutenant Joe Warne
1947	*Christmas Eve*	Mario Torio
1947	*Intrigue*	Brad Dunham
1948	*Race Street*	Dan Gannin
1949	*Johnny Allegro*	Johnny Allegro
1949	*A Dangerous Profession*	Vince Kane
1949	*Red Light*	John Torno
1949	*Outpost in Morocco*	Captain Paul Gerard
1949	*Nous Irons a Paris*	Himself
1951	*Lucky Nick Cain*	Nick Cain
1952	*Loan Shark*	Joe Gargen
1953	*I'll Get You*	Steve Rossi
1953	*The Man from Cairo*	Mike Canelli
1954	*Rogue Cop*	Dan Beaumonte
1954	*Black Widow*	Lieutenant Detective Bruce
1955	*A Bullet for Joey*	Joe Victor/ Earl Steiner
1956	*Around the World in Eighty Days*	Bouncer at Barbary Coast saloon
1959	*Some Like It Hot*	"Spats" Columbo
1959	*Jet Over the Atlantic*	FBI Agent Stafford
1960	*Ocean's Eleven*	Jack Strager
1961	*The Ladies Man*	Himself
1962	*Two Guys Abroad*	(unreleased)
1964	*The Patsy*	Himself
1964	*For Those Who Think Young*	Detective
1966	*Du Rififi a Paname (The Upper Hand)*	Charles Binnaggio
1967	*Casino Royale*	Himself
1968	*Five Golden Dragons*	Golden Dragon
1968	*Skidoo*	Captain Garbaldo
1969	*The Great Sex War*	Himself
1971	*Deadhead Miles* (released in 1982)	Himself

1972 *Hammersmith is Out* ....Guido Scartucci
1978 *Sextette* ....Himself
1980 *The Man with Bogart's Face* .... Petey Cane

Films featuring the character of George Raft

1960 *The George Raft Story* .... Ray Danton
1982 *Mae West* (made-for-TV) .... Nicholas Meyer
1984 *The Cotton Club* .... Richard Gere
1991 *Bugsy* ....Joe Mantegna

Cartoons featuring the likenes of George Raft

1936 .... *The CooCoo Nut Grove*
1940 .... *Ali Baba Bound*
1941 .... *Malibu Beach Party*
1941 .... *Hollywood Steps Out*
1964 -73 .... *Underdog* (Riff-Raff)

Selected Short Subjects

1933 .... *Hollywood on Parade* (2 appearances)
1934 .... *The Fashion Side of Hollywood*
1937 .... *Screen Snapshots* (Series #16 and #17)
1938 .... *Screen Snapshots* (Series #18)
1941 ....*Meet the Stars: Stars at Play*
1949 .... *Screen Snapshots: Vacation at Del Mar*

1937-1937	*Kraft Cheese Program* with Bing Crosby and Bob Burns (2 programs — guest)
1936	*Lux Radio Theatre:* "Cheating Cheaters"
1938	*Standard Brands Hour with Edgar Bergen and Charlie McCarthy* (guest)
	30 Minutes in Hollywood (guest)
1938	*Lux Radio Theatre:* "Spawn of the North" (with Fred MacMurray and Dorothy Lamour
1939	*Proctor and Gamble's Knickerbocker Playhouse:* "Bulldog Drummond"
1940	*Campbell Soup Playhouse:* "A Free Soul" (with Frances Farmer)
1941	*Kraft Music Hall* (guest)
	Lux Radio Theatre: "They Drive by Night" (with Lana Turner and Lucille Ball)
1942	*The Chase and Sandborn Program with Edgar Bergen and Charlie McCarthy* (guest)
	Screen Guild Theatre: "Torrid Zone" (with Paulette Goddard)
	Philip Morris Playhouse: "Brother Orchid"
	Lux Radio Theatre: "Manpower" (with Edward G. Robinson and Marlene Dietrich)
	Lux Radio Theatre: "Broadway" (with Lloyd Nolan and Janet Blair)
1944-1944	*The Abbott and Costello Show* (2 programs — guest)
	Philip Morris Playhouse: "The Glass Key" (with Jeanne Cagney)
	Lux Radio Theatre: "Each Dawn I Die" (with Franchot Tone and Lynn Bari)
	Lux Radio Theatre: "Air Force" (with Harry Carey)
1945	*Texaco Star Theatre with Fred Allen* (guest)
	Lux Radio Theatre: "Action in the North Atlantic" (with Raymond Massey and Julie Bishop)
	The Silver Theatre: "The Sun Field"
1946	*The Bill Stern Sports Show* (guest)
1947	*The Silver Theatre:* "The Private Eye"
	Duffy's Tavern (guest)

1948	*This is Hollywood:* "Mr. Ace" (with Sylvia Sidney)
1949	*Lux Radio Theatre:* "Intrigue" (with June Havoc)
1950	*The Cases of Eddie Ace* (series)
1953-1953	*The Adventures of Rocky Jordan* (series — 58 episodes)
1951-1953	*The Dean Martin-Jerry Lewis Show* (2 programs — guest)
1951-1954	*The Bob Hope Show* (2 programs — guest)

1955	*The Colgate Comedy Hour* (4 episodes — guest)
1956	*What's My Line* (guest)
1957	*I've Got a Secret* (guest)
	I Am the Law (series — 26 episodes)
1954	*The Buick-Milton Berle Show* (2 episodes — guest)
1956	*Texaco Star Theatre with Jimmy Durante* (3 episodes — guest)
1957	*The Tonight Show with Jack Parr* (guest)
1964	*The Ed Sullivan Show* (2 episodes — guest)
1957	*The Gisele MacKenzie Show* (guest)
1959	*The Arthur Murray Dance Party* (guest)
	The Jack Paar Show (guest)
1960	*The Red Skelton Show* (guest)
1961	*Here's Hollywood* (guest)
1965	*The New London Palladium Show*
1966	*Hippodrome Show* (guest)
	The Today Show (interviewed in London at The Colony Club)
1967	*Batman:* "The Black Widow Strikes Again"
1969-1974	*The Tonight Show with Johnny Carson* (4 episodes — guest)
1969-1974	*The Merv Griffin Show* (2 episodes – guest)
1970	*The Dean Martin Show* (guest)
1971	*Rowan and Martin's Laugh-In* (2 episodes — guest)
	The Chicago Teddy Bears: "The Rivalry"
1974	*The American Film Institute Salute to James Cagney* (at table bow)

BIBLIOGRAPHY

Base, Ron: *Starring Roles*, Stoddart Publishing Company, Ltd., Toronto, 1994.

Clarens, Carlos: *Crime Movies*, W.W. Norton and Company, New York, 1980.

Cooper, Jackie, and Kleiner, Dick: *Please Don't Shoot My Dog: The Autobiography of Jackie Cooper*, William Morrow and Company, New York, 1981.

Dietrich, Marlene, translated from the German by Salvator Attanasio: *Marlene*, Grove Press, New York, 1989.

Douglas, Kirk: *The Ragman's Son: An Autobiography*, Simon and Shuster, New York, 1988.

Druxman, Michael B: *Paul Muni: His Life and His Films*, A.S. Barnes, South Brunswick, 1974.

Eels, George, and Musgrove, Stanley: *Mae West: A Biography*, William Morrow and Company, New York, 1982.

Gardner, Ava: *Ava, My Story*, Bantam Books, New York, 1990.

Jennings, Dean: *We Only Kill Each Other*, Prentice-Hall, Inc., Englewood Cliffs, New Jersey, 1967.

Lawrence, Jerome: *Actor: The Life and Times of Paul Muni*, Putnam, New York, 1974.

Lee, Christopher: *Tall, Dark and Gruesome*, Weidenfeld & Nicolson, London, 1997.

McCabe, John: *Cagney*, Knopf, New York, 1997.

Meyers, Jeffrey: *Bogart: A Life in Hollywood*, Houghton Mifflin, Boston, 1997.

Meyers, Jeffrey: *Gary Cooper: American Hero*, William Morrow and Company, New York, 1998.

Parish, James Robert, and Anderson, Earl: *Hollywood Character Actors*, Arlington House, New Rochelle, New York, 1978.

Parish, James Robert, and Whitney, Steven: *The George Raft File*, Drake Publishers, Inc., New York, 1973.

Robinson, Edward G., and Spigelgass, Leonard: *All My Yesterdays*, Hawthorn Books, New York, 1973.

Sklar, Robert: *City Boys*, Princeton University Press, Princeton, New Jersey, 1992.

Sperber, A.M., and Lax, Eric: *Bogart*, William Morrow and Company, New York, 1997.

Thomas, Bob: *Golden Boy: The Untold Story of William Holden*, St. Martin's Press, New York, 1983.

Tosches, Nick: *Dino: Living High in the Dirty Business of Dreams*, Doubleday, New York, 1992.

Tuska, Jon: *The Detective in Hollywood*, Doubleday, Garden City, New York, 1978.

Warner, Jack, and Jennings, Dean: *My First Hundred Years in Hollywood: An Autobiography*, Random House, Inc., New York, 1964.

Warren, Doug, with Cagney, James: *James Cagney: The Authorized Biography*, St. Martin's Press, New York, 1983.

Yablonsky, Lewis: *George Raft*, McGraw-Hill, New York, 1974.

Magazine Articles:

Catsos, Gregory J.M.: "Sylvia Sidney," Filmfax, Issue #23 November, 1990.

Jennings, Dean and Raft, George: "Out of My Past," Saturday Evening Post, September 21-October 19, 1957.

Meienberg, Paul and Gasten, David: "Alison Skipworth: Reluctant Grand Dame," Films of the Golden Age, Issue #38, fall, 2004.

Richards, Brad: "George Raft," Films of the Golden Age, Issue #38, fall, 2004.

Miscellaneous:

FOIPA George Raft FBI File Documents

Websites:

Wikipedia: George Raft: *http://en.wikipedia.org/wiki/George_Raft*

The Internet Movie Database: George Raft: *http://www.imdb.com/*

FOOTNOTES

Prologue

1. Groucho Marx was awarded the well-deserved honor that year.

2. Tay Garnett had made a number of pictures with Lloyd, including the war classic *Bataan*, 1943. In fact, at the time of our talk, Lloyd had just appeared in a tribute episode to director Garnett on *The Merv Griffin Show*.

Chapter Three

3. Fay and Texas had endured an often-tempestuous partnership. The El Fey Club was doing well, but Fay's preference for hoodlum clientele clashed with Texas's Park Avenue crowd. It was like mixing fire with gasoline, and finally the mixture exploded in a series of federal raids that left the doors to the club permanently padlocked.

4. Coll even had the audacity to kidnap Madden's friend and partner "Big Frenchy" DeMange and demand a ransom, which Owney paid. Coll would be ambushed in a telephone booth by the Dutch Schultz mob in 1932. The killing of Coll may have served as the "inspiration" for the similar phone booth demise of Joe Downing's character in *Angels With Dirty Faces* (Warners, 1938).

5. Larry Fay and Texas Guinan are forgotten names in the history of Prohibition, yet they achieved cinematic immortality in the characters of Eddie Bartlett (James Cagney) and Panama Smith (Gladys George) in Warner Brothers 1939 swan song to the era, *The Roaring Twenties*, produced by George's old New York pal, Mark Hellinger.

6. This exchange provides a black comedy fadeout to the movie, but it is appropriate, given the lavish sendoffs afforded "Big" Jim Colosimo and Dion O'Banion, two of Chicago gangland's earliest casualties.

7. Raft and Cagney became famous for two distinctly different dance styles. Where Cagney adopted a stiff-legged, knee-snapping form, best exemplified in his impersonation of George M. Cohen in *Yankee Doodle Dandy*, Raft's dance moves were fluid: sensuous, sinuous and snakelike.

Chapter Four

8. Armitage Trail (born Maurice Coons) died two years previous to the release of *Scarface*. The severely-obese writer was felled by a heart attack in the lobby of a Los Angeles hotel at the age of only 28.

9. This alternate ending can be seen as a Bonus Feature on the MCA/Universal DVD of *Scarface*.

10. Raft was reportedly offered $500 for the role but Hawks claimed he was paid more due to the filming going over schedule.

11. In comparison, the year before, James Cagney signed a contract with Warner Brothers for a weekly salary of $400. Humphrey Bogart, on the other hand, had in 1930 signed a deal with Fox for $750 per week! Bogart, however, would be quickly dropped from Fox.

Chapter Five

12. There is little doubt that Raft was sexually active in Hollywood. In the early 1930s Tallulah Bankhead was hospitalized with an advanced case of gonorrhea she claimed she'd contracted from Raft.

13. Raft was also the inspiration for the criminal character of "Riff-Raff", voiced by Allen Swift, on the *Underdog* cartoon series (1964-1973).

14. George and Bing were friends on the Paramount lot, where Crosby would usually address Raft as "Twinkletoes".

15. The FBI would later report that Raft spent two weeks as a guest at Owney Madden's home in Little Rock, Arkansas that same year and was observed at a baseball game accompanied by Mack Gray.

Chapter Six

16. The role had been performed onstage by Joseph Downing, veteran of many Warner Brothers crime films.

17. *Dead End* was nominated for four Academy Awards, including Best Picture.

Chapter Sevem

18. Norma Shearer would die of pneumonia, brought on by complications from Alzheimer's disease, in 1983.

19. Raft also has two stars on the Hollywood Walk of Fame for his contributions to Motion Pictures, at 6150 Hollywood Boulevard, and for Television at 1500 Vine St.

20. The film commenced shooting on April 22, 1940 with a five-week schedule. Unusual for standard film production, Raoul Walsh shot *They Drive by Night* in sequence, which benefitted all of the performances.

21. With James Cagney the notable exception, most of the stars' grievances against Warners concerned the quality of roles being offered rather than an increase in financial compensation.

Chapter Eight

22. Raft was the only one of Murderer's Row never to have appeared in uniform in a World War II film. Bogart did *Action in the North Atlantic* and *Sahara* (both 1943); Cagney appeared in *Captains of the Clouds* (1942), and even Edward G. Robinson donned combat fatigues in *Mr. Winkle Goes to War* (1944).

23. Mack Gray recalled the night when Siegel, envious over Gray's own thick head of hair, offered him $1000 on the spot if he could cut it off. Gray agreed and Siegel promptly took a pair of scissors and proceeded to butcher Gray's hair. Gray got the grand, but he was not amused. "He must have got some kicks out of it," Gray later said.

24. In the late forties, Raft recreated the Eddie Ace character as a detective in the short-lived *no-irish* radio series *The Cases of Eddie Ace*.

25. Raft was one of many Hollywood "names" who accepted film work in England once Hollywood offers dried up. Others included George Brent, Richard Carlson, Dane Clark, Brian Donlevy and Forrest Tucker.

26. Perhaps the movie — and Raft — might have fared better had director Enright acceded to George's request that he hire Sophia Loren for a part in the movie. Enright turned her down by explaining: "She can't speak enough English."

27. Dietz was probably best known for producing a number of low-budget Bela Lugosi and East Side Kids movies for Monogram Studios in the 1940s.

28. The National was formerly owned by Meyer Lansky.

Chapter Ten

29. Winchell and J. Edgar Hoover had a long association. Winchell, in fact, had acted as the intermediary when Murder Incorporated's Louis Lepke Buchalter personally surrendered to the FBI chief on August 24, 1939.

30. Warner observed of this later Raft in his autobiography: "He is suave, soigne, and impeccably dressed in his public appearances, and he no longer belts people in the chops if he disagrees with anything they have to say. I am happy to see Georgie so mellow in his senior years ..."

31. Some years later at a Variety Club testimonial dinner honoring Frank Sinatra, Richard Burton got up from his table to say a few words. In his tribute to Sinatra, he mentioned the filming of *Hammersmith is Out* and added that in the cast there was an actor, once a big Hollywood star, who had fallen on hard times. Burton recalled asking the actor if there was anything he needed, only to be told: "No. Frank (Sinatra) is taking care of me." Without naming the actor, it was clear that he was referring to George Raft.

32. The same play that many years earlier Mae West had wanted George to do.

33. James Cagney remained, and would even return to acting in *Ragtime* (1980) and the television movie *Terrible Joe Moran* (1984). He would die of a heart attack, on the morning of Easter Sunday, March 30, 1986.

INDEX

Breinigsville, PA USA
05 December 2010
250680BV00003B/35/P